Monitors and Meddlers

Foreign influences on elections are widespread. Although foreign interventions around elections differ markedly—in terms of when and why they occur, and whether they are even legal—they all have enormous potential to influence citizens in the countries where elections are held. Bush and Prather explain how and why outside interventions influence local trust in elections, a critical factor for democracy and stability. Whether foreign actors enhance or diminish electoral trust depends on who is intervening, what political party citizens support, and where the election takes place. The book draws on diverse evidence, including new surveys conducted around elections with varying levels of democracy in Georgia, Tunisia, and the United States. Its insights about public opinion shed light on why leaders sometimes invite foreign influences on elections and why the candidates that win elections do not do more to respond to credible evidence of foreign meddling.

SARAH SUNN BUSH is associate professor of political science at Yale University. She is the author of *The Taming of Democracy Assistance: Why Democracy Promotion Does Not Confront Dictators* (Cambridge, 2015) and has held fellowships at the Perry World House at the University of Pennsylvania, the Harvard Kennedy School, and Uppsala University.

LAUREN PRATHER is associate professor of political science in the School of Global Policy and Strategy at the University of California, San Diego. She is the author of several publications appearing in such journals as *American Political Science Review and International Organization*, and received the Hellman Fellowship from University of California, San Diego in 2018.

T0384502

Monitors and Meddlers

How Foreign Actors Influence Local Trust in Elections

SARAH SUNN BUSH
Yale University

LAUREN PRATHER
University of California San Diego

CAMBRIDGE
UNIVERSITY PRESS

Shaftesbury Road, Cambridge CB2 8EA, United Kingdom

One Liberty Plaza, 20th Floor, New York, NY 10006, USA

477 Williamstown Road, Port Melbourne, VIC 3207, Australia

314–321, 3rd Floor, Plot 3, Splendor Forum, Jasola District Centre, New Delhi – 110025, India

103 Penang Road, #05–06/07, Visioncrest Commercial, Singapore 238467

Cambridge University Press is part of Cambridge University Press & Assessment, a department of the University of Cambridge.

We share the University's mission to contribute to society through the pursuit of education, learning and research at the highest international levels of excellence.

www.cambridge.org
Information on this title: www.cambridge.org/9781009204279

DOI: 10.1017/9781009204262

First published 2022
First paperback edition 2024

A catalogue record for this publication is available from the British Library

Library of Congress Cataloging-in-Publication data
Names: Bush, Sarah Sunn, 1982– author. | Prather, Lauren, 1984– author.
Title: Monitors and meddlers : how foreign actors influence local trust in elections / Sarah Sunn Bush, Lauren Prather.
Description: Cambridge, United Kingdom ; New York, NY : Cambridge University Press, 2022. | Includes bibliographical references and index.
Identifiers: LCCN 2022016959 | ISBN 9781009204316 (hardback) | ISBN 9781009204262 (ebook)
Subjects: LCSH: Election monitoring. | Foreign interference in elections. | Elections – Public opinion. | Democratization – International cooperation. | BISAC: POLITICAL SCIENCE / General
Classification: LCC JF1001 .B778 2022 | DDC 324.6/5–dc23/eng/20220622
LC record available at https://lccn.loc.gov/2022016959

ISBN   978-1-009-20431-6   Hardback
ISBN   978-1-009-20427-9   Paperback

Contents

Figures

Tables

Acknowledgments

This book began at a dinner in 2012 as a part of a conference on election integrity. We were fatefully seated next to each other, and a conversation started about the effects of international actors on individual perceptions of election credibility. The conversation continued over the course of the next ten years and culminated in a book we are both immensely proud of. We will always be grateful to the organizers of the conference, including Susan Hyde and Stephen Stedman, for unwittingly setting in motion this rewarding partnership.

Along the way, the conversation between the two of us evolved to include many friends, mentors, advisors, practitioners, and supporters. As the book developed, we were grateful for early feedback on chapters from Susanna Campbell, Francisco Cantú, Ursula Daxecker, Jennifer Dixon, Daniela Donno, Erin Graham, Merlin Heidemanns, Josh Kertzer, Dov Levin, Aila Matanock, Megumi Naoi, Yael Zeira, and Noah Zucker, as well as participants at the 2019 Annual Meeting of the American Political Science Association and the Election Sciences, Reform, and Administration Conference. We also had the opportunity to present the manuscript and obtain valuable feedback on early versions of chapters at seminars at the College of William and Mary, Columbia University, Electoral Integrity Project Speaker Series, New York University, Perry World House at the University of Pennsylvania, Texas A&M University, University of California San Diego (UCSD), University of Chicago, University of Georgia, University of Minnesota, University of Rochester, University of Wisconsin, and Washington University in St. Louis. Early versions of some of our theory and findings about election monitors in Tunisia were published as articles at the *Journal of Politics* and *International Organization*. We are grateful to the reviewers and editors at those journals for helping us improve our research and to those colleagues who provided comments on the articles when they were in draft forms.

As the book progressed, we were lucky enough to convene an incredible group of scholars who took the time to read and discuss the manuscript at a workshop in November 2019 hosted by Yale University. The workshop was generously funded by the Dean's fund at the School of Global Policy and Strategy at UCSD, and the Edward J. and Dorothy Clarke Kempf Memorial Fund and the Georg Walter Leitner Program in International and Comparative Political Economy at Yale University. We received outstanding logistical support for the workshop from Mike Goldfien. Our esteemed discussants included Dawn Brancati, Alex Debs, Susan Hyde, Nuno Monteiro, Jon Pevehouse, Randy Stone, and Dustin Tingley. Their insightful comments strengthened the manuscript in numerous ways and set us on the path to publication. Of course that path became obstructed when the COVID-19 pandemic hit in early 2020. We therefore solicited a second round of feedback on the manuscript in August 2020 from Steph Haggard and Milan Svolik, who graciously agreed to read and comment on the revised book. We are incredibly grateful for their careful reading of the book and generous feedback that got us back on track.

Our data collection enterprise spanned three continents, where we interviewed more than 6,000 survey respondents across six national elections. This work would not have been possible without funding from the National Science Foundation, grant no. 1456505, "Rapid Response Research (RAPID): International Election Observation and Perceptions of Election Credibility", the Bridging the Gap Policy Engagement Fellowship, and the New Initiatives Grant in Election Science from the Massachusetts Institute of Technology Election Data and Science Lab grant and the Madison Initiative of the William and Flora Hewlett Foundation. Sarah benefited from funding as a Lightning Scholar at Perry World House at the University of Pennsylvania and a Summer Research Award and Seed Grant from Temple University. Lauren received a Hellman Fellowship from UCSD in 2018 that supported our field research in Georgia.

To execute this field work, we worked with a number of fantastic practitioners and colleagues. In Tunisia, we benefited greatly from the advice and support of Chantal Berman and Liz Nugent, the logistical and translation services of Intissar Samarat, and the survey expertise of Mohammed Ikbal Elloumi and the team at Elka Consulting. In Georgia, we again benefited from the advice of colleagues: Jesse Driscoll,

Aaron Erlich, Julie George, and Scott Radnitz; the logistical and translation services of Tinatin Genevashvili; and the survey expertise of David Sichinava, Dustin Gilbreath, and the team at the Caucasus Research Resource Center. For both countries, we were assisted in coding media reports of foreign election interventions by Awadh Al Breiki (Tunisia) and Nika Nasrashvili (Georgia). In the United States, we worked with Survey Sampling International (now Dynata) to field our surveys and are grateful for Frank Markowitz's deft handling of our account across several elections. As we finalized the analysis and text, we received fantastic research assistance from Mingpu Xiao, who assisted with the creation of the online appendix,[1] and Chloe Adda, Milan Vivanco, and Arnold Setiadi, who helped with finalizing the text and bibliography.

Finally, we wish to jointly thank our editor at Cambridge University Press, John Haslam, for shepherding the manuscript through the review process as well as the anonymous reviewers who challenged us in many ways to clarify and sharpen our framing and theory. And just when we thought we were as clear and sharp as possible, Kelley Friel came in with her exceptional copy-editing services and found the words to help us reach a broader audience.

We also offer individual thanks. Sarah began this project while on a postdoctoral fellowship at the Harvard Kennedy School and continued working on it while on the faculty first at Temple University and then at Yale University. She has benefitted from the advice of generous and smart colleagues at each institution, especially Vin Arceneaux, Orfeo Fioretos, Mark Pollack, and Hillel Soifer at Temple University and Alex Debs, Nuno Monteiro, Liz Nugent, and Milan Svolik at Yale University. More than anyone, Sarah is grateful to her family: her parents, Julian and the late Grace; her son, Linus; and her husband, David, who has provided so much love and support throughout this project.

In the ten years this project was in development, Lauren went from a graduate student at Stanford University to an associate professor at UCSD. She is grateful for the wisdom imparted by her advisors, mentors, and colleagues at these institutions, especially Lisa Blaydes, Ken Schultz, and Mike Tomz at Stanford University, and Jesse Driscoll, Steph Haggard, Emilie Hafner-Burton, David Lake, Liz

---

[1] www.cambridge.org/bushprather

Lyons, Megumi Naoi, Christina Schneider, Branislav Slantchev, and Barb Walter, at UCSD. It turns out that a decade is also a long time in one's personal life. She dedicates this book to her partner, Lee, without whom none of this would be possible; to her daughters, Madeleine and Rose; and to her parents, Rich and Denise.

Abbreviations

ACME	Average causal mediation effect
ATE	Average treatment effect
AU	African Union
CEELA	Latin American Council of Electoral Experts
CIA	Central Intelligence Agency
CIS	Commonwealth of Independent States
CPR	Congress for the Republic
DIEM	Data on International Election Monitoring
DOJ	Department of Justice
DRC	Democratic Republic of Congo
EMB	Electoral management body
EO	Election observer
EU	European Union
GD	Georgian Dream
IFES	International Foundation for Electoral Systems
IGO	Intergovernmental organization
IR	International relations
IRI	International Republican Institute
ISIE	Independent High Authority for Elections
NDI	National Democratic Institute
NELDA	National Elections Across Democracy and Autocracy Dataset
NGO	Nongovernmental organization
OAS	Organization of American States
OSCE	Organization for Security and Co-operation in Europe
SCO	Shanghai Cooperation Organization
TI	Transparency International
UAE	United Arab Emirates
UN	United Nations
UNM	United National Movement

1 Introduction

From the earliest days of the republic, American leaders worried about foreign influence in US elections. In a letter to Thomas Jefferson in 1787, John Adams wrote, "You are apprehensive of foreign Interference, Intrigue, Influence. So am I. – But, as often as Elections happen, the danger of foreign Influence recurs."[1]

In *Federalist No. 68*, published in 1788, Alexander Hamilton expressed a similar concern that other countries would interfere in US presidential elections. He warned that foreign powers would seek "to gain an improper ascendant in our councils" by elevating "a creature of their own to the chief magistracy of the Union."[2] When George Washington stepped down after two terms as president in 1797, his Farewell Address famously warned about the threat of foreign entanglements, which he called "one of the most baneful foes of republican government."[3]

Yet, the founding fathers failed to anticipate that foreign powers would routinely intervene in elections around the world by the twentieth century. Indeed, since the end of the Cold War, countries have openly *invited* many types of foreign involvement, such as international election observers (EOs) and various forms of electoral assistance. More nefarious forms of foreign influence, similar to the interventions by France and Great Britain to help support friendly candidates during the early days of the American Republic, also continue. And as recently observed in the United States, foreign efforts to influence election outcomes can sometimes be tolerated – or even encouraged.

This book illuminates a critical, but poorly understood, dimension of foreign electoral interventions: how individual citizens respond to

---

[1] Adams (1787).
[2] Hamilton (1788).
[3] Washington (1793).

them. Although foreign actors frequently get involved in an effort to undermine citizens' trust in elections, we know little about how effective such interventions are. For example, intelligence analysts suggest that delegitimizing elections is a central goal of Russia's recent influence operations in the United States.[4] Meanwhile, publicly released evaluations of elections from high-quality international election monitors explicitly aim to "cut through the fog of disinformation" that foreign and domestic actors sometimes attempt to create among the public.[5] But what are the true effects of both types of involvement? Does foreign meddling undermine public perceptions of electoral credibility? And do monitors' reports reach – let alone influence – citizens?

Focusing on the citizen allows us to unravel two sets of puzzles about contemporary foreign influences on elections. First, why do leaders invite (or acquiesce to) foreign involvement? In some cases, democratic candidates welcome illegal help from outside countries, although we might expect it to prompt a public outcry. Governments that do not hold clean elections also behave in surprising ways: Sometimes they invite credible international monitors that are sure to criticize them, yet at other times they welcome sham monitoring groups from nondemocratic countries that are sure to discredit them within the international community. We explore the conditions under which countries involve different types of foreign groups.

The second puzzle is: Why don't the candidates and political parties that win elections do more to respond to credible evidence of foreign meddling or the electoral deficiencies identified by monitors? Many analysts have declared that a nationalist backlash to meddling is almost unavoidable, and that this explains why foreign electoral interventions are usually pursued covertly despite the obstacles associated with executing such operations. But US President Donald Trump was slow to retaliate against Russia despite credible evidence that Moscow interfered in the 2016 presidential election, and preventing foreign interference in the 2020 election remained firmly on the back burner. Indeed, it seems that Republicans and Democrats perceive Russia's involvement very differently. This divergence appears to represent a more general trend, as many types of foreign electoral interventions – including observers' monitoring missions and reports,

---

[4] Coats (2019, 7).
[5] Merloe (2015, 92).

for example – are viewed positively by some audiences and negatively by others. Why?

We argue that understanding (1) leaders' decisions about whether to invite and respond to foreign influences and (2) foreign actors' decisions about whether to intervene in the first place requires determining how these interventions affect citizens. In terms of the former, government leaders seek to maximize their chance of remaining in power. In most countries that hold elections, government stability and legitimacy are based on citizens' belief that elections are a credible mechanism for choosing leaders. Thus, leaders may invite or accept foreign influence (or fail to respond to it) because they believe it will maximize their chances of winning and will not undermine – or, in some cases, may even increase – the election's credibility. Regarding the latter, foreign actors must base their decisions about whether (and how) to intervene in elections on how their involvement will affect the credibility of the election – and how this helps achieve their ultimate goal of either advancing or undermining democracy. Meddlers may decide to intervene covertly if they think their intervention will undermine the legitimacy of their preferred candidate's victory. Relatedly, monitors may consider how the public will receive their statements when they craft their election reports and take care to avoid sparking instability or violence. We discuss the implications of citizens' beliefs about election credibility for governments' and foreign actors' decisions throughout the book and summarize these causal processes in a simplified model in Figure 1.1.

Although governments' and foreign actors' decisions are likely to be guided by what they expect the public's reaction to be, as suggested in Figure 1.1, few studies have identified what these effects are. This book therefore develops a bottom-up "theory of the citizen" to explain how foreign actors shape public perceptions of the credibility of elections. We define a *credible election* as one in which people trust the results and believe the outcome reflects the will of the people.[6] We draw on insights from political science and other social science disciplines such as psychology to argue that foreign interventions can change individuals' level of trust in their country's electoral institutions, but only under certain conditions. We acknowledge that such interference is not always unwelcome: Some foreign actors, such as international election

---

[6] Bush and Prather (2017, 922).

Governments decide whether to accept/invite foreign electoral interventions

Foreign actors decide whether and how to intervene in the election

Citizens update beliefs about election credibility and decide how to politically engage

Figure 1.1 Key relationships between government decisions, foreign actors' decisions, and citizens' beliefs around election day
Note: We directly theorize and test the relationships indicated by solid lines. Our findings also have implications for the relationships denoted by dashed lines. As we discuss next, some foreign interventions in elections are not invited by governments. In such cases, foreign actors bypass the first step in this chain.

monitors, can enhance individuals' trust, and other foreign actors, such as states that are trying to swing elections in support of favored candidates, do not always diminish it. Three factors determine whether outside influences enhance or diminish trust: (1) *who* is intervening, (2) *which* political party individuals support, and (3) *where* the election takes place. We briefly introduce each factor before describing the study's case studies.

First, foreign actors have their strongest effects when locals believe they have the capability (and willingness) to influence elections. Sometimes it is surprising which foreign actors are perceived as being capable of doing so. For example in Tunisia, observers from the Arab League were the most likely to enhance trust, even though most analysts and international audiences tend to be skeptical of them since they mainly come from undemocratic countries. That undemocratic observers can legitimize elections in the eyes of the public helps us understand why governments invite them despite the risk of international ridicule.

Second, people respond to foreign interventions in highly partisan ways. Those who support winning candidates and parties (i.e., election winners) *never* significantly update their beliefs about the credibility of elections in response to outside interventions. However, election losers are quite receptive to new information that might cause them to lose faith in the election results, whether from international monitors that have criticized the election or from reports about foreign meddling. In other words, foreign interventions tend to polarize citizens' beliefs about election credibility, exacerbating differences in electoral trust between winners and losers.

Third, foreign actors have their strongest effects when there is uncertainty about an election's integrity. Uncertainty is more likely in countries that are holding transitional elections, but it can exist in stable countries as well.

Our findings are based on large, national surveys in three countries with distinct regime types: Georgia, Tunisia, and the United States. We focus on a small number of cases so we can implement in-depth surveys with three key features. First, we interviewed the same individuals immediately before and after elections, which allows us to examine how interventions and election outcomes shape their beliefs about an election's credibility. Second, the surveys include experiments designed to identify the effects of foreign actors; this approach addresses the challenge that monitors may be prone to observe elections with more integrity, and meddlers may be more likely to interfere in elections that have less integrity to begin with. Third, our surveys shed light on the dual role of the United States as both a site of intervention and a key intervener (it sponsored monitors in Georgia and Tunisia and was rumored to have meddled in both countries' elections). Like other countries, including Russia, the US experience as the target of foreign electoral interventions may shape the public's views about instigating electoral interventions going forward.

Our cases differ in terms of culture and institutions but share recent histories as the sites of substantial outside interventions. They allow us to examine how foreign actors shape perceptions of election credibility in a consolidated democracy (the United States, 2016–2020), a transitional democracy (Tunisia, 2014), and a partial democracy (Georgia, 2018). By studying diverse cases, we can investigate the effects of monitors and meddlers in countries that are at least partially democratic. Although our surveys are the heart of the book's empirical contribution, we also analyze other quantitative datasets[7] and draw on qualitative materials identified through desk research

---

[7] These datasets include the World Values Survey, National Elections Across Democracy and Autocracy dataset, and the Data on International Election Monitoring.

(e.g., election monitoring reports and manuals, news articles, and intelligence reports) and field research (e.g., interviews with international and domestic election monitors, election management officials, civil society organizations, and focus groups).

Since citizens' trust in elections affects whether they turn out to vote or participate in post-election protests, among other outcomes, the book's findings help us understand how foreign interventions influence the shape of politics in the countries where they occur. They also advance our understanding of a much broader topic: whether and how international politics affect domestic politics. A great deal of attention has been devoted to studying the international sources of general cross-country trends related to democracy, stability, resistance, and violence. We show that foreign electoral interventions – and perhaps foreign influences more broadly – contribute to the polarization of domestic audiences. Given the threat that polarization is increasingly thought to pose to democracy, our findings suggest new ways in which foreign interventions affect countries' overall trajectories by influencing ordinary citizens' political attitudes.

Our findings also shed light on why policymakers engage with foreign actors near elections in the ways that they do, including sometimes inviting or tolerating outside influence in puzzling ways. Although meddling can cause election losers to question their faith in democratic institutions, it does not appear to shake the faith of election winners enough to prompt policy action. Thus, partisan interventions by outside powers have the potential to undermine core democratic processes.

1.1 How Foreign Actors Intervene in Elections

As John Adams feared in 1787, foreign influences on elections are pervasive. In today's globalized world, events beyond a country's borders influence its economy, politics, and society – and can indirectly shape its elections, too. Indeed, prior studies have explored how foreign influences on domestic politics have the potential to affect elections *indirectly*, for example, through foreign governments' lobbying of elected officials,[8] foreign aid programs and loans,[9] and the actions of

[8] Pevehouse and Vabulas (2019).
[9] Stone (2004); Jablonski (2014).

intergovernmental organizations (IGOs) like the European Union (EU) that are engaged in promoting and enforcing democratic norms over the long term.[10] The evolving ways in which countries are interconnected make this strand of the literature an important and interesting area for future inquiry, particularly as foreign interventions relate to citizens. This book focuses on how foreign actors' *direct* interventions in elections affect citizens' perceptions of an election's credibility. Thus, we exclude various indirect forms of foreign influence that have the potential to significantly influence domestic politics but are not focused on elections *per se*.

Past research on direct interventions in elections typically focuses on either *democracy-promoting* or *democracy-undermining* interventions. Scholars of the former have examined why and how states pursue democracy promotion, including election monitoring and its effects on election quality.[11] Prior studies of the latter have assessed the supply and effects of partisan electoral interventions, which seek to undermine democracy by influencing citizens' free and fair choice of elected representatives.[12]

Few scholars have combined both types of interventions under the same theoretical umbrella. The most recent example is Johannes Bubeck and Nikolay Marinov's research on foreign electoral interventions, which investigates foreign actors' decisions to intervene in other countries' elections.[13] They argue that such decisions represent a combination of two choices: (1) whether to intervene in the democratic process and (2) whether to support a specific candidate or party. Both decisions can either enhance or undermine democracy. Their emphasis on foreign actors' decisions to intervene in the process, for a candidate, or both has shed considerable light on questions about interveners' strategies. Our work builds on the foundation of their research with a focus on how foreign actors intervene in the democratic process in diverse ways (which can make the electoral playing field either more or less fair) as we develop a theory of citizens' perceptions of elections.

We argue that understanding the effects on citizens requires considering the domestic government's choice to invite, accept, or reject

---

[10] Kelley (2004); Pevehouse (2005); Vachudova (2005).
[11] See, for example, Pevehouse (2005), Hyde (2011), Kelley (2012b), Donno (2013), Bush (2015), and von Borzyskowski (2019a).
[12] See, for example, Levin (2020).
[13] Bubeck and Marinov (2019).

Table 1.1 *Types of foreign influences on elections*

	Invited by the Government	Not Invited by the Government
Makes playing field fairer	Example: high-quality international election observers	Example: IGO punishment of countries violating electoral integrity norms
Makes playing field less fair	Example: "zombie" international election observers	Example: foreign disinformation campaigns that occur without invitation

the intervention. As Susan Hyde has argued in the context of election monitoring, inviting monitors can signal to the international community that the incumbent intends not to cheat in an election.[14] We extend this logic, noting that domestic governments play a role in inviting, accepting, or rejecting all types of outside electoral interventions, which serves as a signal to citizens of their commitment to democracy (or lack thereof).

We therefore classify direct foreign electoral interventions along two dimensions (Table 1.1 describes them in more detail). First, such interventions make the electoral playing field either more or less fair. Second, some foreign electoral interventions are invited by the government, whereas others are not. While foreign influences on elections could be classified in other ways, such as according to the type of actor involved or the point in the electoral cycle at which they occur, these two dimensions are the most relevant for our theory of the citizen.

The first dimension along which we classify foreign influences on elections is how fair or unfair that influence makes the electoral playing field. In a fair electoral playing field, the electoral outcome reflects the will of the people.[15] Many domestic institutions and practices can contribute to a fair electoral playing field, from those that ensure citizens have a genuine choice in the election to those that govern vote counting and guarantee that citizens can vote freely and safely. Foreign actors also play a role.

[14] Hyde (2011).
[15] Birch (2011, 14).

Given how important competitive elections are to democracy, we consider any foreign intervention in an election that seeks to make the playing field fairer to be a form of *democracy promotion* and any foreign intervention to make the playing field less fair to be a form of *meddling*.[16]

The second dimension that is important to understanding foreign influences on elections is whether the government invites or accepts the intervention. As we elucidate in the summary of our argument, this characteristic is central to our theory because such an invitation can provide information to citizens about whether incumbents intend to cheat.

A quintessential example of a foreign intervention that helps make the playing field fairer and is invited by the government is high-quality international election observation.[17] Most countries today invite international EOs to monitor their elections.[18] The first international EOs were perhaps a group of European representatives that observed elections in the disputed territories of Moldovia and Wallachia in 1857 as part of the Treaty of Paris.[19] It was a long time before inviting international EOs became a global norm.

The number of national elections monitored by international EOs increased significantly during the second half of the twentieth century and especially after the end of the Cold War. During that time, the proportion of elections being observed by international monitors grew significantly, reaching around 80 percent in 2015, the most recent year for which we have reliable data.[20] The rising demand for international

---

[16] Both terms represent much broader categories that encompass many other activities that are not directly related to elections. For instance, other democracy promotion activities include most forms of democracy assistance and many actions taken by IGOs (Vachudova 2005; Bush 2015), and other examples of meddling include longer-term efforts to support a favored political party, such as through economic relations and diplomacy (Bush and Prather 2020). Others may also use "meddling" as a pejorative to describe more or even *all* types of foreign influences on elections and domestic politics.

[17] Other examples of activities that fall into this quadrant of Table 1.1 include some forms of international electoral assistance. For example, Nigerian President Goodluck Jonathan welcomed technical assistance from the UN Development Programme to create a much-needed new voter registry in advance of the 2011 elections (Lührmann 2019, 9).

[18] Hyde (2011); Kelley (2012b).

[19] Kelley (2012a, 205).

[20] See Chapter 4 for more details.

election observation is related to the "third wave of democratization" as well as the increase in rewards since the end of the Cold War for countries recognized as adhering to democratic norms, such as foreign aid and IGO membership.[21]

Governments invite high-quality EOs to monitor their elections from IGOs such as the Organization for Security and Co-operation in Europe (OSCE) or the Organization of American States (OAS) and from nongovernmental organizations (NGOs) such as the Carter Center or the International Republican Institute (IRI), both of which are headquartered in the United States. These organizations send both long- and short-term teams that observe and report on the quality of elections. Multiple international organizations often observe a single election.[22] Although high-quality EOs are not without their biases and flaws,[23] they generally contribute to a fairer electoral playing field by making it more difficult for incumbents to steal an election. They do so by collecting information about election integrity, reporting on any irregularities they find, and increasing the costs of cheating through publicizing electoral malpractice. For example, observers from the OSCE and other organizations are commonly thought to have played an important role in the early 2000s in the post-Soviet Color Revolutions, helping to expose fraud and mobilize citizens in the post-election protests that led to regime change in previously authoritarian countries such as Georgia and Ukraine.[24] Yet, there are no direct analyses of how monitors affected public attitudes in these (and other) influential cases. Our work sheds light on whether foreign organizations were likely to have influenced citizens' perceptions of election credibility in a way that led to the collapse of these regimes.

A good example of a foreign intervention that helps make the playing field fairer but is not specifically invited by the government is IGO enforcement of electoral integrity norms in countries that violate them. Countries sometimes join IGOs such as the EU or OAS that have stated commitments to democracy and are later punished when their elections do not meet international standards for being free and fair. IGOs can attempt to enforce election integrity norms

---

[21] Huntington (1991); Kelley (2004); Vachudova (2005).
[22] Kelley (2009b).
[23] Kelley (2009a); Kavakli and Kuhn (2020).
[24] Fawn (2006, 1139–1140); Beissinger (2007, 261); Bunce and Wolchik (2007); Tucker (2007).

via conditionality (i.e., actual or threatened sanctions), diplomacy and mediation missions, and shaming.[25] Under the right conditions, IGO enforcement around elections seems to have the potential to influence citizens' perceptions of election credibility. By loudly criticizing the flawed 1994 general election in the Dominican Republic, for example, the OAS "validated the opposition's claims that tens of thousands of its voters had been disenfranchised," ultimately prompting the incumbent president Joaquín Balaguer to hold early (cleaner) elections and step down.[26]

Other examples of activities that fall into this quadrant of Table 1.1 include some forms of democracy assistance that do not involve cooperation with the government, such as training high-quality domestic EOs. Some people criticize activities in this quadrant as being a form of outside interference since they are not invited by the government, whereas others object to such a characterization on the grounds that such activities are consistent with international norms (Melia 2018; National Democratic Institute 2018a).

Foreign interventions that undermine the fairness of the electoral playing field can also vary according to whether the government invites them. Although some governments opt to invite high-quality international EOs to monitor their elections as described earlier, others ask low-quality international EOs that seek to undermine the democratic process. These "zombie" EOs are sent by groups such as the Commonwealth of Independent States (CIS), a Russia-led IGO that has monitored elections in authoritarian countries such as Azerbaijan and Belarus. Although zombie observers attempt to mimic higher-quality EOs, they are better understood as a form of foreign election meddling since they seek to tilt the playing field in the government's favor.[27] Zombie international EOs monitor elections in authoritarian countries with the goal of strengthening the position of the incumbent nondemocratic government by being present and issuing and publicizing positive reports about the highly flawed elections they observe. Incumbent governments may invite them to enhance public perceptions of an election's credibility.[28]

---

[25] Donno (2010, 597).
[26] Donno (2013, 3).
[27] Walker and Cooley (2013).
[28] Debre and Morgenbesser (2017).

Election meddling also occurs in a variety of other forms. States play a larger role in election meddling, while nonstate actors are active in many domains of democracy promotion such as high-quality election observation. It is very difficult to determine how frequently meddling occurs since it is often done secretly, but it is almost certainly less common than monitoring. However, it is not a rare event. Some of the best data on this topic come from Dov Levin. According to his calculations, "Between 1946 and 2000, the United States and the Soviet Union/Russia have intervened in about one of every nine competitive national-level executive elections."[29] His data show that election meddling was common during the Cold War; well-known examples include interventions by both the United States and the Soviet Union during elections in Italy in 1948 and Chile in 1964. Since the end of the Cold War, the United States has remained active in some Latin American countries, such as its opposition to Chavismo in Venezuela since 1999, and Russia has meddled in numerous European democracies' elections and in its near abroad.[30] Election meddling goes back at least to the 1796 US presidential election, in which France expressed its disappointment in the victory of (pro-Britain) John Adams over (pro-French) Thomas Jefferson with a decree ordering the French navy to prevent US trade with Europe.[31]

Other forms of election meddling are also invited by the government they are intended to help. For example, the Russian government provided support to incumbent Ukrainian Prime Minister Viktor Yanukovych in 2004 in a variety of ways, including by directly funding his campaign. This campaign also featured government-invited zombie monitors; CIS observers (and Russian President Vladimir Putin) prominently endorsed the results of an election that other, more reputable, international observers had criticized.[32] Zombie monitors thus obscured the clear signal that reputable monitors sent to citizens about the poor quality of the election.

---

[29] See Chapter 5 for more details.
[30] Gill (2018); Way and Casey (2018).
[31] DeConde (1958).
[32] McFaul (2007, 70).

A good example of a foreign intervention that makes the playing field *less* fair and may not be invited is a disinformation campaign.[33] A disinformation campaign during an election entails spreading false information about a candidate or the election as a whole. Disinformation was part of the US intervention in Chile's 1964 presidential election, which has been described as the "peak" of electoral interventions by the Central Intelligence Agency (CIA). The CIA authorized a range of covert and illegal activities from propaganda and disinformation to vote buying in support of the United States' favored candidate, Eduardo Frei Montalva, who was running against the socialist candidate Salvador Allende in an election to replace outgoing President Jorge Alessandri.[34] This effort is estimated to have cost a total of $3 million (or $25 million in 2020 dollars), including covering over half of Frei's campaign expenses.[35] The US Senate's Church Committee later acknowledged that the US government's disinformation campaign in support of Frei included "'black propaganda' – material which purported to originate from another source, such as the Chilean Communist Party."[36] If disinformation campaigns are discovered and become public knowledge, they have the potential to decrease the credibility of elections among citizens.

Given these myriad types of foreign influences on elections, the same election can often feature competing and complementary foreign interventions. The same country can use multiple tools, and multiple countries can use the same (or competing) tools.

Sometimes, states or IGOs use multiple tools of influence at the same time to influence the electoral playing field in a similar way. For example, a state might support a high-quality international EO mission (an invited intervention) *and* provide funding for domestic nongovernmental efforts designed to promote electoral integrity (an intervention that is not necessarily invited by the government, though it may be legal and thus permitted by the government). During Moldova's 2019 parliamentary election, for example, the US government provided funding to the National Democratic Institute (NDI), an international NGO,

---

[33] Disinformation campaigns may also be invited. Another activity that fits into this category is attempting to harm a disfavored candidate, such as by physically attacking them.
[34] Shimer (2020, 48, 52).
[35] Ibid., 53.
[36] Church Committee (1975, 15).

for two purposes: to provide high-quality EOs and to maintain a long-term presence in the country. Prior to the election, the NDI office there "supported nonpartisan groups in promoting the integrity of elections through monitoring and advised youth initiatives on solving community problems and increasing the turnout of young voters."[37] NDI also encouraged women's participation in the election as candidates and voters. All of these efforts could be considered as supporting the overall goal of a fair electoral playing field in Moldova, though they varied in their relationship with the government.

The same country occasionally uses multiple tools of foreign influence in *competing* ways to affect the fairness of the electoral playing field. For example, during the 2006 Palestinian legislative election, the US government took steps to both advance the general democratic process (i.e., to make the electoral playing field fairer) and to support the electoral chances of a particular party (i.e., to tilt the playing field and thus make it less fair). The American government initially pressured the Palestinian National Authority (PNA) to hold democratic elections, as "US policymakers were convinced that the [earlier] Oslo [peace] process had failed because Palestinians were not democratic enough."[38] US government-funded NGOs, such as NDI, were present alongside the EU and other international observers seeking to encourage a fair electoral process at the invitation of the PNA. Yet, the US government also clearly had a favored side: the ruling party Fatah, not Hamas, the militant faction that ended up winning. To increase Fatah's electoral odds in advance of the election, the US Agency for International Development spent around $2 million on "dozens of quick projects...to bolster the governing Fatah faction's image with voters."[39] The Bush administration recognized Hamas's electoral victory, reflecting international observers' largely positive assessments of the integrity of the electoral process. Yet soon afterwards, the United States coordinated with other members of the international community to impose economic sanctions against Palestine and took further covert steps to try to return Fatah to power.[40]

---

[37] National Democratic Institute (2019).
[38] Jamal (2012, 192).
[39] Erlanger (2006, A11).
[40] Rose (2008).

Competing foreign actors may also try to influence the same election in opposite ways, in what has been called an "election war."[41] Whereas election wars between the United States and the Soviet Union were rare during the Cold War,[42] they have since become more frequent between the United States and Russia – for instance over multiple post-Soviet elections in Ukraine.[43] They have also featured as elements of other regional and global power struggles. In elections held since the Arab uprisings of 2011, Qatar has used its economic influence to support Islamist parties in Egypt and Tunisia, while Saudi Arabia and the United Arab Emirates have sought to support secular parties and leaders there.[44] In addition to foreign countries taking opposing sides in the same election, there are also cases in which one set of foreign actors seeks to make the electoral playing field fairer, and a different set of foreign actors attempts to have the opposite effect. For example, the 2004 Ukraine election mentioned earlier included high-quality international monitors such as the OSCE that sought to expose fraud and make the election more democratic, while Russian meddling sought to undermine the electoral playing field to benefit Yanukovych.

1.2 Why Interveners Seek to Influence Citizens

This book explores how the foreign electoral interventions described previously affect citizens' perceptions of election credibility. In addition to accepting or inviting foreign electoral interventions, domestic political actors can take various actions to influence citizens' perceptions; Americans need only to think of Donald Trump's efforts to undermine the credibility of the 2020 election that Joe Biden won and the January 2021 insurrection that followed. We concentrate here, however, on domestic political actors' decisions vis-à-vis foreign actors. This shift in focus is needed due to the prevalence of foreign electoral interventions, which governments and foreign actors themselves believe have potentially significant effects on citizens. Although domestic actors' attempts to shape public opinion may sometimes be more powerful than foreign actors' efforts, we do not expect that this is always the case, and

[41] Bubeck and Marinov (2017, 536).
[42] Levin (2019a, 99).
[43] Bubeck and Marinov (2017, 547–548).
[44] Cherif (2014, 2017); Trager (2017); Bush and Prather (2020).

our analysis of election monitors supports this assumption. The public may (sometimes accurately) view domestic leaders' efforts to promote or undermine credibility skeptically due to domestic actors' recognized stakes in the election outcome.

As Figure 1.1 models, both domestic governments' and foreign actors' actions related to monitoring and meddling have the potential to influence citizens' beliefs about election credibility. Domestic governments often invite or accept foreign electoral interventions to increase public perceptions of credibility.[45] In uncertain electoral environments, governments that do not intend to cheat may seek the assistance of high-quality EOs that can communicate to citizens (and to the international community) that an election was free and fair. Governments that *intend* to cheat may invite low-quality EOs. If citizens cannot distinguish between high- and low-quality monitors, a cheating incumbent can attempt to use zombie monitors to convince the public that a flawed election was fair. Chapters 2 and 4 provide examples of governments strategically publicizing election monitors' activities.

Both monitors and meddlers seek to influence citizens' beliefs about an election's credibility. According to the Declaration of Principles for International Election Observation, high-quality international EOs believe they influence both the electoral playing field and citizens' perceptions of it:

International election observation has the potential to enhance the integrity of election processes, by deterring and exposing irregularities and fraud and by providing recommendations for improving electoral processes. It can promote public confidence, as warranted, promote electoral participation and mitigate the potential for election-related conflict.[46]

These are not just empty words. Chapter 4 discusses numerous examples of high-quality EOs from Europe and the United States declining invitations to monitor elections because they do not want to promote public confidence in an election when it is not warranted. Moreover, monitors tend to blunt their criticism of elections that they anticipate

---

[45] Doing so could have unintended effects, for instance, if the government invites a foreign actor to covertly meddle in the election to maximize the incumbent's chance of winning and the meddling inadvertently becomes public knowledge and undermines the legitimacy of his or her victory.
[46] *Declaration of Principles for International Election Observation* (2005, 2).

could involve violence to avoid emboldening citizen groups that seek to challenge the regime by reinforcing perceptions that an election was not fair.[47]

Although meddlers, by definition, generally seek to swing an election in favor of their preferred candidate or party, they often do so as part of a concerted effort to undermine citizens' trust in the electoral process. Or they may be indirectly interested in the credibility of the election because they want an ally to win without jeopardizing the legitimacy of the election. Meddlers may therefore interfere covertly and may be directly interested in influencing the credibility of fair elections. Indeed, diminishing citizens' trust in elections is a welcome outcome for autocratic meddlers even if their desired election result is not achieved. For instance, Way and Casey (2018, 1) demonstrated that the Russian government's electoral interventions in the West since 2015 have sought to undermine democracy, and one mechanism for achieving that aim is to cause ordinary citizens to question the credibility of elections that are generally free and fair. As we discuss in Chapter 5, US intelligence agencies have concluded that these goals characterized Russian meddling in the 2016 US election in particular. More recently, after the 2021 summit between Presidents Biden and Putin, Russian media analysts reported that Russian state media claimed that the January 6, 2021, insurrection was evidence that Russian meddling had successfully sown distrust in elections, and that Moscow should continue to try to influence American public opinion.[48]

Governments and foreign actors thus seek to influence public attitudes. But do they succeed? Given the significance of citizens' perceptions of election credibility, it is important to find out if they do, as we explore in Section 1.3.

1.3 Why Citizens' Perceptions of Election Credibility Matter

As noted previously, we conceptualize perceptions of election credibility as reflecting both individuals' trust in the results of the election and their belief that the outcome reflects the will of the people. This two-part definition recognizes that an election with integrity requires both a fair process on election day *and* a fair environment and political

---

[47] Kelley (2009a).
[48] Davis (2021).

institutions over the longer term. For example, citizens might believe the announced election winner is consistent with the public's preferences but question whether the reported margin of victory is accurate. This dynamic may reflect how the public thinks about elections in popular authoritarian regimes, such as that of the Partido Revolucionario Institucional (PRI) in Mexico or Putin's Russia, as well as in consolidated democracies where the public nevertheless has concerns about vote tabulation.[49] By contrast, if election day occurs without fraud but takes place within a fundamentally closed political environment, citizens might rightfully perceive it to lack credibility given that the free will of the people could not be expressed, even though the votes may have been counted accurately in the strictest sense. For example, international observers positively evaluated Armenia's election day procedures in 2007 and 2008[50] but concluded that the pre-election campaign and media environment were skewed in favor of the ruling party.

Therefore, to measure perceptions of election credibility in practice, we use surveys that ask respondents two separate questions (described further in Chapter 3): One asks about their trust in the election result and the other about their belief that the outcome reflects the will of the people. We could ask these questions in a straightforward manner because our cases do not include authoritarian regimes where respondents might consider them sensitive. Although conceptually distinct, the responses to these questions are highly correlated. We average the answers to both questions to create a single measure of election credibility to use in our main analysis, noting instances where our results are stronger on one dimension of election credibility than the other. Chapter 3 discusses our measurement approach and its strengths and limitations in more detail.

Although individuals' perceptions of election credibility are related to more objective measures of election *quality*,[51] these two concepts are distinct. Sometimes individuals question the integrity of a largely free and fair election, while at other times, people may accept the results of an election characterized by widespread fraud. Illustrating

---

[49] Robertson (2017, 602).

[50] For example, the OSCE said they were "largely in accordance with OSCE commitments" in 2007. Quoted in Simpser and Donno (2012, 502).

[51] Norris (2013a).

the potential disjuncture between perceptions and reality, we show later in this book (in Chapter 4) that Americans in our surveys tended to express less confidence in their elections than Tunisians did, even though the United States is widely considered to have democratic (though by no means perfect) elections, whereas Tunisia was a transitional democracy at the time of our surveys. Thus, we do not assume that it is necessarily normatively desirable to convince citizens that elections are credible, as it might entail instilling confidence in a flawed contest.

For many political outcomes that matter to governments (and foreign actors), citizens' *perceptions* of election credibility are the most important because they shape citizens' degree of acceptance of the political system and decisions about when (and how) to participate in politics.[52] A substantial body of research finds that individuals' trust in elections affects their likelihood of participating in politics in two ways: through *regular* means such as voting and through *irregular* means such as protesting. Perceived credibility thus has at least three important effects.

The first is that when citizens believe elections are credible, they are more likely to turn out to vote and to engage in the regular political process in other ways as well, such as by volunteering for a campaign or contacting an elected official. Surveys in a variety of global settings have established a positive correlation between perceptions of election quality and voter turnout.[53] The causal logic is intuitive: If people think the outcome of an election has already been determined, there is less reason for them to go to the effort of campaigning for a candidate, voting, and so on.

The second important effect of perceived credibility is that when citizens believe their elections are *not* credible, they are more likely to participate in postelection protests. Although elections perceived to be untrustworthy can lead to political disengagement by decreasing voter turnout, they can also encourage people to look for ways to make their voice heard outside the normal political system. Again, the causal logic is straightforward: When people believe elections are not credible, they are less likely to perceive the government as legitimate and therefore become more willing to protest against it.

---

[52] Daxecker, Salvatore, and Ruggeri (2019).
[53] Birch (2010); Norris (2013b, Ch. 7).

Analysts often cite the Color Revolutions that erupted in the early 2000s in multiple former Soviet-bloc countries as examples of this phenomenon, although perceptions of election credibility are also linked to protest willingness in the Arab world[54] and sub-Saharan Africa.[55] The Color Revolutions involved the diffusion of a similar model of protests in Serbia (Bulldozer Revolution in 2000), Georgia (Rose Revolution in 2003), Ukraine (Orange Revolution in 2004), and Kyrgyzstan (Tulip Revolution in 2005).[56] Although these and other countries in the region had held flawed elections for some time, newfound opposition tactics enabled antiregime activists to gain more ground than in past election cycles.[57] The revolutions were triggered by large-scale public demonstrations after major election fraud, which focused on public attention and helped dissatisfied citizens overcome the collective action problem.[58] In Serbia, for example, internationally supported domestic observers provided credible evidence that opposition candidate Vojislav Koštunica had secured enough votes to defeat Slobodan Milošević in the September 2000 presidential election; official tallies had declared Milošević the winner. Believing the election had been stolen, Serbians began to demonstrate, culminating in more than a million protesters gathering in Belgrade on October 5. Milošević admitted defeat the next day.[59]

The third and final important effect of perceived credibility that we consider follows from the first two. Because perceptions of election credibility shape individual-level political behaviors such as voting and participation in protests, they also have knock-on effects for democracy. Regular political participation through voting is critical for democratic quality (not to mention election outcomes). That is one reason why growing public concerns about election integrity in several advanced industrial democracies, including the United States, have prompted worries about the future of democracy there.[60]

Meanwhile, election-related protests can have both positive and negative effects on democracy, as they can oust corrupt regimes but

---

[54] Williamson (2021).
[55] Daxecker, Salvatore, and Ruggeri (2019).
[56] Beissinger (2007).
[57] Bunce and Wolchik (2007).
[58] Tucker (2007).
[59] Donno (2013, 138–139).
[60] Norris (2018); Norris, Cameron, and Wynter (2018); Berlinski et al. (2021).

also unleash processes that lead to repression and violence. On the one hand, the threat of protest is crucial to the idea of self-enforcing democracy[61] and can lead to democratic revolutions, as the Serbia case illustrates. On the other hand, governments that fear losing power are more likely to violently suppress election-related protests.[62] For example, the government of Azerbaijan cracked down violently on opposition supporters who protested the results of the country's flawed 2005 parliamentary election to prevent a revolution.[63] These dynamics of protest and violence are especially likely in competitive authoritarian regimes, as demonstrated by the crisis that occurred in Kenya after its flawed election in 2007 led to widespread killings and displacement. The popular mobilization that flawed elections can spur is therefore linked to both normatively desirable outcomes (ousting corrupt regimes that rig elections) as well as troubling ones (government repression, large-scale violence, and even civil war).

Thus far, we have considered the effects of perceptions of election credibility through a review of previous research. We can also consider this topic using evidence from our own surveys. Since none of the elections we studied for this book were followed by significant post-election protests, we focus on more regular forms of political participation.

In all three countries, we asked people after the elections about their perceptions of election credibility and their plans to engage in various political activities in the future, including voting. Despite significant differences in intentions to participate across the cases, when people perceived the recent election to be more credible, they were always significantly more likely to report planning to engage in future political activities, even when controlling for other factors that could confound this relationship.[64] In Tunisia, for example, we conducted our first survey after the 2014 parliamentary election and the second using the

---

[61] Weingast (1997); Przeworski (2006); Fearon (2011). For a discussion of how international actors can contribute to this process, see Hyde and Marinov (2014).

[62] Daxecker (2012); von Borzyskowski (2019b).

[63] Hafner-Burton, Hyde, and Jablonski (2014, 149–150).

[64] These factors include age, gender, education, political knowledge, income, party identification, and satisfaction with democracy. The online appendix (www.cambridge.org/bushprather) includes a table containing this analysis as well as a description of the political participation measure. For a fuller explanation of how we measure perceived election credibility, see Chapter 3.

same sample a few months after the presidential election held later the same year. A one-standard-deviation increase in the perceived credibility of the parliamentary election was associated with a 28 percent increase in the odds of having reported voting a few months later in the presidential election.[65]

The relationship between perceived credibility and voting is not unique to the transitional environment of Tunisia in 2014. We also conducted a survey before the 2018 US Congressional election in which we asked all respondents how credible they thought it would be, and if they would be willing to sign an online pledge to vote in the election. US political campaigns and NGOs often use voting pledges as mobilization tools because they are thought to commit individuals to vote. For respondents who expressed an interest in making such a pledge, we provided links to three nonpartisan American organizations with online voting pledges at the end of the survey.[66] Our survey platform tracked whether respondents clicked on these links. We found that a one-standard-deviation increase in perceived election credibility increased the odds of clicking on at least one of the voting pledge campaign links by 25 percent.[67] This positive effect is precisely what we expected: People are more likely to want to participate in a political process if they believe their participation will matter.

When we examine a broader set of cases, similar patterns emerge. Figure 1.2 uses data from the seventh wave of the World Values Survey, which polled representative samples of the public in forty-nine diverse countries between 2017 and 2020 on a variety of political and social topics. It shows that people who reported that they trusted their

---

[65] $p < 0.01$. This analysis controls for the same variables referenced in the previous footnote. Respondents could have overreported voting in the presidential election because voting is socially desirable. However, the 65 percent turnout rate in our nationally representative survey was identical to that reported by the Independent High Authority for Elections in Tunisia for Tunisians in the country at the time, and the reported vote share for the winning candidate in our survey closely matched the official result. See Instance Supérieure Indépendante pour les Élections (Tunisia) (2014c). A table containing this analysis is in the online appendix (www.cambridge.org/bushprather).

[66] These organizations included two youth-oriented campaigns (Inspire US and Rock the Vote) and one senior-oriented campaign (AARP, formerly an abbreviation for the American Association of Retired Persons).

[67] $p = 0.05$. This analysis controls for the same variables referenced earlier. A table containing this analysis is in the online appendix (www.cambridge.org/bushprather).

country's elections (on a scale of 1–4 that captures part of our concept of election credibility) were more likely to report that they were satisfied with its political system (on a 1–10 scale). They were also more likely to report that they tended to vote in their country's national elections (coded from 1 to 3).[68] There are important limits to these data and analysis. For instance, the surveys were not generally conducted close to election day, and it is difficult to establish causal relationships between variables measured in the same survey. Nevertheless, Figure 1.2 supports the logic that perceptions of election credibility affect how legitimate citizens perceive their political system to be, and therefore how willing they are to turn out to vote – and likely how willing they are to engage in protests as well.

In summary, the book's theory and findings about foreign actors' effects on perceptions of election credibility have important implications for our understanding of countries' long-term trends related to democratization and democratic backsliding. Foreign interventions can contribute to democratic progress in at least two ways. First, incumbents who are sincerely committed to democracy can invite high-quality foreign election monitors to elections. Their presence may improve the quality of the election, engage the international community in the country's democratic trajectory in supportive ways, and increase citizens' perceptions of election credibility, leading to more engagement of the type that is likely to consolidate democracy. Second, high-quality foreign election monitors can provide information about flawed elections that triggers irregular forms of political engagement, such as protests demanding pro-democracy institutional changes. In this way, some foreign interventions can move public perceptions of election credibility closer to the actual level of election quality and spur democratization and democratic consolidation.

---

[68] The specific questions were Q222 ("When elections take place, do you vote always, usually or never? Please tell me separately for each of the following levels: National level"), Q224 ("In your view, how often do the following things occur in this country's elections? Votes are counted fairly"), and Q252 ("On a scale from 1 to 10 where '1' is 'not satisfied at all' and '10' is 'completely satisfied', how satisfied are you with how the political system is functioning in your country these days?"). In the figure on trust in elections and voting, we exclude countries with enforced compulsory voting between 2017 and 2020 (the years of the World Values Survey). Information on compulsory voting comes from International IDEA (2021).

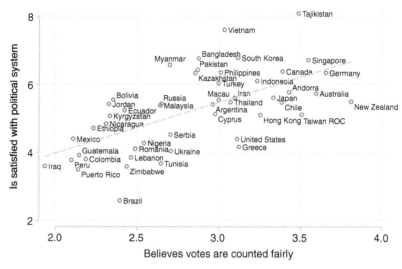

(a) Trust in elections and political satisfaction

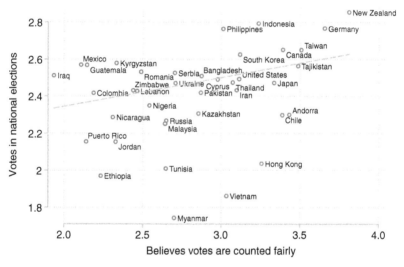

(b) Trust in elections and voting

Figure 1.2 The correlations between (a) trust in elections, political satisfaction, and (b) voting, 2017–2020
Note: Data are from Inglehart et al. (2020).

However, foreign interventions can also undermine democracy. Meddling is an anti-democratic intervention by definition, but all types of interventions have the potential to jeopardize democracy through their effects on perceptions of election credibility. We find that interventions increase the gap between winners' and losers' perceptions of election credibility, which contributes to polarization and thus poses challenges for democracy.[69] Polarization is not an exclusively negative force, as it can "strengthen party brands and clarify voters' choices"[70] and "produce stronger party organizations," especially in developing democracies.[71] At the same time, polarization makes it more difficult for elites to cooperate – an essential task, especially in transitional democracies – and may insulate them from getting voted out for violating democratic norms.[72] Although accurately informing at least some individuals about election credibility (as credible election monitors do) may be considered valuable in and of itself, this dynamic is not an unalloyed good insofar as it contributes to polarization.

Interventions can also widen the gap between election quality and perceptions of election credibility in ways that are problematic for democracy. For example, if nondemocratic incumbents are worried about citizens' negative reactions to flawed elections, they may invite low-quality zombie election monitors to boost the credibility of the election. In this way, low-quality foreign monitors allow autocrats to undermine the competitiveness of elections without eschewing them altogether. Alternatively, election winners may tolerate election meddling. Foreign meddling therefore degrades the quality of an election without necessarily undermining its credibility in the eyes of citizens who voted for the winner. Because winners have less incentive to enact policies to punish past meddling and prevent future meddling once they take office, foreign meddlers have license to continue interfering. In both cases, governments can exploit the effects of foreign interventions on citizens' perceptions of election credibility to undermine democratic progress.

For all these reasons, it is essential to understand how citizens form beliefs about election credibility. We now present our argument about how foreign actors influence those beliefs.

[69] Carothers and O'Donohue (2019).
[70] Lupu (2015, 332).
[71] LeBas (2018, 60).
[72] Svolik (2019); Nugent (2020).

1.4 The Argument in Brief

People form their beliefs about election credibility through two processes that map onto two general models of public opinion formation. To build our "theory of the citizen," we start by describing these general processes and then consider how foreign actors might exploit them to cause individuals to update their beliefs. First, people want to hold *accurate* beliefs about an election's credibility. They rely on their personal experiences of voting and what they have learned about the election from politicians and the media.[73] A country's electoral institutions, such as its electoral management body and campaign finance laws, can offer especially important clues about whether an election was free and fair.[74] In a second process, people desire to hold beliefs about election credibility that are *consistent* with their partisan attachments. For that reason, the people who support the winning party or candidate typically perceive an election as more credible than those who support the losing party or candidate.[75] This winner–loser gap reflects individuals' emotional responses to election outcomes, as well as their search for information about election integrity that will confirm their partisan biases.

Although these processes can lead people to have strong opinions about election credibility, in many cases, some uncertainty remains. It is difficult for citizens to observe and assess election credibility themselves, since many forms of malpractice are committed behind closed doors (both literally and figuratively). Moreover, the political elites to whom citizens might look for information about election credibility have incentives to misrepresent the true level of malpractice: Election winners have reason to portray themselves as having won fairly, and election losers are motivated to declare the election was stolen. The extent of uncertainty depends on both the political environment (transitional countries tend to have more uncertainty than more stable regime types, whether democratic or autocratic) and individual characteristics.

---

[73] Claassen et al. (2013); Kerr (2013, 2018); Berman et al. (2019).

[74] Birch (2008); Hall, Monson, and Patterson (2009); Rosas (2010); Kerr (2013); Erlich and Kerr (2016); Jochem, Murtazashvili, and Murtazashvili (2020).

[75] Anderson et al. (2005); Alvarez, Hall, and Llewellyn (2008); Ansolabehere and Persily (2008); Moehler (2009); Rose and Mishler (2009); Beaulieu (2014a); Cantú and García-Ponce (2015); Sances and Stewart (2015); Robertson (2017); Wellman, Hyde, and Hall (2017).

In this context, foreign actors can provide valuable information to citizens about an election's credibility. Their actions – if people learn about them – can help citizens assess whether political candidates are committed to the rules of the game and whether fraud was likely to have been committed on election day. Citizens are unlikely to have extensive information about foreign interventions around elections, although they may encounter EOs at polling stations. Even if they have limited firsthand knowledge about foreign interventions, they can obtain at least basic information via the media and use it as a heuristic with which to assess the electoral playing field. Our theory considers several ways in which foreign actors affect citizens' perceptions of election credibility on average. More importantly, it proposes several new ways that foreign actors' effects depend on the characteristics of foreign actors, individual citizens, and the countries where elections occur.

We call the expected average effects of foreign actors the *conventional wisdom* because they are the effects that the monitors and meddlers believe themselves to have (as described earlier), and that previous scholarly studies assume they have. For example, research on how international monitors affect patterns of post-election protest typically hypothesizes that they do so via their effects on citizens' perceptions of election credibility but does not test this effect directly.[76] To the best of our knowledge, our study is the first to provide a theoretical logic at the citizen level to explain how individuals change their beliefs about election credibility. By developing this logic, we can specify: (1) the mechanisms linking foreign election interventions to election credibility, (2) the variables most likely to condition the relationship between foreign interventions and election credibility, and (3) the most plausible alternative explanation.

According to the conventional wisdom about the effects of foreign interventions, the expected direction of the effect depends on the type of intervention and can be understood primarily through the accuracy mechanism discussed earlier. Whereas international monitoring is expected to increase trust, meddling is expected to have the opposite effect. Foreign actors could affect individual perceptions of elections in this way because of the uncertainty individuals often have about election integrity. Information about international monitors' presence or

---

[76] Daxecker (2012); Little (2012); Donno (2013); Hyde and Marinov (2014); von Borzyskowski (2019a).

their positive reports may reassure individuals that the electoral playing field is fair and that elites are truly committed to democracy. By contrast, information about foreign meddling may imply that fraud has occurred and, especially if meddling is welcomed, that local politicians are merely pretending to respect the rules of the game. Therefore, it may cause citizens to lose trust.

Yet, we can also construct a richer theory that accounts for individual psychology, which can drastically change how citizens interpret information about foreign interventions in two ways. First, in order for foreign actors' interventions to provide new information to the public about the electoral playing field, citizens must believe these actors are able and willing to influence it. For example, if individuals believe international monitors are biased toward a particular candidate, then their presence does not suggest the playing field is fair and is unlikely to enhance individuals' perceptions of election credibility. Thus, foreign actors' effects are conditional on characteristics associated with their identity. When individuals want to hold accurate beliefs about election integrity, they will only revise their opinion about elections in response to credible foreign interventions. We argue and find that the foreign actors that citizens perceive as capable are not always those that experts regard as such.

Second, individuals' vote choice and uncertainty about the election moderate the effect of foreign actors. Accuracy and directional motivations both point to vote choice as an essential moderating factor. Based on accuracy motivations, foreign actors' interventions are more likely to affect citizens' trust in elections when they reveal information that is different from individuals' existing beliefs and when individuals are uncertain. Uncertainty is especially likely in certain electoral contexts, such as countries that are transitioning from autocracy to democracy, and where politicians' true intentions are unknown. Based on directional motivations, however, foreign actors' interventions are more likely to affect citizens' trust in elections when they reaffirm their partisan biases. For example, election losers may be receptive to information about foreign meddling because they are more open to the possibility that they lost an election unfairly.

Our predictions contrast sharply with an alternative perspective on foreign interventions around elections that expects citizens to respond with hostility to any outside intervention. Nationalism "maintains that peoples with a powerful sense of collective identity should be allowed to govern themselves" and is currently thought to be "on the march" in the United States and beyond.[77] And what could be a more essential element of self-government than elections? Yet, we argue that nationalism does not offer the best lens through which to understand citizens' views about foreign electoral interventions.

This argument contrasts with recent research, which finds that nationalism's emotional power makes it ripe for deflecting external pressure related to issues of democracy and human rights.[78] In fact, there is mounting (but not uniform) evidence that individuals respond negatively to foreign interventions in these domains that are perceived to violate their country's sovereignty.[79] More broadly, researchers argue that nationalism is a key source of blowback from foreign interventions and the legitimacy problems that plague politicians installed by outside powers in their wake.[80] The nationalism perspective we consider is closely related to the narrative – common among both academics and political commentators – that "foreign threats facilitate partisan unity."[81]

Based on these arguments, one might expect norms of national self-determination to encourage a backlash against all forms of foreign influence on elections – monitoring, meddling, and everything in between.[82] Certainly, according to this perspective, one would at least expect meddling to always diminish citizens' trust. Many studies of the topic have taken this point for granted; in a recent book on election meddling, for example, historian David Shimer writes, "Overt interference *inevitably* provokes a backlash."[83] Likewise, Levin considers the potential for backlash to be a key reason why interveners opt for covert instead of overt interventions and provides evidence that policymakers worry about it when planning operations.[84] Our theory instead proposes that even if meddling has negative effects on trust, many citizens are quite tolerant of – if not receptive to – foreign influence in their elections as long as it helps their preferred party win.

---

[77] Mearsheimer (2021, 1).
[78] Snyder (2020).
[79] Gruffydd-Jones (2019); Grossman, Manekin, and Margalit (2018); Terman (2019); Chapman and Chaudoin (2020). For exceptions or partial exceptions, see Corstange and Marinov (2012), Bush and Jamal (2015), Lupu and Wallace (2019), and Anjum, Chilton, and Usman (2021).
[80] Edelstein (2011); Lake (2016).
[81] Myrick (2021, 5).
[82] Shulman and Bloom (2012).
[83] Emphasis added. Shimer (2020, 27).
[84] Levin (2020, 40–41).

1.5 Plan of the Book

Chapter 2 develops our theory. Chapter 3 then describes the research strategy we use to test its observable implications. Since talking to citizens directly is the best way to determine how foreign actors influence perceptions of election credibility, we rely heavily on evidence gathered in nationally representative surveys that we conducted for this project, which we supplement with other forms of evidence. We administered a total of ten large-scale surveys across elections in three countries at different levels of democracy. We studied citizens' perceptions of the 2014 parliamentary and presidential elections in Tunisia (a transitional democracy); the 2016, 2018, and 2020 general elections in the United States (a consolidated democracy); and the 2018 first- and second-round presidential elections in Georgia (a partial democracy). Chapter 3 describes our survey methodology, including our approach to embedding experimental vignettes designed to identify the effects of foreign actors, discusses our case selection rationale, and provides background information on each case.

Chapters 4–7 present our main empirical analyses and findings. We organize the book thematically around our theory's explanatory variables – monitoring, meddling, intervener identity, and individual vote choice – rather than around the three country cases. This decision reflects our core interest in explaining the effects of foreign electoral interventions and showcasing commonalities (as well as variation) in the interventions' effects across three diverse cases.

In Chapter 4, we begin testing the theory with respect to election monitoring. After discussing the ecology of international election monitors and demonstrating general public acceptance of them, we find limited support for the hypotheses related to their average effects. In none of our cases did information about the *presence* of international monitors increase trust in elections. We find more support for the conventional wisdom about the effects of monitors' reports: Positive reports increased trust relative to negative reports in Tunisia (somewhat tentatively) and the United States (more clearly). The substantive effects in both cases were fairly modest, however, and we find no evidence that they had the same effect in Georgia.

We turn to election meddling in Chapter 5. Like Chapter 4, it begins with descriptive information about this phenomenon and its prevalence and shows there is substantial public concern about it. We further demonstrate that across all three countries, individuals who believed foreign actors had a negative influence on elections had lower levels of trust in their elections. But our experiments again offer only limited support for the conventional wisdom. Our treatments priming individuals about election meddling either had no effect on perceptions of election credibility or only had an effect when we were able to reassure them that meddling had *not* occurred.

In summary, Chapters 4 and 5 do not offer a great deal of support for the conventional wisdom. As we discuss in more detail in the conclusion (Chapter 8), the null effects in these chapters not only challenge prior assumptions about foreign actors' effects, they also contribute to the broader movement within the social sciences to recognize how null effects contribute to scientific understanding and progress.

We show in Chapters 6 and 7 that these analyses of the *overall* effects of foreign interventions mask considerable variation. Chapter 6 focuses on how the effects of foreign interventions depend on the identity of the intervener. We show that in Tunisia and the United States, the presence of *capable and unbiased* monitors (not any monitors) increased election credibility. In Georgia, an unusually certain electoral environment, the same was true when we focused only on individuals with significant uncertainty in their beliefs about election credibility. Intriguingly, in Tunisia, the monitors perceived as capable and unbiased were those from the Arab League, while in the United States, international observers were not perceived very warmly unless their positive traits were mentioned.

Most survey respondents did not believe election meddling was likely to affect the results of their country's election. If they did believe meddlers were capable of having such an effect, however, then we observe the predicted negative relationship with election credibility. Moreover, using a hypothetical experiment in which we told people that a foreign actor *successfully* meddled in a future election, we find the expected decrease in election credibility. Overall, Chapter 6 illustrates how dependent the effects of foreign meddling on election credibility are on beliefs about the meddler's capabilities.

Chapter 7 explores how monitors' effects are conditional on individuals' vote choice. We show across our three case studies that winners were much more likely than losers to view an election as credible. The question then in terms of theory is whether winners and losers responded differently to the information we provided about foreign electoral interventions. We find that positive information about monitors' presence and complimentary reports did not reassure losers, who were much more receptive to negative information from monitors' critical reports. The evidence can be interpreted as consistent with individuals forming beliefs in both accuracy-driven and directionally-driven ways. Similarly, our meddling experiments never caused election winners to lose trust, although they did have such an effect on election losers. Election losers were also much more likely to believe in the existence of foreign meddling and its success to begin with. Overall, these results are somewhat sobering since democracy depends on the consent of election losers and a commitment among election winners to the rules of the game.

Chapter 8 concludes by considering the implications of the theory and findings for both political behaviors that are important to democracy, including voter turnout, and for scholarship on international relations and democratic backsliding. We discuss how the evidence presented in the book complicates the narratives that scholars and others have developed about how foreign actors shape local trust in elections. Without assessing citizens' psychology, we cannot understand which members of society are the most vulnerable to the influence of foreign actors. This chapter also explores how our theory could be expanded to incorporate the role played by elites and political parties in amplifying or diminishing foreign actors' effects on domestic politics writ large. Finally, we close the book with thoughts on how foreign electoral interventions contribute to polarization – and thus to current threats to democracy – around the world.

2 | How Foreign Actors Influence Election Credibility

Kenya's December 27, 2007, presidential election resulted in a humanitarian disaster. When President Mwai Kibaki was proclaimed the winner and inaugurated on December 30, supporters of his challenger, Raila Odinga, began protesting. Violence spread throughout the country, often along ethnic lines. Nearly 1,200 people died and 500,000 were displaced.[1] Violence raged until February 2008, when an international group of mediators helped broker a deal that kept Kibaki as president and created the position of prime minister for Odinga.

This election illustrates *why perceptions of election credibility matter* and *how foreign actors help shape those perceptions.* According to Gibson and Long, who conducted a definitive exit poll at the election, the violent aftermath of the election was rooted in the failure of Kenya's electoral commission to "maintain confidence in the vote."[2] Journalists' interviews with Kenyans at the time supported this interpretation. For example, James Onyango, a resident of Nairobi, spoke to a reporter from the US National Public Radio a few days after the election about why he and others were continuing to back Odinga. As protests and violence raged, he said, "We have been rigged out, we are not going to accept defeat...We are ready to die and we're ready for serious killings."[3] As Onyango's comments show, citizens' trust in elections (or lack thereof) is extremely important.

Foreign actors may have contributed to the postelection chaos in Kenya through their effects on citizens' attitudes. Observers from the European Union (EU) and the International Republican Institute (IRI) released positive preliminary reports, in line with their tendency to avoid condemning elections where negative comments could lead to

[1] Gibson and Long (2007, 497).
[2] Ibid., 501.
[3] Thompkins (2007).

33

violence.[4] As hostilities spread, however, both organizations quickly downgraded their assessments, which fueled citizens' suspicions and bolstered Odinga's challenge.[5] A 2012 EU-sponsored report on election violence later concluded that one of their mission's critical comments "may have reinforced the narrative (of a vote stolen by the election commission on behalf of President Kibaki) which was driving violence."[6] As IRI East Africa Director Kenneth Flottman wrote in an e-mail to a colleague at the time, "Supporting democracy and managing political outcomes are two different objectives for a nonpartisan, foreign-based organization or country... and sometimes there is a conflict."[7]

Understanding whether election observers (EOs) really did alter citizens' attitudes and contribute to violence in Kenya is important for the lessons that organizations such as the EU and IRI draw about how to issue reports in conflict-prone societies. Despite the negative assessments of the role of foreign actors in this case, it is possible that violence would have occurred regardless of international observers' statements. Indeed, Kenya had a history of election-related violence and several other characteristics – including an incumbent under threat and a lack of democracy – that are known to be correlated with election violence.[8] Thus, we require a firm understanding of the conditions under which foreign actors are likely to influence citizens' electoral trust.

This chapter develops our argument about how foreign actors such as those in Kenya influence individual perceptions of the credibility of elections. In Chapter 1, we defined a credible election as one in which *the people trust the results and believe the outcome reflects the will of the people.* In this chapter, we outline the two main reasons why individuals may be uncertain about the credibility of elections. First, election integrity is often difficult to observe. Second, the political leaders who have insider knowledge about electoral conduct also have incentives to misrepresent the true nature of the election. In Kenya, for example, malpractice occurred during the vote tallying

---

[4] Kelley (2012b, 73).
[5] von Borzyskowski (2019a, 112–114).
[6] Atwood (2012, 22).
[7] Quoted in McIntire and Gettleman (2009, A1).
[8] Hafner-Burton, Hyde, and Jablonski (2014).

process, which is difficult to directly verify except by comparing the official results with a high-quality exit poll.[9] Meanwhile, President Kibaki's party repudiated Odinga's accusations of malpractice, but this move was perhaps to be expected given that it had been declared the winner.[10] In addition to these two potential sources of uncertainty, the overall context in which elections occur further shapes individuals' degree of confidence in their assessments of elections. For instance, when elections are held in transitional environments, such as after a revolution or civil conflict, individuals' beliefs about their credibility tend to be less certain. Individuals' personal characteristics matter too: Some people have more confidence than others even in the same election because of their political knowledge or another factor.

Because individuals often harbor some level of uncertainty about election credibility, even in democracies, foreign actors' interventions in elections may cause people to update their beliefs about the electoral playing field. The assumption by many pundits, policymakers, and practitioners – which we call the conventional wisdom – is that EOs' presence and positive evaluations of elections enhance individuals' perceptions of election credibility, whereas negative EO evaluations and individuals' perceptions of foreign meddling diminish it. We build a theory grounded in the psychology of individuals to explain this conventional wisdom. This discussion yields a set of hypotheses about how foreign actors influence perceptions of election credibility *on average*.

This theoretical grounding then allows us to propose several variables that *moderate* or *condition* the effect of foreign actors on individuals' beliefs about election credibility. The conditional hypotheses point to some of the limits on foreign actors' effects, which previous research and policy analysis about foreign electoral interventions have not explored. Building on general theories about how people update their opinions when confronted with new information, we argue that foreign actors' effects depend on two factors in addition to the electoral context. The first is the identity of the foreign actor, which shapes individuals' perceptions of whether it has the capacity (and motivation) to alter the electoral playing field. The second is the content and

---

[9] Gibson and Long (2007, 497).
[10] Gettleman (2007).

certainty of individuals' beliefs about election credibility, which are closely linked to whether their preferred candidate or party won or lost. This approach contrasts with a simple model of foreign actors' domestic effects that lacks a theory of the citizen and therefore fails to capture the psychological factors that affect a person's susceptibility to influence from external interventions. Put differently, the conventional wisdom overlooks several important factors that must be present for foreign actors to influence local trust in elections.

Our approach, which emphasizes the role of information and uncertainty, also contrasts with an alternative theory of the citizen that is centered on the role of nationalism. Many analysts suspect that citizens are prone to regard *any* form of foreign influence suspiciously as a form of outside interference that has the potential to undermine their confidence in elections. This perspective is rooted in studies that demonstrate how nationalism generates opposition to foreign influences on domestic politics. It offers alternative predictions about how foreign actors influence local trust in elections, as our framework implies that even meddling – the most objectionable type of foreign influence – does not always diminish individuals' trust. Indeed, we argue, and show in subsequent chapters, that individuals are often quite receptive to foreign influence in their elections.

2.1 Perceptions of Election Credibility

The vast majority of general research on election credibility focuses on how domestic factors such as local political elites and electoral institutions shape local trust in elections. We review this literature later.

On the specific topic of foreign actors and perceptions of election credibility, however, our research joins a small but growing literature that examines how monitoring and meddling affect citizens. Four studies are closely related to ours. The first three concentrate on election monitoring. First, Dawn Brancati randomized citizens' information about the activities of European EOs during the 2009/2010 municipal elections in Kosovo and found that they enhanced trust.[11] Second, Graeme Robertson found that Russian citizens who reported being familiar with Golos, a domestic EO that is critical of the government, were less likely to trust the results of the 2011 Duma election

---

[11] Brancati (2014a).

if they were opposition supporters.[12] Third, Lindsay Benstead, Kristen Kao, and Ellen Lust examined how knowledge of international EOs affected trust in elections in Jordan and Tunisia fifteen and seven months afterwards, respectively, and found null effects.[13]

The fourth related study examines how perceptions of meddling influence citizens' trust in elections. Michael Tomz and Jessica L.P. Weeks surveyed Americans about a hypothetical future election in which a foreign country (China, Pakistan, or Turkey) did or did not intervene in favor of a preferred candidate.[14] The authors found that information about electoral interventions significantly decreased respondents' trust in the integrity of the hypothetical election.

We draw on valuable insights generated by these studies to advance the literature in three ways. First, we develop a theory of the citizen detailed later in this section that helps us understand the individual-level effects of *multiple* types of foreign influences on elections, from monitoring to meddling. Our theory allows us to compare the effects of different types of interventions on public attitudes. Second, our bottom-up theory identifies intervener- and individual-level characteristics that can be expected to *condition* the effect of foreign actors on perceptions of election credibility. Finally, our study is explicitly *comparative*. Previous research generally draws on single cases, while this book includes evidence from three countries with different regime types, as we discuss in more detail in Chapter 3. Drawing on evidence from multiple cases is essential for understanding the generalizability of claims regarding how foreign actors affect individuals' perceptions of election credibility. For example, the effect of monitors and meddlers on trust may depend on whether the country in which an intervention occurs is a democracy.

In contrast to this small literature on monitors and meddlers' effects on election credibility, there is substantial research on the domestic determinants of citizens' perceptions of elections. We draw on this larger literature to help us explain why individuals trust elections

---

[12] Robertson (2017). Note that familiarity with Golos is self-reported rather than experimentally manipulated in this study, although the author carefully attempts to control for potentially confounding variables. Robertson also describes the results of a survey experiment exploring the factors that motivate people to trust EOs' reports.

[13] Benstead, Kao, and Lust (2020).

[14] Tomz and Weeks (2020).

before foreign actors enter the picture. Previous studies emphasize how individuals' information about the electoral playing field and vote choice shapes their opinions. Yet, considerable uncertainty about election credibility remains for many people and in many elections.

2.1.1 The Domestic Sources of Trust in Elections

People form their impressions of election credibility based on a variety of information, ranging from firsthand experiences to expert accounts reported in the news. They must then make sense of the information they gather. Understanding this process requires appreciating individuals' goals when interpreting evidence.

Citizens hold two (potentially conflicting) desires: (1) to have *correct* beliefs about an election's credibility and (2) to hold beliefs about election integrity that are *consistent* with their preferred party's or candidate's success in an election. The social science literature refers to these two desires as individuals' "accuracy" and "directional" (or "partisan") motives, respectively.[15]

When individuals are motivated mainly by accuracy, they want to know whether an election was free and fair and will rely on the best available information to form their opinion. People may be motivated to reach the "correct" conclusion about election credibility as an end in and of itself and to inform future political decisions such as whom to vote for or whether to protest an election outcome.

Yet when individuals are motivated mainly by partisan goals, they mostly seek out and respond to information that supports their partisan views of the election. Their desire to confirm their existing beliefs can lead people who support a winning party to ignore credible information about electoral malpractice. The same desire can cause people who support a losing party to ignore clear signs that an election was fair. People may be directionally motivated because of emotional considerations (it feels better to hold beliefs that are consistent) or threats to their partisan identities.[16] Partisans want to believe good things about their group and bad things about other groups, and most people disapprove of cheating in an election.

[15] Kunda (1990, 480).
[16] Flynn, Nyhan, and Reifler (2017, 133).

In building our theory and conducting our empirical analyses, we do not seek to prove or disprove the accuracy or directional logics. Instead, we use them as theoretical lenses to think about how citizens respond to new information. Both goals suggest that two key individual-level factors shape perceptions of election credibility: (1) information about the electoral playing field and (2) vote choice.

Information about the Playing Field

Some individuals witness fraudulent behavior firsthand, or hear about it from their family and friends, which causes them to lose trust.[17] Personal experiences on election day, such as with new forms of voting technology, can shape trust even in consolidated democracies.[18]

What individuals know (or believe) about the country's institutions also influences their beliefs about the electoral playing field. Many institutions can level (or tilt) the playing field and thus may affect individuals' perceptions of it. The academic literature has focused heavily on the autonomy and capacity of electoral management bodies (EMBs). Although the average citizen does not always agree with scholars' assessments of the significance of autonomous EMBs,[19] survey data show that voters do think EMBs' capacity, as measured by individuals' beliefs about poll workers, is important.[20] Other electoral institutions that affect the playing field – and therefore have been shown to affect individual trust – include the electoral system, campaign financing rules, and voting technologies.[21] The link between a citizen's beliefs or knowledge about the electoral playing field and his or her beliefs about election credibility holds across a variety of regime types and regions, from the United States and Western Europe to sub-Saharan Africa and Latin America.

Vote Choice

Individuals also want their beliefs about election credibility to be aligned with their partisan goals. Therefore, individuals' beliefs about

---

[17] Kerr (2013, 2018); Berman et al. (2019). But this is not a universal finding. For example, see Wellman, Hyde, and Hall (2017).
[18] Claassen et al. (2013).
[19] Birch (2008); Rosas (2010); Kerr (2013); Erlich and Kerr (2016).
[20] Hall, Monson, and Patterson (2009).
[21] Alvarez, Hall, and Llewellyn (2008); Birch (2008); Jochem, Murtazashvili, and Murtazashvili (2020).

election credibility depend on whether they supported the winning or losing party.[22] Supporters of winning (losing) parties are more likely to view elections positively (negatively).

Of course, vote choice could shape perceptions of election credibility through the accuracy mechanism. For example, election winners may perceive elections more positively because they are more likely to reside in areas of the country where the government commits less malpractice since those are the locations where its supporters are based. However, the directional mechanism also suggests two additional ways that individual vote choice affects perceptions of election credibility.

First, people often have intense emotional reactions to their party winning or losing. In our research for this book, we asked Americans how they felt after the 2016 election; their survey responses illustrate the extremes that post-election emotions can reach. Whereas one respondent reported that she was "thrilled beyond words," another said, "I was crushed, dismayed, angered, and embarrassed." These positive (or negative) emotions then spill over to individuals' assessments of the electoral institutions that produced the victory (or defeat). Individuals' initial emotional responses to winning or losing are often complicated by their parties' histories of wins and losses, which shape how people react to future wins and losses.

Second, and further compounding the winner–loser gap, individuals may be reluctant to adjust their initial views of an election. Winning or losing an election creates powerful incentives for people to seek out information that confirms their biases about its credibility, while ignoring information that contradicts these biases. For example, election winners tend to obtain their political information from sources that support the winning party, whereas the opposite is true for election losers. These information sources contribute to individuals' beliefs about whether the electoral playing field is fair and whether candidates intended to cheat. Ironically, this dynamic can lead politically engaged people to hold less accurate views about politics, since they are more likely to consume biased media.[23]

---

[22] There is a large literature on this topic. See, for example, Anderson et al. (2005), Alvarez, Hall, and Llewellyn (2008), Ansolabehere and Persily (2008), Moehler (2009), Rose and Mishler (2009), Beaulieu (2014a), Cantú and García-Ponce (2015), Sances and Stewart (2015), Robertson (2017), Wellman, Hyde, and Hall (2017).

[23] Taber and Lodge (2006).

2.1.2 The Role of Uncertainty

Thus far, we have suggested reasons why people may form strong opinions about the credibility of their country's elections. Yet, many individuals remain uncertain about elections' integrity, even in democracies. This point relates to the broader idea that individuals often lack quality information about government performance, which several recent studies have explored.[24]

Roots of Uncertainty

There are two general reasons why people may be uncertain about election credibility. The first reason is that election credibility is often difficult to observe and assess. In some cases, individuals do witness fraudulent behavior firsthand. Violence, such as attacks on election workers or candidates, is an easily observable form of electoral malpractice. Some other types of election day manipulations are also readily apparent to voters. For example, some voters showed up to polling stations during the 2018 presidential election in the Democratic Republic of Congo (DRC) only to find that they had been eliminated from the voter rolls or that the electronic voting machines were missing or broken.[25] These irregularities raised immediate suspicions of electoral fraud.

Yet, other types of electoral malpractice are deliberately difficult for citizens to track, from ballot box stuffing to the manipulation of electoral infrastructure and institutions. Even in countries that few would consider to be democratic, political leaders go to great lengths to disguise their efforts to steal elections. During the 2004 presidential election in Ukraine that preceded the Orange Revolution, for example, election officials distributed ballots and pens with disappearing ink to voters in areas known to support the opposition. Although international observers eventually discovered this trickery, the government's goal was to generate the appearance of a democratic election while in fact rigging it in favor of Prime Minister Viktor Yanukovich.[26] Given leaders' desires in most cases to present themselves as committed to democratic norms (an idea developed later), the absence of blatant

---

[24] Ferraz and Finan (2008); Chong et al. (2015); Winters and Weitz-Shapiro (2017); Dunning et al. (2019).
[25] Gavin (2019).
[26] Associated Press (2004).

electoral fraud is not the same as evidence of a clean election. Just because citizens did not observe electoral malpractice firsthand does not mean it did not occur. Violations of election integrity resulting from covert foreign meddling may be especially difficult to rule out. These dynamics can contribute to uncertainty.

The overall effect of electoral malpractice is also difficult to assess. Recall that a credible election is one in which the people trust the results and believe the outcome reflects the will of the people. Thus, even if there is clear evidence of *some* electoral fraud, it may not have been systematic or comprehensive enough to alter the overall election outcome. Assessing election credibility thus requires making a judgment about whether any irregularities were serious enough to call the overall outcome into question and undermine the will of the people. As a study on election annulment for practitioners published by the International Foundation for Electoral Systems notes, evaluating the effect of a voter intimidation campaign on an election outcome is quite different from estimating the impact of a known number of irregularities at an isolated polling place.[27] Given these complexities, citizens may be justifiably uncertain about whether an election they believe had some flaws truly lacked credibility.

The second reason why people are uncertain about election credibility is that they may lack what they consider to be a high-quality source of information on this topic. Political elites sometimes deliberately mislead the public about election integrity to advance their own agendas. For example, it is not uncommon for losing candidates to question the legitimacy of their opponents' victories. After the 2018 presidential election in the DRC, for example, runner-up Martin Fayulu was quoted as saying, "These results have nothing to do with the truth of the polls…It's a real electoral coup, it's incomprehensible."[28] Sometimes, as in the DRC, election losers' complaints are justified, and do not constitute the mere grousing of people who wish they had won.[29] Yet, that is not always the case. Indeed, Fayulu's language was similar to Donald Trump's claims of a "rigged" 2020 election in the United States, which was not supported by the evidence.

---

[27] Vickery et al. (2018, 2).
[28] Gonzales and Schwartz (2019).
[29] See, for example, the *Financial Times* analysis of voting data from this election (Wilson, Blood, and Pilling 2019).

Amidst conflicting sources of information about election credibility, citizens may find it difficult to know who to trust. Losing candidates have a clear incentive to undermine their opponents' victories, while winners have reasons to downplay concerns. For example, election losers may believe that if they claim election fraud convincingly enough, they will be able to remain in or gain office by winning legal challenges or encouraging their supporters to participate in protests or riots. Though election losers are sometimes justified in these claims, at other times they are engaging in "sore loser" protests. It can be difficult to determine which dynamic is at play, which creates substantial uncertainty if there is no neutral party such as credible international observers.[30] Although it is perhaps intuitive that well-known domestic politicians would be more trustworthy messengers than foreigners in communications about election credibility, the public may discount domestic political elites' endorsements or criticisms of election credibility given their incentives to spin election results in their favor. After all, ordinary people are privy to neither the details of the electoral process nor the true intentions of the incumbent government or opposition candidates. They therefore have reason to question statements regarding election credibility made by political candidates and reported in partisan or government media. As such, citizens may have further cause for uncertainty.

How Uncertainty Varies
Thus far, we have suggested reasons why people might be uncertain about election credibility *in general*, despite any information they may have about the electoral playing field and the influence of vote choice. While there will probably be at least a few people who are uncertain about a given election's level of integrity, certain contextual and individual factors increase the likelihood of this uncertainty.

Regime type is an important *contextual factor*. Citizens use their beliefs about the overall state of democracy as a heuristic to assess election integrity. For example, they are more likely to be certain that their votes are counted fairly in consolidated democracies than in stable autocracies. Countries at both ends of the spectrum have lengthy track records of either clean or fraudulent elections, which strengthens

---

[30] Hyde and Marinov (2014, 352–353).

citizens' confidence in their assessments of political leaders' true intentions regarding election quality. Moreover, in stable regimes, losing political candidates may respond consistently over time to election results, which enhances public certainty; for example, losing candidates usually concede and accept the election results in consolidated democracies. By contrast, transitional elections, elections that follow a previous suspension of elections, and a country's first multi-party election all tend to exhibit varying degrees of uncertainty[31] and to have more unknowns than elections in more stable regimes.

Another relevant contextual factor relates to cues from the media and political elites regarding election integrity. The United States is a stable democracy, but Americans' confidence in their elections has dropped steadily and precipitously in recent years. Whereas 52 percent of those surveyed in 2006 reported having confidence in the honesty of elections, already a fairly low proportion for a consolidated democracy, that number had dropped to 30 percent just 10 years later.[32] This trend is related to, but distinct from, broader declines in public trust in the United States. It should also be understood as the result of widely publicized problems with ballots in Florida during the 2000 presidential election and repeated allegations since then by Republican politicians of electoral fraud.

Individual characteristics also determine levels of uncertainty about election integrity. The large literature on the determinants of individuals' trust in elections is almost exclusively focused on what affects the *content* of those beliefs (i.e., do people trust the election?) rather than their *certainty* (i.e., if people say they trust the election, how sure are they about that?). It is plausible that an individual's proximity to the hypothesized malpractice may be relevant, since people who have personally witnessed fraud may be more certain about an election's lack of integrity than those who have merely heard reports about such fraud in the news. Empirical research paints a more complicated picture, however, as personal exposure to fraud does not always decrease individual trust, which also calls into question the extent to which it influences individual certainty.[33] An individual's level of political interest and sophistication, as well as her general tendency to have

[31] Hyde and Marinov (2014, 340).
[32] Norris, Cameron, and Wynter (2019, 11).
[33] Wellman, Hyde, and Hall (2017).

confident opinions, could also plausibly shape whether she is certain in her beliefs about an election. In fact, uncertainty about politics in general can be understood as an individual state as much as a feature of the information itself.[34] But here, too, the empirical evidence is somewhat ambiguous; it is difficult to identify factors that consistently make people susceptible to changing their minds about election quality, which is a likely indicator of uncertain beliefs.[35]

2.2 How Foreign Actors Influence Trust on Average

When people are uncertain about the quality of elections, they are more likely to change their minds. If individuals desire to hold accurate opinions about election credibility, then being confronted with new information may cause them to update their beliefs. Of course, some conditions make updating more likely, such as when the information comes from a credible source, as we discuss later. However, a general prediction is that when individuals are uncertain about election credibility, they may rationally update their beliefs in response to new information. This type of accuracy-driven updating is known as the Bayesian model of public opinion formation in the political science literature.[36]

Foreign interventions offer one pathway to such updating. We begin by developing a theory about the effects that foreign actors have *on average*. As we explain later, we term this theory the conventional wisdom because the average effects it predicts have been assumed by foreign actors themselves as well as by many analysts. We build upon their arguments to more fully specify the logical mechanisms that could underpin their assumptions that foreign actors (both monitors and meddlers) substantially affect citizens' opinions. Foreign actors engage in potentially trust-*enhancing* interventions (monitoring, positive evaluations contained in publicized reports) as well as potentially trust-*diminishing* activities (negative EO reports, meddling). Foreign

---

[34] McGraw, Hasecke, and Conger (2003).
[35] Sinclair, Smith, and Tucker (2018, 866).
[36] It is known as "Bayesian" because it draws on Bayes' theorem, a mathematical formula used to calculate conditional probabilities, to understand who is likely to update his or her opinion in response to new information. For discussions of (and debates about) this model, see Gerber and Green (1999), Bartels (2002), and Bullock (2009).

actors can influence citizens' perceptions of election credibility by providing them with new information about the electoral playing field and whether candidates are committed to democracy.

2.2.1 Learning about Interventions: Monitors vs. Meddlers

Most international EOs are public and transparent in their activities. Monitors draw attention to their presence because they believe doing so will help deter fraud and, when warranted, enhance election credibility. They issue public reports, hold press conferences to deliver their initial findings, involve famous people as monitors, and pursue targeted strategies to reach the domestic and international media. Citizens are one of the multiple targets of these publicity efforts, which also include domestic and international journalists, elected officials, aid donors, and diplomatic personnel. According to a report prepared by the National Democratic Institute to offer advice to the West Africa Election Observers Network, "Conducting outreach is inherent in any election monitoring effort... All information that you collect, including your findings, is useless if you do not and cannot communicate it effectively to your stakeholders and the general public."[37]

Yet, monitors are not always successful at drawing attention to their activities. International EOs can directly communicate with citizens by posting their reports on their websites and publicizing them via social media. Most citizens, however, learn about their findings from the domestic media, which may be partisan or government controlled – and therefore have ulterior motives to bury stories about EO reports.

Of course, domestic political elites may seek to draw attention to international EOs' activities under some conditions. For example, incumbents may publicize their decision to invite monitors because they think it gives them legitimacy, and opposition parties may have their own reasons to publicize EOs' efforts at elections.[38] Critical reports can bolster losers' protests, while positive assessments can legitimize a government's victory. Prior studies have found that international monitors' activities can affect patterns of protest and violence. For instance, the heavy publicity surrounding international observers' condemnation of Peru's fraudulent 2000 presidential

---

[37] National Democratic Institute (2013, 4).
[38] Beaulieu and Hyde (2009); Kelley (2011).

election is thought to have galvanized the protests that led to President Alberto Fujimori's escape to Japan.[39]

By contrast, foreign meddling is much less transparent and often covert. For example, foreign actors may provide secret funding or other forms of campaign assistance to a favored side in an election. That does not mean, however, that meddling does not receive public attention. In some cases, such as US interventions against the Communist Party in the 1948 Italian election and in favor of the Christian Democratic Union in the 1953 West German election, meddlers make their actions public, or at least easily detectable, to allow them to interfere in more (and more in-depth) ways.[40] In other cases, government agencies, journalists, or international monitors may discover and publicize covert meddling.[41] Election losers may also strategically publicize meddling (real or alleged) to undermine an election's credibility. As with election monitoring, domestic elites and foreign actors' attempts to influence election credibility can interact dynamically over time: Meddlers are likely to intervene more in future elections if domestic elites seem to tolerate or even welcome their past actions.

In the absence of high-quality information about meddling, citizens can still be influenced by rumors or a history of meddling in the country. Given the difficulties associated with observing meddling directly, citizens may have substantial uncertainty about its existence (or lack thereof). In this way, meddling is distinct from monitoring. As we discuss later in the book, the greater uncertainty that surrounds meddling offers a plausible explanation for why we find its effects to be slightly less consistent than those of monitoring.

2.2.2 *Types of Information Supplied by Foreign Actors*

As discussed earlier, domestic populations are more certain about the credibility of some elections than others; thus, the likelihood that foreign actors will shape individual perceptions based on domestic elites' claims about election credibility also varies. In many cases, however, some uncertainty about election credibility remains. Election integrity

---

[39] Daxecker and Schneider (2014, 74); Hyde and Marinov (2014, 352).
[40] Levin (2016, 189–191).
[41] Awareness of meddling may therefore be greater in more democratic countries, which have greater freedom of the press and stronger systems of checks and balances.

reflects decisions made by both national political leaders – especially the incumbent government – and local officials who are responsible for carrying out election fraud.[42] Thus, it is important to explore how foreign interventions provide two types of information to the public about both levels of government.

The first type of information that foreign actors can provide is about the candidates in an election. Foreign interventions can convey information to voters about whether candidates are likely to play fair or cheat – whether they are what Susan Hyde calls "true" democrats (who never cheat in elections) or "pseudo-democrats" (who sometimes do).[43] As Hyde explains, "Although pseudo-democrats agree to hold elections, and will even hold free and fair elections if they believe they are popular enough to win outright, they manipulate the election or the electoral process when they are not otherwise sure of their victory."[44] Pseudo-democrats wish to appear to be true democrats and will make considerable efforts to conceal their cheating.

This argument about foreign actors and candidate type draws on signaling theories within international relations (IR) and, before that, economics. According to these theories, imperfectly informed audiences seek to distinguish between "good" and "bad" types of individuals or goods but are unable to do so because much relevant information is hidden from view. The challenge for citizens who are attempting to evaluate political candidates is that both true democrats and pseudo-democrats have incentives to convince voters that they will not cheat for two reasons. The first is that citizens prefer democratic institutions and may withdraw their support from elected officials who violate democratic principles. The second reason relates to the international benefits associated with a reputation for democracy, which increased with the end of the Cold War and range from foreign aid to international organization membership and prestige.[45]

Despite these incentives not to cheat, pseudo-democrats will take actions to undermine the will of the people in order to get elected. They can violate the rules and norms associated with free and fair elections at any stage of the electoral cycle. The more likely voters

---

[42] Rundlett and Svolik (2016).
[43] Hyde (2011, 7).
[44] Ibid., 32.
[45] Ibid., Ch. 3.

are to believe candidates are pseudo-democrats, the less likely they are to believe an election is credible. Given the public's uncertainty about whether candidates are cheating or fair types, foreign interventions have the potential to send an important signal to the public. The presence of monitors, whether they have endorsed the election, and whether meddling has occurred can all cause citizens to update their beliefs about candidates in positive or negative ways, which in turn affects the perceived credibility of elections. We describe the logic for both monitoring and meddling in more detail later.

The second type of information that foreign interventions can provide relates to the quality of electoral institutions on and around election day. Foreign actors can affect electoral institutions in ways that make elections either more or less likely to reflect the will of the people. These effects are related to, but theoretically distinct from, the signaling effects described previously. For example, although the presence of EOs potentially signals to citizens about whether the incumbent is a true democrat, the presence of high-quality EOs also makes fraud less likely on election day.[46] Similarly, foreign meddlers can take actions that directly undermine the fairness of electoral institutions. For example, Russia's attempts to hack Bulgaria's Central Election Commission during its 2015 referendum and municipal election could have understandably raised public concerns that the electoral playing field was not fair, regardless of whether pro-Russian candidates invited this action.[47] Thus, learning about foreign actors' interventions provides a variety of information to the public about the quality of the electoral playing field, both because of what foreign interventions reveal about politicians and because of what they reveal about the day-to-day operations of the election.

In developing this general theoretical model, we do not assume that all people in a country are committed democrats. The comparative politics literature has long maintained that citizens in democracies share a "civic culture" that supports democracy.[48] These values can

---

[46] It is possible that EOs could instead cause citizens to worry that fraud exists, whereas previously they had been confident about an election's integrity. We address this question empirically in Chapter 4 in our analysis of providing information about election observation in the United States, a consolidated democracy with relatively clean elections.

[47] Dorell (2017).

[48] Almond and Verba (1963).

help consolidate democracy since the government knows that if it violates democratic principles, it will lose power, and they motivate pseudo-democrats to imitate true democrats, as discussed earlier.[49] In highly polarized societies, however, some citizens prioritize their partisan interests over their support for democracy.[50] Yet as long as at least some voters care about democratic values, pseudo-democrats have a domestic incentive (in addition to international incentives) to represent themselves as true democrats. This incentive contributes to the uncertainty that foreign actors help solve. At the same time, in polarized environments, being certain that an election lacks credibility may not be enough to discourage voters from supporting a candidate who they believe violated democratic norms. Insofar as citizens' responses to monitors and meddlers are partisan (a possibility that we explore later in this chapter), foreign interventions pose a threat to democracy. We evaluate the nature of this threat in Chapter 8.

2.2.3 The Effects of Monitors

The type of foreign influence that we examine in this book that has the greatest potential to enhance trust is monitoring. We consider both monitors' presence and reports.

Monitors believe they have potentially significant effects.[51] The small body of previous research on how monitors' presence affects public attitudes has reported mixed findings. For instance, Brancati found that European EOs had positive effects in Kosovo, and Robertson similarly discovered that domestic EOs in Russia improved citizens' perceptions of election credibility.[52] However, Benstead, Kao, and Lust administered post-election surveys in Jordan and Tunisia and found that monitors did not improve citizens' perceptions that elections reflected the will of the people.[53] Many scholars have posited that international monitors affect patterns of post-election protest

---

[49] Weingast (1997).
[50] Svolik (2019); Graham and Svolik (2020).
[51] Merloe (2015).
[52] Brancati (2014a); Robertson (2017).
[53] Benstead, Kao, and Lust (2020).

and violence via their impact on individuals' attitudes, though these relationships are seldom tested at the individual level.[54]

Monitors' Presence

Rare events such as COVID-19, which blunted some criticism when the authoritarian government in Burundi reversed its decision to allow international observers to monitor the May 2020 presidential election, occasionally limit the supply of monitors.[55] However, these groups are generally available to monitor elections all over the world. When high-quality international EOs accept a government's invitation to monitor an election, they engage in a number of activities. At the very least, they are likely to be present at polling stations to observe voting. Longer-term observers may monitor the EMB, the political environment, and the media. Although observers vary in their capabilities and biases – which we discuss later – we begin by thinking about how they might affect citizens' perceptions in general.

The presence of observers has the potential to enhance perceptions of election credibility through two mechanisms. First, citizens may assume that governments would not invite observers to monitor an election if they intended to cheat. Governments request election monitoring to demonstrate their commitment to democracy, meet their obligations as members of democratic intergovernmental organizations (IGOs), and access the rewards (e.g., foreign aid, prestige) associated with a democratic reputation. Given the value of such benefits, governments often experience at least indirect pressure from foreign governments to invite observers. This pressure can be more direct, as in the case of US officials' statements about the importance of inviting monitors to observe the 1999 Algerian presidential elections.[56] Yet, the 55 high-quality nongovernmental organization (NGO) and IGO monitors who have signed the Declaration of Principles for International Election Observation have affirmed the principle that "An international election observation mission... should not be organized unless the country holding the elections takes the following actions,"

---

[54] Daxecker (2012); Little (2012); Donno (2013); Hyde and Marinov (2014); von Borzyskowski (2019a).
[55] Mudge (2020).
[56] Hyde (2011, 85).

including "unimpeded access," "freedom of movement" for monitors, and "freedom [for monitors] to issue without interference public statements."[57] While citizens are unlikely to be familiar with the details of the declaration, if governments open themselves up to outside scrutiny by inviting international EOs to monitor an election, citizens may interpret this action as a positive signal of the candidate's type. As such, they may be more likely to perceive an election as credible when they are aware of the presence of observers.[58]

Authoritarian governments sometimes invite sympathetic observers, known as "zombie EOs," which monitor undemocratic elections in order to generate the appearance of a level electoral playing field. While often greeted with derision internationally,[59] autocrats believe zombie monitors will increase citizens' trust in elections. Pseudo-democrats may do so to balance their competing desires of complying with the norms of holding elections and inviting monitors, as well as staying in power. Such governments would be unlikely to win an election that meets the standards laid out in the Declaration and do not want to subject themselves to the criticism and scrutiny a fair election would entail.

The second mechanism is that citizens may believe it is harder for governments to commit fraud when international observers are present. Again, there is some basis for this belief, since high-quality international EOs do attempt to deter fraud – and are often successful. For example, experimental studies in Armenia, Ghana, and Russia have demonstrated that credible EOs significantly affect vote shares at local polling stations.[60] As with the signaling mechanism, EOs' effects on the electoral playing field are somewhat more complex in practice, since not all monitors are high quality or even attempt to deter fraud. Cheating governments may also pursue electoral malpractice

---

[57] *Declaration of Principles for International Election Observation* (2005, 4–5).

[58] It is now so common for countries to invite international EOs to monitor their elections that the act of inviting them may have lost its signaling power for experts (i.e., there is a "pooling" equilibrium; see Hyde [2011, 44–45]). The presence of *high-quality* EOs could still be an informative signal for experts, as could *not* inviting any international EOs, since only truly authoritarian countries do not invite observers.

[59] On how associating with authoritarian countries can contribute to a bad international reputation, see Gray (2013).

[60] Hyde (2007); Ichino and Schündeln (2012); Enikolopov et al. (2013); Asunka et al. (2019).

that is harder to detect.[61] For citizens, however, the presence of international monitors may serve as a simple heuristic to indicate the quality of electoral institutions.

Monitors' Reports

Monitors' reports also provide information about election integrity to both the public in the observed country and international audiences. High-quality observers' costly efforts allow them to render detailed judgments not only about the level of fraud in which candidates engage but also the extent to which electoral institutions and rules meet broader international standards. As such, their reports contain information about candidates' types as well as the conduct of elections. Zombie monitors may also weigh in on these issues, though their reports are grounded more in fiction than in fact.

While credible EOs tend to write lengthy reports that contain both positive and negative information, it is often possible to infer from them an overall endorsement, condemnation, or ambiguous assessment, which the public can use as a heuristic. The media often covers EOs' evaluations in its reporting on elections, helping to transmit their headline findings to the public. Politicians may also draw attention to EOs' evaluations, choosing to strategically publicize reports that either legitimize their election victories or question their losses.

The judgments in EO reports have the potential to significantly affect citizens' beliefs about election credibility; positive evaluations are more likely to instill trust than negative evaluations. There is ample evidence that policymakers and practitioners believe their reports have such effects. For instance, Cameroon's autocratic government prepared a television news report the day after the fraudulent October 7, 2018, presidential election which featured actors pretending to represent Transparency International who proclaimed the election "extremely good." (Transparency International later issued a statement that it had not monitored the election.)[62] While this action was risky and had a high chance of backfiring, it demonstrates the considerable influence that EO reports are expected to have on citizens' perceptions of election credibility.

[61] Simpser and Donno (2012).
[62] O'Donnell and Gramer (2018).

2.2.4 *The Effects of Meddling*

Election meddling has the potential to diminish trust. Like many monitors, election meddlers may also seek to affect citizens' perceptions of election credibility. Some analysts believe this effect motivates contemporary Russian election meddling in the United States and its near abroad, for example.[63] Consistent with this logic, in a unique experimental survey of how outside meddling affects citizens' attitudes, Tomz and Weeks found that it diminished Americans' trust in a hypothetical future election.[64]

When it is known to have occurred, election meddling conveys information to the public about election integrity because it involves an attempt to tilt the playing field in favor of a foreign country's preferred parties or candidates. Yet unlike monitoring, election meddling is often done covertly. Consequently, citizens' *perceptions* of meddling are often crucial. Like monitoring, meddling may undermine perceptions of election credibility via two mechanisms. It has the potential to convey information to the public about (1) candidates' types as well as (2) the quality of electoral institutions.

For the first mechanism, when meddling has occurred – or when people *believe* that it has – citizens may update their beliefs about whether candidates are true or pseudo-democrats. International EOs are always *invited* to monitor elections, whereas meddling does not require candidates to accept – let alone invite – support from foreign actors. Nevertheless, meddling sometimes involves candidates' acceptance, whether tacit or explicit.

It is not unreasonable for citizens to conclude that meddling may have been accepted by the candidates it is designed to help. According to Dov Levin, a "great power will 'sit out' an election, even in the face of an intervention by an unfriendly great power and even if it sees such a situation as highly threatening to its interests, unless it can find a significant domestic actor willing to accept its assistance."[65] Accepting illegal foreign assistance signals that a politician is not truly committed to a fair electoral playing field. Some forms of meddling – such as attempting to hack voting machines – clearly involve electoral malpractice and violate domestic laws. A candidate who welcomes this

---

[63] Grier (2017); Fandos and Wines (2018); Way and Casey (2018).
[64] Tomz and Weeks (2020).
[65] Levin (2016, 190).

kind of help has cheated. Yet, even forms of meddling that involve less direct actions – such as soliciting statements from a foreign country that future economic relations will depend on the electoral outcome – could raise questions about candidates' true intentions. Given the norm of national self-determination, citizens may not understand why candidates who do not intend to cheat would invite even these lesser forms of foreign interference. Thus, information that a candidate accepted help from a foreign actor signals that he or she is a pseudo-democrat. Individuals may therefore update their beliefs about a candidate's type when a candidate is linked to meddling.

For the second mechanism, citizens may similarly update their beliefs about the electoral playing field if meddling occurs. Even if meddling does not alter individuals' opinions about candidates, it could cause them to update their beliefs about the country's electoral institutions. An outside country could gather and spread disinformation to help a party without encouragement from that party. In the United States, for example, Iran has reportedly engaged in this type of activity with the aim of harming Republican candidates and especially President Trump around the 2018 and 2020 elections, but Democratic politicians are not generally thought to have invited this involvement.[66] Nevertheless, such actions could raise concerns about the integrity of US elections. After all, meddling often succeeds at tilting elections.[67] Consequently, information about election meddling may diminish citizens' trust, similar to the effect of negative EO reports hypothesized earlier. Either type of information – indications of meddling and negative monitor reports about other aspects of election integrity – can demonstrate to citizens that candidates are cheaters, that the playing field is unfair, or both.

2.3 Factors that Condition Foreign Actors' Effects

Thus far, we have considered how foreign interventions could affect citizens' perceptions of election credibility, on average. Yet, these effects are apt to vary according to the characteristics of the intervener and the individual. These conditional effects of foreign actors have not been sufficiently appreciated in the past and therefore represent a key theoretical contribution of our study. To identify which characteristics

[66] Fabian (2018); Perlroth and Sanger (2019).
[67] Levin (2016).

of the intervener and the individual are most relevant theoretically, we return to an earlier idea: that individuals are motivated by both accuracy and directional goals when responding to new information about election credibility. Recognizing these two goals encourages us to evaluate the identity of the intervener and individuals' vote choices and uncertainty, as we explain later in this chapter.

2.3.1 Identity of the Intervener

For information about the electoral playing field to be persuasive, it must come from a credible source. Thus, the identity of the intervener matters. This insight is consistent with a model of Bayesian updating, which assumes that citizens desire to have accurate beliefs about election credibility, although the model makes no assumptions about which sources they are likely to perceive as credible.[68] We focus on interveners' perceived *capabilities* and monitors' perceived *biases*. We expect these characteristics to condition how foreign interventions influence credibility.

Perceived Capabilities

The first relevant characteristic is whether citizens believe a foreign actor is capable of influencing an election. For foreign actors to convey new and valuable information about candidates' types and the likelihood of malpractice, they must have the capacity to influence the electoral playing field in practice.

For monitors, being capable means being able to detect and deter fraud. If monitors are not perceived to be capable, then we would not expect inviting them to signal a government's commitment to holding clean elections. Moreover, if they are not perceived as being able to detect fraud, then their presence should not suggest to citizens that they are deterring it. Finally, if monitors cannot detect fraud, then their reports are unlikely to be persuasive. In summary, for EOs to provide persuasive information, they must be perceived to be capable.

For meddlers, being capable means being able to increase the odds that a preferred candidate or party will get elected. If meddlers cannot influence an election outcome, then their efforts will not affect the

---

[68] Bullock (2009, 1111). Note also that different people may assess the credibility of the same source differently.

electoral playing field. Incompetent meddling arguably still sends a signal that a candidate is a pseudo-democrat if citizens believe he or she invited or accepted the intervention. Even so, we expect meddling that is perceived to be distorting the playing field enough to affect an election outcome will be more likely to cause individuals to update their beliefs about candidates and the playing field.

The variation in foreign actors' capabilities that citizens perceive is real, and not merely theoretically possible. Although powerful countries such as the United States and Russia/the Soviet Union have meddled in the elections of several weaker states,[69] weaker countries sometimes attempt to influence an election in a more dominant country, such as Iran in recent US elections. And even relatively formidable election meddlers do not always succeed at helping their favored candidates win. Reflecting on Russia's election meddling in its near abroad between 1991 and 2014, Lucan Way and Adam Casey concluded, "[T]hese interventions often did more to undermine than to bolster Russia's geopolitical interests."[70] When Moldova's ruling Communist Party had a dispute with Russia over the breakaway territory of Transnistria in 2005, for example, Russia provided direct support to opposition candidates in the parliamentary election and threatened the incumbent government with economic sanctions.[71] Yet, the intervention was not enough: The Communist Party won the election handily.

International election observation is even more complex, since many different organizations with varying capacities often monitor the same elections.[72] International EOs include highly professional teams from organizations such as the Carter Center, the EU, and the Organization for Security and Co-operation in Europe (OSCE), as well as zombie missions from organizations that are much less interested in democracy promotion such as the Commonwealth of Independent States and the Shanghai Cooperation Organization. We therefore anticipate that some organizations are likely to be perceived as being capable of detecting and deterring fraud, while others are not.

---

[69] Levin (2019a).
[70] Way and Casey (2018, 1).
[71] Chivers (2005, A8); Way (2016, 69).
[72] Kelley (2009b); Pratt (2018).

Perceived Biases

The second relevant characteristic is whether the foreign actor is perceived as willing to influence an election. This trait is primarily relevant for international EOs, who may be viewed as either neutral democracy promoters or partisan actors. Yet meddlers, by definition, are willing to influence an election. They will never be viewed as neutral, although they may support a variety of political parties.

International observers' perceived biases affect their ability to instill trust through the same mechanisms as their perceived capabilities. Some international EOs are – or are perceived to be – biased. This is clearly the case for zombie election monitors, but even reputable groups have been shown to sometimes offer more generous assessments of elections than would otherwise be expected because of political considerations.[73]

If international EOs are perceived to be biased in favor of the incumbent government, then their presence may not offer persuasive information to citizens about election credibility. The act of inviting them does not necessarily reveal any information to citizens about the government's type, because their presence is not costly to the incumbent. Moreover, if EOs do not make genuine efforts to detect and deter fraud, then their presence is unlikely to alter the electoral playing field. Therefore, we do not expect the activities of international EOs that are perceived to be biased to significantly enhance trust in elections. Supporting this argument, evidence from Russia confirms that citizens' trust in observers heavily shapes their beliefs about EOs' partisan biases.[74]

If international EOs are perceived to be biased, then their reports may also affect citizens' perceptions of election credibility in heterogeneous ways. A positive report may be expected to have the greatest trust-enhancing effect when an observer group that is expected to condemn an election because of its perceived bias actually endorses it. In other words, when observers deliver an unexpectedly positive report, it may send a stronger signal than when they give an expected positive report based on their political biases.[75] A similar dynamic would be expected when observers release an unexpectedly negative report.

---

[73] Kelley (2009a); Dodsworth (2019); Kavakli and Kuhn (2020).
[74] Robertson (2017).
[75] Chernykh and Svolik (2012).

The Origins of Citizens' Perceptions of Foreign Actors

Thus far, we have taken individuals' perceptions of international actors as given. While it is not one of the book's main objectives to theorize and identify the origins of such perceptions, it is important to note that they are subject to the same accuracy and directional goals as citizens' perceptions of the electoral playing field.

When citizens' perceptions of foreign actors are motivated by *accuracy* goals, they rely on their general knowledge of or personal experiences with the foreign country that is intervening – such as how powerful or wealthy it is, and its cultural and geographic proximity. For example, the intervener's actions related to previous elections in the country or region provide clues about its capabilities and biases. Some international monitors, such as the Carter Center or the OSCE, have sent missions to the same country for many years, if not decades, which contributes to their local reputations. Overt instances of election meddling may be even more salient than election monitoring and likely remembered for a long time.

People also consider foreign actors' histories beyond electoral interventions, such as their involvement in regional conflicts or their colonial histories. In some cases, the foreign actors are IGOs or international NGOs, as in the case of many international election monitors. Individuals may have limited information about such actors, but the organization's most powerful member country or main sponsoring country can indicate which party, if any, it is likely to support. This can often be a reliable heuristic, since powerful countries influence international organizations in various ways, including their enforcement of norms related to election integrity.[76]

When individuals are more motivated by *directional* goals, their partisan biases are likely to shape their perceptions of foreign interveners' capabilities and biases. Such biases may cause election losers to perceive international EOs that are present or that issue positive reports as less capable than election winners.[77] Similarly, election losers may be more likely than election winners to perceive foreign meddlers as capable. As noted previously, there are greater ambiguities surrounding election meddling: It can be hard to assess whether it

---

[76] Stone (2011); Donno (2013).
[77] This phenomenon could resemble what Little (2019, 675) describes as "the distortion of related beliefs."

has occurred, and if it *has* taken place, it is often difficult to determine whether it ultimately affected the election result. Individuals may therefore be especially susceptible to partisan biases when evaluating the capabilities of election meddlers.

2.3.2 Individual Characteristics

As noted earlier in the chapter, a substantial body of research examines how individuals' election day experiences, political knowledge and sophistication, and various demographic factors shape their trust in elections.[78] It is possible that a number of these characteristics *could* condition how foreign actors influence perceptions of election credibility. However, our theoretical framework suggests we should focus first on individuals' vote choice and the uncertainty of their prior beliefs. Later, we explain how recognizing citizens' accuracy and directional motives suggests that these variables are the most theoretically relevant individual characteristics. To account for the possibility that additional individual characteristics could shape perceptions of election credibility and interact with foreign actors' interventions, our surveys asked about several other characteristics, which we address in our discussion of the research design (Chapter 3) and in the analysis (Chapters 4–7).

Whereas accuracy motives are associated with the Bayesian model of information processing, directional motives are associated with the motivated reasoning model, which is drawn from psychology.[79] IR scholars have explored a wide array of psychological models that seek to explain how people make biased decisions due, for example, to groupthink or framing effects.[80] However, the motivated reasoning model is particularly relevant for this study. As applied within political science, it has explored the "drive to process information to buttress one's preferred party's policy positions and endorsed candidates."[81]

---

[78] For example, see Anderson et al. (2005), Alvarez, Hall, and Llewellyn (2008), Birch (2008), Rosas (2010), Beaulieu (2014b), Cantú and García-Ponce (2015), Sances and Stewart (2015), Erlich and Kerr (2016), Kerr and Lührmann (2017), Wellman, Hyde, and Hall (2017), Kerr (2018), and Jochem, Murtazashvili, and Murtazashvili (2020). On the role of political sophistication in information processing more generally, see McGraw, Lodge, and Stroh (1990).

[79] Kunda (1990); Taber and Lodge (2006).

[80] Hafner-Burton et al. (2017, S13–S14).

[81] Leeper and Mullinix (2018).

Given that elections are, by definition, partisan events, many prior studies of citizens' trust in elections have emphasized this type of biased information processing.[82] Our study is the first to apply these insights to analyze how foreign actors affect trust at the individual level.

It is beyond the scope of our study to adjudicate between the Bayesian and motivated reasoning models, which have been debated extensively in the public opinion literature. Doing so would be very challenging, if not impossible; it is difficult to ascertain individuals' real motives, and the same empirical pattern can often be interpreted as supporting either model, depending on what one assumes about an individual's prior beliefs and other factors.[83] We instead suggest ways that both models can be used to shed light on the conditioning effect of individual characteristics.

Vote Choice

There are reasons to believe that both accuracy and directional motivations could lead vote choice to condition the effects of foreign actors on local trust in an election. As discussed earlier, vote choice is an important determinant of perceptions of election credibility: Election winners are more likely to have confidence in an election than election losers. Whether an individual supported an election's winner or loser influences the information they have about the electoral playing field and shapes his or her emotional and cognitive processes surrounding elections. We do not theorize *ex ante* about whether winners vs. losers or good news vs. bad news should be associated with larger effects, although we explore this topic empirically in Chapter 7, and it has been the subject of prior research on information processing.[84]

From an *accuracy* perspective, if people are somewhat uncertain about whether an election has integrity, and holding constant the source of new information, individuals' prior beliefs will determine the effect of new information. All else equal, trust-enhancing information is expected to have a stronger positive effect on people who initially believed an election lacked credibility. Thus, people who support losing candidates and parties – who tend to have lower trust in

---

[82] We review this literature in Section 2.1.2.

[83] For a discussion of the challenges, see Coppock (2021, Ch. 7). Recent game theoretical models have also explored ways in which both models may be integrated into a game theoretic framework (e.g., Little 2019).

[84] For example, Eil and Rao (2011).

the credibility of elections to begin with than those who support the winners – will be more likely to be reassured by international monitors' presence and positive reports because EOs are providing new information to them. By contrast, people who already believe an election is clean will be less likely to update their assessment of the electoral playing field in response to such information because it is reinforcing what they already (think they) know. Meanwhile, people who support winning candidates and parties are more likely to have less trust in an election if they hear about monitors' criticisms or become aware of foreign meddling via a credible source of information.

From a *directional* perspective, however, partisan biases shape how new information affects beliefs. Thus, if an individual's vote choice motivates his or her beliefs about the election, then vote choice will condition the effect of foreign actors on perceived credibility. The logic of motivated reasoning suggests that trust-enhancing foreign interventions may not increase trust among supporters of the losing party who are already motivated by their partisan commitments to believe an election lacks credibility. We would expect any positive effects from trust-enhancing interventions (such as the actions of international EOs) to be concentrated among supporters of the winning party or candidate. The reverse prediction can be made about trust-diminishing foreign interventions such as election meddling, which should have their strongest effects on election losers but may not diminish the trust of election winners.

Although it is not the focus of our later analysis, this logic could be extended to hypothesize that individual vote choice interacts with intervener characteristics to determine how foreign actors shape election credibility. For example, a person who voted for the challenger could be especially worried about the effects of a capable pro-incumbent meddler. Whereas the incumbent's supporters might be skeptical of whether capable meddling has truly tilted the electoral playing field in favor of the government, the opposition's supporters might be directionally motivated to seek out or be influenced by information concerning trust-diminishing interventions or hold stronger priors about meddlers' capabilities.

Uncertainty

Earlier in the chapter, we established that individuals' uncertainty about election credibility is a key condition that makes it possible for new information to persuade them, especially according to a Bayesian model. For people to update their beliefs about election credibility in the search for greater accuracy, they must generally have at least some degree of uncertainty about the election. Individuals who already possess a wealth of information or are strong partisans are likely to have durable preexisting beliefs about the electoral playing field; even direct exposure to a foreign intervention might not change their minds.

As discussed previously, both contextual and individual factors influence the probability of uncertainty. In less certain electoral environments, such as transitional elections, foreign actors are more likely to influence perceptions of election credibility since they are more likely to provide new, persuasive information to citizens. We explore this empirical expectation by investigating variation *across* countries in the effects of foreign actors. In addition, some individual characteristics, such as exposure to malpractice, political interest and sophistication, or personality traits, may shape an individual's confidence in her evaluation of election credibility. It is thus possible to measure individual uncertainty as well as variation *within* countries in the effects of foreign actors.

2.4 An Alternative Perspective

Finally, nationalism may cause citizens to view *all* forms of foreign influence on their elections negatively. According to one summary of the literature, "nationalism is expected to produce a fairly uniform response to threatening outsiders: resistance."[85] For instance, a study of public attitudes in Ukraine found that citizens' reactions to foreign electoral interventions were processed through a nationalist lens.[86] A recent history of covert electoral interference called resistance to outside interference "inevitabl[e]."[87] Scholars of foreign interventions argue that fear of such a backlash is a key reason why powerful countries opt to intervene covertly in elections[88] and often fail in their attempts at occupation and statebuilding.[89] Nationalist blowback is now an important concern: Nationalism appears to be on the rise, with

---

[85] Kocher, Lawrence, and Monteiro (2018, 118).
[86] Shulman and Bloom (2012).
[87] Shimer (2020, 27).
[88] Ibid.; Levin (2020, 40–41).
[89] Edelstein (2011); Lake (2016).

events such as Trump's victory and Brexit illustrating its far-reaching and concrete implications.[90]

The norms of sovereignty and noninterference in states' domestic affairs are among the most longstanding in international politics. Though it is perhaps obvious that election meddling violates those norms, other foreign influences on elections have also been accused of doing so. While the practice of international election observation has gradually become accepted at the United Nations and within other international institutions, it was only after considerable contestation about whether monitoring infringed upon state sovereignty.[91] Broader democracy promotion efforts (i.e., support for international monitors and other activities that help level the electoral playing field, see Chapter 1) that practitioners insist neutrally support democratic values, such as international efforts to support civil society around the 2000 Bulldozer Revolution in Serbia, have frequently been criticized on the grounds that they involve inappropriate outside interference in states' sovereign affairs.[92]

Despite its formal acceptance, the widespread practice of international election monitoring may be unwelcome among certain audiences and could be perceived as a form of foreign interference. In fact, political leaders often accuse critical international monitors of violating their country's sovereignty. Ahead of the disputed December 2018 election in the DRC, for example, the government used the language of foreign interference to discredit international observers. After rejecting the appointment of former South African President Thabo Mbeki as special envoy, DRC Communications Minister Lambert Mende was reported as saying that observers "tend to behave like proconsuls. They don't respect the DRC's autonomy. We want to mark our sovereignty."[93]

Civil society organizations seeking to advance democracy often worry that citizens' concerns about foreign influence will undermine their work. A 2009–2010 survey asked almost 1,500 individuals working in leadership roles in civil society organizations and state institutions that had received democracy assistance about the greatest risks

---

[90] Mearsheimer (2021, 1).
[91] Kelley (2012b, 34–36).
[92] For a discussion, see Melia (2018).
[93] Agence France-Presse (2018).

associated with receiving such aid. More than one-third (37 percent) of all respondents "felt that the greatest risk was being labeled an 'agent' or 'stooge' of outside forces"; this proportion increased to nearly one-half (48 percent) of respondents in countries classified as "not free" by Freedom House.[94] These figures may be even higher today given the rise in populist nationalism associated with the backlash against liberal internationalism.[95] One reason why international actors were encouraged in the 1990s to do more to support domestic EOs (which they subsequently did) is that domestic monitors were deemed likely to circumvent some of these nationalist concerns. As Thomas Carothers explained, "they embody the crucial idea that the society in question should take primary responsibility for improving its own political processes."[96]

When governments like the DRC's use nationalist rhetoric to discredit international EOs, this suggests such rhetoric could be a powerful force. For example, the Chinese Communist Party has unexpectedly *publicized* international human rights monitors' negative reports, because doing so enhances the regime's support among citizens who are eager to defend their country from outside criticism.[97] Indeed, there is growing evidence from a range of countries of nationalist backlash against international pressures related to issues of gender equality and human rights.[98] This dynamic seems especially likely when foreign actors criticize or want to change the behavior of a target state, as these actions can provoke emotional responses such as anger and resistance.[99]

If the public considers all forms of foreign electoral influence to be inappropriate violations of the principle of national self-determination, then we might expect that even interventions that we classified earlier as potentially trust enhancing will diminish perceived election credibility. This logic can be integrated with our theory regarding the reasons why election meddling may cause people to perceive elections as less credible, but it can be applied to *any* form of foreign influence on an

---

[94] Barkan (2012, 134).
[95] Copelovitch and Pevehouse (2019, 169–170).
[96] Carothers (1997, 26).
[97] Gruffydd-Jones (2019).
[98] Grossman, Manekin, and Margalit (2018); Terman (2019); Chapman and Chaudoin (2020); Chaudhry (2021); Chaudhry, Dotson, and Heiss (2021).
[99] Snyder (2020).

election. If candidates invite interventions by foreign actors, this would indicate that they are not committed to a fair electoral playing field. Moreover, if an intervention by foreign actors with bad intentions is ongoing, it could also undermine the fairness of the electoral playing field through various mechanisms. For both reasons, all foreign influences could depress trust.[100] This alternative perspective, which emphasizes the negative reception of *any* form of foreign intervention, makes predictions about foreign actors' overall (as opposed to conditional) effects.

Some evidence already cuts against this alternative explanation. Governments all over the world willingly invite international EOs to monitor elections. And countries that have been the target of foreign meddling – presumably the worst form of outside interference – do not always retaliate. The coming chapters provide further direct evidence that few countries' citizens seem to process foreign influences on elections primarily through a nationalist lens. Indeed, we find that many individuals respond neutrally or positively to foreign interventions – even those that have the potential to diminish an election's integrity.

2.5 Conclusion

In this chapter, we developed a bottom-up theory of how foreign actors shape citizens' perceptions of election credibility by providing information about candidates' types and the electoral playing field. Our framework allows us to develop predictions about both the average effects of foreign interventions on citizens' beliefs (which is more consistent with the conventional wisdom) and their more conditional effects (which scholars and practitioners have underappreciated in the past). The hypothesized conditional effects depend on the intervener's identity and the individual's vote choice and uncertainty. Table 2.1 lists our empirical expectations and which chapter we test them in.

Our theory makes four broad contributions. First, it unifies the study of diverse forms of foreign interventions within a single framework. We argue that both monitors and meddlers – types of foreign actors that

---

[100] Drawing on Gruffydd-Jones (2019)'s findings, we could also hypothesize that citizens will respond especially negatively to outside criticism in the form of monitors' negative reports.

Table 2.1 *Observable implications*

	Variable	Prediction (Location Tested)
Average effects (conventional wisdom)	Monitors present	Increases credibility (Chapter 4)
	Monitors' reports	Positive reports increase credibility more than negative reports (Chapter 4)
	Meddling	Decreases credibility (Chapter 5)
Conditional effects (new theory)	Foreign actors...	
	-Perceived as capable and unbiased	Accentuates effects of monitors (Chapter 6)
	-Perceived as capable	Accentuates effects of meddlers (Chapter 6)
	Individuals...	
	-Vote choice	Accentuates or diminishes effects of foreign actors (Chapter 7)
		Shapes perceptions of foreign interventions (Chapter 7)
	-Uncertain	Accentuates effects of foreign actors (Chapters 4–7)
Nationalist backlash (alternative theory)	Any foreign influence	Decreases credibility (Chapters 4–7)

are often studied in isolation – have the potential to influence domestic politics through their effects on individuals' beliefs about the fairness of the electoral playing field. Although these diverse forms of foreign influences on elections differ markedly – in terms of when and why they occur, and whether they are even legal – they have a common effect on a critical, but understudied, audience: citizens in the countries where elections are held.

Second, and relatedly, our theory makes the case that it is not the *foreignness* of foreign influences on elections that causes individuals to update their beliefs about election credibility. The alternative perspective we outlined in the preceding section posits that the norms of sovereignty and noninterference imply that citizens will respond negatively to *all* forms of foreign influence, even activities such as reputable international election monitoring designed to advance democracy rather than meddle in other countries' elections. By contrast, our framework posits that foreign actors can provide information about election integrity to citizens in much the same way that other sources of information – including domestic ones – do. As such, we expect vote choice to condition responses to foreign interventions. Our finding that individuals' partisanship conditions their response to foreign influences on elections is consistent with recent findings about responses to an even more extreme type of outside influence: foreign occupation.[101]

In a third contribution, our theory draws on prior findings on public opinion from the subfields of American and comparative politics to study the effects of foreign actors. It builds on the insight that individuals are motivated by both accuracy and directional goals. Previous IR research on the effects of foreign interventions in elections has often posited individual-level effects without directly theorizing or testing them.[102] Yet, there are reasons to think the effects of foreign interventions may be considerably more conditional than has previously been recognized. Thus, our theory identifies some of the conditions under which the effects of foreign actors will be *limited*. For instance, the activities of credible international EOs will not always enhance trust; nor will foreign meddling always undermine it. Previous research and policy debates about foreign influences on elections have not sufficiently appreciated this point. Our insight joins other recent research applying theories from political psychology to understand IR. This literature, however, has focused more on the dynamics of international

[101] Kocher, Lawrence, and Monteiro (2018).
[102] Examples include Daxecker (2012), Hyde and Marinov (2014), and von Borzyskowski (2019a). As we explain in Chapter 3, one advantage of our survey-based research design (and of other studies that use related methods) is that it allows us to directly test for individual-level effects.

security than on transnational issues such as democracy promotion; thus, we build a theoretical bridge to these other issue areas.[103]

Finally, our theory acknowledges and allows for the idea that capabilities and biases are not objective characteristics of foreign actors. For example, in earlier work, we argued that citizens' perceptions of international EOs' capabilities are rooted as much in their beliefs about the observers' perceived local knowledge and resources as in the observers' historic familiarity with and commitment to democracy.[104] Yet, the international community values democratic credentials most of all. Our approach therefore draws on a perspective that is dominant in fields such as science and technology studies but not in political science: that expertise is socially constructed and subjective. Thus, and despite applying ideas from rationalist models such as Bayesian updating and psychological models such as motivated reasoning, we engage ideas that might be more commonly associated with a postpositivist theoretical approach to IR. This synthetic theoretical approach may be useful for understanding a range of phenomena in world politics, an idea we explore in Chapter 8.

---

[103] For examples, see Yarhi-Milo (2014), Hermann (2017), and Kertzer, Rathbun, and Rathbun (2020). For a review of political psychology in IR, see Kertzer and Tingley (2018). They note that most of this literature has focused on international security and foreign policy (Kertzer and Tingley 2018, 325).

[104] Bush and Prather (2018).

3 | Research Strategy

We developed a theory in Chapter 2 that predicts the conditions under which foreign actors can be expected to enhance or diminish citizens' trust in elections. This theory could be tested in a variety of ways. We use multiple research methods and data sources – most importantly original surveys that we conducted in Tunisia, the United States, and Georgia between 2014 and 2020. Although every research strategy involves trade-offs, we maintain that these surveys represent the best opportunity to test our theory, especially when supplemented with other forms of evidence. In this chapter, we explain why we believe this is the case and address other crucial questions about our methodology. The chapter has three sections.

In the first section, we explain why we decided to collect individual-level data for this book. Adopting a survey-based approach allows us to measure citizens' trust precisely and at the points in time that are most relevant for our theory. It also enables us to use survey experiments, in which the researcher randomly assigns a "treatment" (in our case, information about foreign actors) to respondents who are taking the public opinion survey. Yet, we acknowledge that relying on surveys has drawbacks. For example, it requires us to focus on a small number of cases, which makes it more difficult to draw general conclusions. We address this limitation in various ways, including by relying on other forms of data when possible and carefully selecting our case studies.

In the second section of the chapter, we discuss our approach to data collection, emphasizing how the surveys we conducted were designed and implemented. Our surveys were shaped by qualitative data gathered through field research, and prior survey findings informed the design of subsequent surveys. All surveys employed a common approach to conceptualizing and measuring perceptions of election credibility and similar experiments, which we explain in this chapter.

In the third section, we describe our approach to case selection. We chose three diverse cases that were substantively important and varied in regime type. This type of variation is relevant for our study since our theory predicts that foreign actors will have more influence on perceptions of election credibility if the electoral environment is uncertain, as we would expect in a transitional setting such as Tunisia in 2014. In this section, we also provide brief overviews of electoral integrity and foreign influences on recent elections in each of our cases.

3.1 Focusing on Citizens

Many prior studies argue that foreign actors influence countries' domestic politics, including through their effects on and around election day.[1] Past research on election-related protests and violence hypothesizes that the mechanism linking foreign actors to these effects is that they shape citizens' perceptions of election credibility. However, these analyses generally overlook the citizen: Instead of showing how monitors or meddlers change citizens' perceptions, they look for evidence that patterns of protest and violence change with the involvement of foreign actors and assume that the mechanism is through effects on individual beliefs.[2]

But to understand whether citizens perceive an election to be credible, it makes sense to ask them. Previous research on foreign actors has been unable to study the citizen due to a lack of public opinion data

---

[1] A large literature examines how foreign actors influence domestic politics in general, which international relations scholars refer to as the tradition of research on "the second image reversed." See Gourevitch (1978). The election credibility literature contains several studies on how international monitors influence local dynamics of protest and violence. For example, see Daxecker (2012), Little (2012), Donno (2013), Hyde and Marinov (2014), and von Borzyskowski (2019a).

[2] There are a few important exceptions, as described in more detail in Chapter 2. See Brancati (2014a), Robertson (2017), Benstead, Kao, and Lust (2020), and Tomz and Weeks (2020). Like us, these scholars study how monitors and meddlers affect citizens' attitudes. Yet, our study departs from theirs in three ways. First, we theorize and empirically test the effects of multiple types of foreign influence rather than a single type. Second, we examine intervener- and individual-level characteristics that condition foreign actors' effects, while most prior studies focused on foreign actors' overall effects. Third, our study is comparative *and* cross-regional, while previous research was generally focused on single cases or cases within the same region.

on the topic. The World Values Survey started to examine citizens' perceptions of election integrity using a large (though far from comprehensive) set of forty-one countries in its sixth wave between 2010 and 2014.[3] However, these surveys are generally not conducted around election day and contain few questions regarding perceptions of foreign influence. As such, they are of limited utility for understanding how foreign actors affect citizens' perceptions, both because they lack sufficient questions about perceptions of foreign influence and because too much time has generally passed since the election. Post-election events and governance often cause people to reassess earlier elections, making retrospective answers about elections potentially unreliable.

Our research focuses on the period immediately before and after election day, which enables us to measure individual attitudes at the time when foreign influence is likely to be highest. Otherwise, it is difficult to rule out potential counterarguments about foreign actors' effects. This is the first challenge our research design addresses. For example, consider the finding that international monitors' negative reports are correlated with post-election protests. People may be more likely to protest when election observers (EOs) issue critical statements because they think the international community is paying attention and will support opposition groups – not because they have updated their beliefs about the election's credibility. Therefore, it is essential to complement macro-level analyses of trends *among* countries with micro-level analyses of individuals' perceptions *within and across* countries. It is not enough to assume that observable patterns of protest and violence reflect changes in citizens' electoral trust; we must directly measure that trust.

Our survey research design also addresses a second challenge that any study of the effects of foreign influences on domestic politics faces: Foreign actors do not intervene in elections at random. Credible international EOs tend to get invited – and accept invitations – to elections that are already of relatively high quality. Similarly, it is plausible that meddling is more likely to occur in elections that already have questionable integrity, since they are more vulnerable to foreign influence. Thus, finding a correlation between foreign influence and perceptions of election credibility in several countries may not indicate causation.

---

[3] Haerpfer et al. (2014). The seventh wave also included a relevant battery of questions. See Inglehart et al. (2020).

This problem is known as selection bias. Foreign actors could indeed be increasing or decreasing citizens' trust in elections, or they could simply choose to intervene in elections that have higher or lower levels of baseline integrity.

To address concerns about potential selection bias, we adopt an experimental research design, following other recent studies in international relations.[4] As explained in detail in the empirical chapters (Chapters 4–7), we randomly created a subsample of respondents in our surveys who received information about the activities of foreign actors and then asked them about their trust in elections; the other respondents (those in the control group) did not receive such information. Respondents who heard information about foreign actors were therefore identical to those who did not. This approach enables us to accurately estimate the effect of knowledge and awareness of foreign interventions on citizens' perceptions of election credibility without controlling for any other variables that might confound these relationships.[5] It therefore enhances our study's internal validity or its ability to confidently understand cause-and-effect relationships.

By choosing to focus on individual attitudes, we make three main sacrifices. The first is that conducting original, representative surveys is resource intensive, so we could not pursue our research strategy in more than a handful of cases. To address this limitation, we chose the cases carefully to promote the study's generalizability, as we discuss below. We also supplement our analysis of original survey data with analysis of other cross-national surveys (including the World Values Survey and Global Barometers project) and other global datasets (including the National Elections Across Democracy and Autocracy

---

[4] Hyde (2015) describes the experimental turn in international relations research. The experiments in Georgia were preregistered with the Evidence in Governance and Politics registry (20181102AC) following recent conversations within political science about the design and analysis of experiments. The online appendix (www.cambridge.org/bushprather) contains the remaining pre-specified analyses that we do not include in the book, which mostly pertain to additional conditional hypotheses that we do not theorize and test here.

[5] The main exception to our general approach of not including any control variables is in Chapter 7, where most of our analyses do include them because we focus on how vote choice moderates the effect of foreign interventions on perceptions of election credibility. Since vote choice is not randomly assigned and several factors could affect both vote choice and perceptions of election credibility (e.g., educational attainment), our analyses include measures for those variables.

dataset and the Data on International Election Monitoring). Although these excellent datasets are not ideally constructed for answering our research questions, they shed valuable light on trends in a larger set of countries.

The second sacrifice is that our survey experiments, by design, informed people about the activities of foreign actors, but in the real world, people acquire this information in a variety of ways. As detailed in Chapters 4–7, we tracked news coverage about foreign actors and interviewed people involved in trying to transmit information about them to the public; this information helped us craft experimental treatments that mimicked what people might encounter in the real world. Yet in practice, politicians use and publicize the types of information we provided to respondents for their own ends, and their messages could enhance or diminish the effects we identify in our survey. The ability to translate an experiment's findings to the real world is known as its "external validity."[6] One way of interpreting our findings is that they help us understand why political elites choose to publicize information about foreign actors in the ways that they do, including in some ways that might seem strange, such as politicians publicizing the presence of fake or zombie EOs. Doing so makes sense given that many citizens in our study responded favorably to information about election monitors, including those from relatively undemocratic countries. We return to this issue in Chapter 8.

The third sacrifice is that focusing on individual citizens means that we do not focus on other, very important outcomes such as the incidence of protests following elections. As discussed above, we believe the shift to studying citizens directly is a necessary move in the literature and a complement to previous studies. We further maintain that individuals' perceptions of election credibility are intrinsically important. And as we showed in Chapter 1, they are linked to crucial individual-level political behaviors, including one of the most essential forms of political participation, voting. Focusing on individuals also raises a variety of intriguing theoretical questions about the conditional effects of foreign actors, as we discussed in Chapter 2. However, determining how individuals' beliefs about election credibility aggregate into decisions made by groups of people about, for example, whether to engage in protests or violence is beyond the scope of our study.

---

[6] Gaines, Kuklinski, and Quirk (2007).

While it seems safe to assume that individuals' preferences shape those more-collective decisions, we leave it to future research to investigate how exactly that process works.[7]

3.2 Data Collection

We conducted ten large-scale surveys across elections in three countries (see Table 3.1). We studied citizens' perceptions of the 2014 parliamentary and presidential elections in Tunisia; the 2016, 2018, and 2020 general elections in the United States; and the 2018 first- and second-round presidential elections in Georgia.

Although the surveys form the core of our empirical research strategy, our case studies were informed by other types of data. For each country, we read a variety of qualitative materials, including documents produced by international and domestic EO teams (e.g., their reports and training documents), civil society organizations, the news media, and academics. We also conducted fifteen interviews in Georgia and Tunisia with elites knowledgeable about issues related to election integrity, including representatives of electoral commissions, leaders of international and domestic election monitoring missions, and local academics.[8] In Tunisia, we further led two focus groups with interested university students. This qualitative information guided some of our design choices in the surveys and our interpretation of the results, as we note in the empirical chapters to come (Chapters 4–7).

Overall, our research process resembles what Jason Seawright describes as an "integrative research sequence,"[9] in which scholars cycle between multiple methods. Our surveys also represent an integrative research sequence, as the results of each set of surveys and experiments informed the design of subsequent surveys and

---

[7] Similar to other research on public opinion in international relations, one might think of the broader research agenda we propose as following the "boxes-within-boxes" framework. Future research could connect the findings in this book's "box" (about individual attitudes) to a meso-level "box" (perhaps the actions of a social network or political party) to a more macro-level "box" (national patterns of protest or violence, which others have studied, such as Lake and Powell [1999] and Hafner-Burton et al. [2017, S18–S19]).

[8] We made one research trip to Georgia and two research trips to Tunisia, each for a period of 1–2 weeks.

[9] Seawright (2016, 10).

Table 3.1 *Summary of cases*

Country	Year	Election	Survey Timing	Survey Format	Country Context
Tunisia	2014	Legislative	Post-election	Face to face	Transitional democracy
Tunisia	2014	Presidential (second round)	Post-election	Face to face	Transitional democracy
United States	2016	Presidential	Pre-election	Online	Consolidated democracy
United States	2016	Presidential	Post-election	Online	Consolidated democracy
United States	2018	Legislative	Pre-election	Online	Consolidated democracy
United States	2018	Legislative	Post-election	Online	Consolidated democracy
United States	2020	Presidential	Pre-election	Online	Consolidated democracy
United States	2020	Presidential	Post-election	Online	Consolidated democracy
Georgia	2018	Presidential (first round)	Pre-election	Face to face	Partial democracy
Georgia	2018	Presidential (second round)	Post-election	Face to face	Partial democracy

experiments. Our later surveys did not merely attempt to replicate our earlier findings in new settings. They also sought to improve upon some of our earlier survey analyses and findings, for example by testing additional observable implications of our theory or by making our empirical tests more direct or precise.

3.2.1 Measuring Perceptions of Election Credibility

Each of our surveys included two very similar questions about citizens' perceptions of election credibility – the main outcome we seek to explain. Using the same question wording in all of our surveys facilitated comparisons across the different contexts. Asking the questions in a similar way despite the diverse cases made sense since earlier research had shown that there are shared global norms about what a free and fair election looks like.[10]

As explained in Chapter 1, we define a credible election as one in which people (1) trust the results and (2) believe the results reflect the will of the people.[11] This conceptual approach represents somewhat of a departure from previous research, as some prior studies on citizens' attitudes focus only on the first dimension – for instance by asking citizens whether they think an election was fraudulent or whether they trust the results.[12]

However, both dimensions reflect how many people contemplate the topic of election credibility in real life and help test our theory about whether individuals think the electoral playing field was fair. On the one hand, it is possible for votes to be counted correctly but for the playing field to be so skewed that it is difficult to say that an election truly reflected the will of the people. On the other hand, some votes might be counted incorrectly even in a consolidated democracy, but this is unlikely to have changed the overall result, which still reflects the wishes of the majority. Given these complexities, we asked all respondents whether they trusted the election results and believed they reflected the will of the people.

Nevertheless, we note that individuals' responses to both questions about election credibility were highly correlated in all of our surveys,

---

[10] Norris (2013a).
[11] See Bush and Prather (2017, 922) for our first articulation of this definition.
[12] For example, Robertson (2017) and Tomz and Weeks (2020).

illustrating how they capture the same underlying concept in most elections. Since the two dimensions are both key elements of our conceptualization of election credibility, our default approach is to analyze responses to both together by creating a single measure of election credibility. In robustness checks located in the online appendix, we analyze each outcome measure separately. When respondents perceived an election as slightly more credible on one dimension than the other, we note that. For example, in Tunisia, a minority of our survey respondents said they did not trust the results of the parliamentary election but still believed the outcome reflected the will of the people. This conclusion is similar to that of the EOs, who noted some problems with the election but did not believe fraud had altered the overall outcome.

Since the cases have varying levels of democracy, we varied the specificity of the response options for these questions depending on the context. For example, in the United States, a consolidated democracy, we used a 10-point scale to capture subtle shifts in trust, and a 4-point scale in Tunisia, a transitional democracy. To facilitate comparisons throughout the book, however, we standardized our credibility indicators to range from 0 (least perceived credibility) to 2 (most perceived credibility).

When we standardize the variable and compare across the countries studied, the average level of election credibility in our case studies mirrors other surveys' findings about perceptions of elections in these countries. For instance, just as we find strong trust in elections in Tunisia, the Arab Barometer survey fielded there in 2013 found incredible enthusiasm for the country's new elections: More than 75 percent of respondents assessed the most recent parliamentary elections as either completely free and fair (56.7 percent) or free and fair with some minor breaches (18.6 percent).[13] We find somewhat weaker trust in the US election outcomes in 2016, 2018, and 2020 when our survey results are standardized, but our results are similar to what other researchers have found when studying confidence in US elections.[14] Finally, using the standardized measure, our surveys showed that Georgians have the least confidence in their elections of the three cases, which is

---

[13] Arab Barometer (2015).

[14] See, for example, the results of Gallup polls from 2004 to 2018 (McCarthy 2018), in which only 66 percent of Americans expressed being very or somewhat confident in the accuracy of US elections in 2016.

consistent with the country's generally lower level of democracy. Our Georgia results are similar to findings from other surveys such as those carried out by the International Republican Institute in 2017, which found that only 40 percent of Georgians were confident in the 2016 parliamentary election results.[15]

As with responses to any survey questions, an important consideration is whether our measures of citizens' perceptions of election credibility reflect respondents' true beliefs. Because questions about election credibility are not particularly sensitive outside of authoritarian contexts, the responses to them should not have been subject to common problems such as social desirability bias.[16]

A more pressing concern is perhaps whether respondents engaged in "expressive responding." It is possible that winning partisans told us they thought an election was credible (and that losing partisans did the opposite) *not* because they truly believed that was the case, but because they wanted to engage in partisan "cheerleading."[17] A number of studies have attempted to document the prevalence of expressive responding among Americans using surveys that incentivize correct responses using monetary payments and other techniques.[18] Since our surveys did not use these methods, we cannot confidently estimate the extent of expressive responding, although we note that election credibility is intrinsically a more subjective concept than the factual topics on which expressive responding has usually been studied.[19] Thus, we

---

[15] Center for Insights in Survey Research, International Republican Institute (2017).

[16] In addition, the US surveys were online, which should further reduce any social desirability bias concerns since respondents did not have to share their opinions directly with enumerators.

[17] Bullock et al. (2015, 521).

[18] Ibid.; Prior, Sood, and Khanna (2015); Berinsky (2018); Schaffner and Luks (2018).

[19] For example, Berinsky (2018) examined beliefs about whether Barack Obama is a Muslim, while Schaffner and Luks (2018) studied beliefs about whether President Obama or Trump had a larger inauguration crowd. As we detail later in the chapter, even in the United States, a consolidated democracy with high levels of election integrity, various events and elite statements have plausibly fostered sincere doubts about election credibility among the public in recent decades. By contrast, the electoral environment in Tunisia in 2014 was uncertain (since it was a transitional election) and it was of middling integrity in 2018 Georgia (since it was a partial democracy), meaning that in both cases a range of responses about election credibility might be considered reasonable (as opposed to cheerleading).

acknowledge it is possible that responses about election credibility in our surveys reflected expressive responding. Yet if that is the case, it is not obvious that the downstream political behaviors (e.g., voting or protesting) that make citizens' trust in elections so important would only be correlated with their "true" beliefs. Indeed, the studies linking citizens' trust in elections to turnout rely on survey measures similar to ours, which implies that these expressed beliefs are indeed politically important.[20]

3.2.2 Survey Design

Our research design entailed making five consequential decisions about how to structure the surveys. First, it was important for us to survey a large number of respondents (at least 1,000 individuals) in each country and to ensure that the people we interviewed were broadly representative of their countries as a whole. Surveying representative samples of each country's population enhances the external validity of our study by allowing us to draw conclusions about how the public is likely to behave as a whole in response to foreign interventions around elections.

To obtain representative (or at least diverse) samples, we implemented the surveys in formats tailored to the context. In Tunisia and Georgia, we worked with respected local survey research firms – ELKA Consulting and the Caucasus Research Resource Center Georgia respectively – to administer the surveys in person. The interviewers used either pen and paper or tablets to record respondents' answers.[21] The survey interviewers were carefully trained in person by both us and the local survey research firms. They conducted the interviews in the relevant local languages and generally in the regions of the country where they lived or were from.[22] All of these surveys were nationally representative based on the most recent national census. The US surveys were conducted online, since it is possible to conduct a quality (though not fully nationally representative) survey

---

[20] See, for example, Birch (2010) and Norris (2013b).
[21] For more on the survey mode in Tunisia, see Bush and Prather (2019).
[22] In Tunisia, interviews were conducted in the Tunisian Arabic dialect. In Georgia, they were conducted in Georgian, Azeri, and Armenian.

of Americans using this format.[23] We worked with Survey Sampling International to conduct the US surveys. The online appendix contains detailed information about the representativeness of the samples in each country.

The second decision relates to timing. We conducted surveys immediately before and after election day in all three countries. It was essential for us to conduct our surveys close to elections, because that is when citizens' beliefs about election credibility are most in flux – and thus when foreign actors are most likely to shape individuals' decisions about whether to accept or reject the results. Because the US surveys were conducted online, they were completed in just a few days before and after election day. The Tunisia and Georgia surveys took longer, generally 1–2 weeks, since they involved sending interview teams throughout the country, including to rural and hard-to-reach locations.

Third, we conducted *panel* surveys – that is, we interviewed the same people multiple times.[24] By conducting the surveys around elections, we could see how individuals' perceptions of election credibility changed as they learned more – who won the election, what foreign actors said and did in real life – and explore how beliefs about one election informed opinions and actions before and after later elections. In Tunisia and Georgia, our panel surveys examined individuals' changing beliefs over periods of weeks or months. In the United States, we tracked some individuals' opinions over several years, and the rest over one week before and after the election.

Fourth, each of our surveys included randomized experiments. To address the problem of selection bias discussed above, we randomly selected a subset of respondents to be told truthful information about the activities of foreign actors. For the surveys conducted online or using tablets, the survey software randomly chose this subset; for the surveys conducted using pen and paper in Tunisia, randomization was accomplished by rolling dice, an approach we pretested to ensure it

---

[23] The US national samples met demographic targets in terms of region, age, and gender. Numerous studies have explored whether online political science survey experiments produce similar treatment effects to other, more representative survey samples. The findings are generally optimistic. See Berinsky, Huber, and Lenz (2012) and Mullinix et al. (2015).

[24] Some individuals did not accept our invitations to participate in follow-up surveys. The online appendix (www.cambridge.org/bushprather) contains a discussion of when attrition was most likely.

was culturally appropriate. This design facilitated comparisons across groups of respondents who were otherwise identical, except for the unique information they had been given about foreign actors.

Fifth, and as we describe in later chapters in more detail, a primary concern was to treat our survey respondents ethically, which informed our design of the experiments. In general, we sought to design informational treatments that would test the observable implications laid out in Chapter 2 without being dishonest or having such a large impact on individuals' political attitudes that we could inadvertently spark risky protests or other harmful outcomes. Ethical considerations also informed our other research practices, such as ensuring that participation was voluntary, that respondents gave informed consent to participate in the research, and that we carefully safeguarded their survey responses, although most of the content of our surveys was not particularly sensitive or risky.[25] All surveys complied with the laws of the relevant country and received approval from our universities' institutional review boards and, as needed, the appropriate local institutions.

3.3 Case Selection and Background

Given the expense of conducting original and representative panel surveys, we focused on a small number of cases. Beyond our own expertise and practical considerations, our case selection strategy focused on ensuring variation in our explanatory variables and providing a fair test of other potential explanations.[26]

To ensure variation in our explanatory variables, we chose three cases with different regime types at the time of our research: The United States was a consolidated democracy, Tunisia was a transitional

---

[25] No deception was used in the surveys. Each survey firm that we worked with compensates individuals for participating in its surveys at a standard rate that is large enough to encourage participation but not so large that it might compromise the voluntary nature of individuals' participation. The US surveys, which were conducted online, were anonymous; thus, no information was collected that could have identified respondents. The Tunisia and Georgia surveys, which were conducted face to face, were confidential since our interviewer teams retained some information about respondents' locations in order to recontact them given the panel survey format. This information was destroyed at the conclusion of the surveys.

[26] For a discussion of the importance of selecting cases based on explanatory variables, see King, Keohane, and Verba (1994, 137–138).

democracy, and Georgia was a partial democracy. Consequently, they had different electoral environments and levels of uncertainty about the electoral playing field, which is a key variable highlighted in our theory. Our theory predicts that Tunisia is a relatively "easy" (or "most likely") case for detecting significant effects of foreign actors on perceived credibility given the uncertainty around its transitional elections, and that the United States and Georgia are relatively "hard" (or "least likely") cases given their consistent democracy ratings before the elections we study.

In addition to cross-case variation in regime type, the cases also provide within-case variation in three ways that were relevant for our theory. First, since all three cases hold at least somewhat competitive elections, we knew that individuals' vote choice and uncertainty about the electoral playing field would differ. Second, because multiple monitors have observed elections in all three countries, and each has experienced at least some rumors about foreign meddling, we could examine how variation in intervener identity conditions the effects of foreign actors. Finally, in the United States, we examine perceptions of election credibility over a number of years, conducting surveys around the 2016, 2018, and 2020 general elections. In the 2016 and 2018 US elections, as well as the Tunisian and Georgian elections, domestic actors largely conceded defeat. The 2020 US election represents a case in which the losing candidate called the election's credibility into question, and his supporters largely accepted this criticism. These shifts over time provide an interesting opportunity to explore how domestic actors' influences on election credibility change, creating different conditions in which foreign actors operate.

Our cases also allow us to consider an important alternative theory about foreign interventions: that norms of national self-determination will cause citizens to respond negatively to all forms of foreign influences on elections. Since the publics in all three countries are fairly nationalistic, it should be relatively easy to find support for this alternative perspective if it is correct. We assess public levels of nationalism using responses to a World Values Survey question from its sixth wave (2010–2014), which asked representative samples of citizens in forty-one countries: "How proud are you to be [nationality]?"[27] Response options ranged from 1 ("not proud at all") to 4 ("very proud").

---

[27] Question 211. See Haerpfer et al. (2014).

The average score across all surveyed countries was 3.48, indicating that most people have substantial national pride. Scores ranged from 3.49 in the United States (in 2011) to 3.50 in Tunisia (in 2013) and 3.72 in Georgia (2014). Also relevant for testing the nationalism argument fairly is that the Middle East is commonly perceived as a region where the public may be suspicious of foreign countries engaged in democracy promotion.[28]

We also chose cases that would enhance the study's generalizability. Our study was designed to illuminate how foreign actors affect election credibility for the broader population of countries that hold at least partially competitive elections. To this end, we selected a *diverse* trio of countries. This case selection strategy "has as its primary objective the achievement of maximum variance along relevant dimensions."[29] Our three cases vary in many ways, including degree of global power, region, level of economic development, religion, and cultural heritage. They also have varying levels of party institutionalization: Several new parties competed in Tunisia's transitional election (as explained below) and relatively long-standing parties contested the US and Georgian elections we study. At the time of our surveys, the three cases were somewhat more polarized than the average country.[30] Although we do not have clear expectations about whether such variables would accentuate or diminish the effect of foreign actors on trust, part of our motivation in choosing diverse cases was to reflect the reality that foreign actors intervene in many types of countries' elections. To the extent that we find similar patterns across these diverse settings, we can be more confident that we would find them elsewhere, too.

Finally, the cases are also important and, we hope, interesting on their own terms. Until recently, Tunisia has served as the key success story from the Arab Spring. Georgia sits at the crossroads of conflict

---

[28] Bush (2017b).

[29] Seawright and Gerring (2008, 300).

[30] The Varieties of Democracy (V-Dem) project codes countries from 0 ("serious polarization") to 4 ("no polarization"). See Coppedge et al. (2019). Looking across our cases in the years of their surveys, V-Dem coded the United States as the most polarized (0.324 in 2016) and Tunisia as the least polarized (0.984 in 2014), although all three countries scored between 0 and 1 ("moderate polarization"); the world average is 1.65. We do not have a strong intuition that societal polarization would make us more or less likely to find significant results in our study, although these dynamics seem most plausible for our analysis of the conditional effects of foreign actors on vote choice (Chapter 7).

between Russia and the West. The United States has been the target of recent high-profile external meddling and is an active intervener in other countries' elections. As the discussion in Chapters 4 and 5 elaborates, our experiments allow us to examine the United States' dual role as both an intervention target and an intervener, as we explore the effects of American monitors on perceptions of election credibility in Georgia and Tunisia and consider rumors of US meddling in both cases. Although the United States is arguably the most prominent instigator of both monitoring and meddling, it is not unique in its experience as both an intervention target and intervener; other countries such as France, Russia, and the United Kingdom have also played both roles in recent years.

Together, our three cases allow us to draw more general conclusions about how foreign actors influence trust in elections in countries that are at least partially democratic. We leave applications of our theory to fully autocratic countries that nevertheless hold elections for future research. We focus on the types of countries we did, given resource constraints, for three reasons: (1) consolidated autocracies represent a minority of countries[31]; (2) countries that are at least partial democracies offer a more open and comfortable context for conducting social science research and surveys; and (3) consolidated autocracies tend to have a smaller variety of foreign actors present. For example, they may only invite zombie observers, and we explore how various foreign actors' identities shape their effects on local attitudes.

To illustrate the countries' diverse histories of foreign influence around elections, we provide brief overviews of each case below. Readers who do not require this background may proceed to the end of the chapter.

3.3.1 Tunisia

Tunisia gained independence from France in 1956 and was a largely stable autocracy until a popular revolution in 2011. Nationalist leader Habib Bourguiba initially governed after independence and was elected

---

[31] They are also a declining portion of the world's states. Lührmann, Tannenberg, and Lindberg (2018, 9) used V-Dem data to classify regimes as liberal democracies, electoral democracies, electoral autocracies, or closed autocracies. Only 12 percent of countries were classified as closed autocracies in 2016.

"president for life" by his supporters in the legislature in 1975. In 1987, the recently appointed Prime Minister Zine El Abidine Ben Ali replaced Bourguiba in a bloodless coup d'état. Ben Ali's initial gestures toward democratization did not lead to deeper reforms.[32]

Ben Ali's rule unexpectedly ended in the span of roughly a month starting at the end of 2010. On December 17, Mohamed Bouazizi, a street vendor, set himself on fire to protest local police corruption and harassment. His death sparked protests in his hometown of Sidi Bouzid that spread throughout the country. The situation escalated quickly. Although Bouazizi's self-immolation was the immediate cause, the deeper issues were years of stagnation and corruption.[33] By January 14, 2011, Ben Ali stepped down, and protests quickly spread to other Arab countries.

After the revolution, Tunisia began a transition to democracy. Freedom House has considered it "free" since 2015, though events in 2021 (which are still unfolding at the time of writing) will likely alter this rating.[34]

The initial promise of the transition included national elections in 2014 that a variety of observers agreed were free and fair. According to Freedom House, Tunisians "enjoy[ed] unprecedented political rights and civil liberties" through 2020.[35] The Constituent Assembly that oversaw the transition was led by a coalition of three parties known as the Troika. Ennahda, an Islamist party founded in 1981, secured a plurality of seats and governed in alliance with two secularist parties, Ettakatol and Congress for the Republic (CPR).

A period of transition followed that was often characterized by questions about the role of religion in politics. Secularists supported the tradition of laïcité adopted by Bourguiba and Ben Ali, while Islamists sought to incorporate Islam into public life. After a period of debate, the Constituent Assembly wrote and passed a new constitution in January 2014 and a new electoral law in May 2014. According to these documents, Tunisia is a semi-presidential republic that holds elections for both president and a unicameral parliament. The first parliamentary election was set for October 2014, with presidential

---

[32] Angrist (1999); Sadiki (2002).
[33] Beissinger, Jamal, and Mazur (2015).
[34] Freedom House (2021b).
[35] Ibid.

elections following soon after. Despite Ennahda's earlier success in the Constituent Assembly elections, it performed worse than expected. Nidaa Tounes, a secularist party formed in 2012, instead won a plurality of seats. Its presidential candidate, Beji Caid Essebsi, an official in the Ben Ali government, also beat Moncef Marzouki of CPR, who had served as the interim president. Despite a good showing in both elections, without a parliamentary majority, Nidaa Tounes governed in coalition with Ennahda. Scholar Elizabeth Nugent attributes these parties' ability to compromise and cooperate during the transition period to their shared experience of repression during the Ben Ali era.[36]

Foreign actors intervened in Tunisian politics in multiple ways during the transition. American and European democracy assistance was limited in Tunisia prior to 2011.[37] Although there were some links between activists in Tunisia and veterans of the Color Revolutions,[38] Tunisian protester and academic Tarek Kahlaoui argues that these connections have been overstated.[39] Indeed, few analysts have emphasized the role of international actors in the revolution. After 2011, however, Tunisia became a locus for international democracy promotion.[40] Given the country's recent trajectory, the 2014 parliamentary and presidential elections that we examined afforded us an unusual opportunity to study how international observers affect beliefs about election credibility without having to account for citizens' prior experiences with observers. At the same time, the elections featured a wide array of foreign actors attempting to support the democratic transition.

Foreign countries have intervened in Tunisia to support specific parties. Arab regional powers have intervened in favor of both secularists and Islamists, reflecting the broader regional divide in which Saudi Arabia and the United Arab Emirates (UAE) support secularists and Qatar supports Islamists. Qatar has used its television station *Al Jazeera* to provide favorable coverage of Ennahda and signed ten agreements with the Ennahda-led transitional government designed to support the country's economy.[41] When the Ennahda-led

---

[36] Nugent (2020).
[37] Bicchi (2009, 73); Bush (2015, 191–192).
[38] Kirkpatrick and Sanger (2011).
[39] Kahlaoui (2013, 151–152).
[40] Freyburg and Richter (2015, 7).
[41] Cherif (2017).

transitional government came to power, the UAE halted investments, cooled bilateral relations, and signaled its support for Nidaa Tounes politicians prior to the 2014 elections, prompting "[f]igures from or close to Nidaa Tounes [to] often imply that once Ennahda is ousted, Emirati (and other) funds would pour into Tunisia."[42] By contrast, American and European actions since 2011 have included substantial support for democracy, regardless of the party in power. Yet, Western powers have to some extent remained conflicted about working with Islamists; given their history of cooperating with secular Arab leaders at the expense of democracy, locals often perceive Western countries as being hostile toward political Islam.[43] These policies are an important driver of anti-Americanism in Tunisia, as in the rest of the Arab world.[44] Tunisia is therefore a plausible case to identify the sort of nationalist backlash to foreign interventions around elections that we proposed in Chapter 2 as a counterargument to our theory.

At the time of writing, Tunisian democracy is under threat. After the death of President Essebsi in July 2019, the presidential election was moved forward to September 2019. Independent candidate and constitutional lawyer Kaïs Saïed, who "rose to power on [a] wave of anti-partisanship," won the election.[45] In July 2021, after months of violent protests following a period of economic turmoil and a rise in COVID cases, Saïed invoked the president's emergency powers as detailed in the constitution and suspended parliament and dismissed the prime minister; his actions went beyond what is permitted by law. International actors' public reactions to the events have been fairly muted: Most countries and institutions have called for stability and expressed concern without condemnation.[46] Although Saïed described these actions as provisional in nature, his office announced a lawmaking system in September 2021 that would allow him to make decisions by decree and bypass the constitution. These changes were met with significant opposition by domestic parties and organizations as well as by demonstrators in the streets.[47]

---

[42] Cherif (2014).
[43] Hamid, Mandaville, and McCants (2017).
[44] Jamal (2012); Jamal et al. (2015, 59).
[45] Grubman and Şaşmaz (2021).
[46] Al Jazeera (2021).
[47] Yee (2021).

3.3.2 *The United States*

The United States is a consolidated democracy with a two-party system that Freedom House has rated as "free" since the start of its reports in 1972.[48] Yet, a growing number of Americans lack trust in their elections. The 2000 *Bush vs. Gore* US Supreme Court case over the recount of presidential election ballots in Florida was a "seismic" event that alerted Americans to the problems with their electoral system.[49] Since then, various politicians have made statements that encouraged the public to question election integrity, especially as it relates to voter fraud. Donald Trump went even further, warning on the campaign trail that the 2016 election that he ended up winning could be "rigged" and calling on his supporters to be "Trump Election Observers."[50] This rhetoric escalated around the 2020 presidential election and culminated with a violent insurrection at the US Capitol building in Washington, DC on January 6 perpetrated by supporters of Donald Trump, the election loser. His supporters believed the winner, Joe Biden, and his campaign had engaged in election fraud and unsuccessfully sought to prevent the US Congress' certification of Biden's victory on that day.

The United States is known to intervene in other countries' elections. It routinely supports international EOs and provides democracy assistance and has taken sides in many countries' elections. Yet, it also has experience as the *target* of foreign electoral interventions. For instance, the main contenders in the 1796 US presidential election were Secretary of State Thomas Jefferson, an admirer of the French Revolution who sought to improve relations with France, and Vice President John Adams, whose Federalist Party preferred close economic and political relations with Great Britain. When Adams won, the French ambassador ordered his navy to prevent US trade with Europe.[51]

More recently, the Soviet Union sought to intervene in US elections to bring friendly presidents to power throughout the Cold War. In 1984, the Soviets feared the reelection of President Ronald Reagan, who the USSR perceived to be an enormous threat. According to declassified KGB documents, Soviet leaders ordered KGB agents to

---

[48] Freedom House (2021c).
[49] Norris, Cameron, and Wynter (2019, 3).
[50] Martin and Burns (2014); Morin (2016).
[51] DeConde (1958).

initiate a propaganda campaign against him, which entailed spreading the slogan that "Reagan Means War" and increasing the salience of some of Reagan's domestic political shortcomings, such as his alleged discrimination against American minority groups and corruption in his administration. These efforts were ultimately unsuccessful.[52]

The United States was once again the target of electoral interventions when the Russian government supported Donald Trump's campaign for president in 2016. Russia used a variety of tactics according to US intelligence agencies, including hacking the Democratic National Committee's computer network and disseminating and promoting fake news on social media.[53] Unlike the more long-standing foreign interventions in Tunisia related to the Islamist–secularist cleavage, Russian side taking in the US election reflected a relatively short-term commitment due to the candidacy of Donald Trump. According to former Federal Bureau of Investigation Director James Comey, a major goal of Russia's intervention was to reduce political trust. As he testified to the House Intelligence Committee, "One of the lessons they [Russia] may draw from this is that they were successful because they introduced chaos and division and discord and sowed doubt about the nature of this amazing country of ours and our democratic process."[54]

Many Americans may be surprised to discover that international EOs also monitor US elections. Teams from the Organization for Security and Co-operation in Europe (OSCE) have been quietly observing US elections since 2002, when President George W. Bush first invited them. In addition, observers from the Organization of American States (OAS) accepted an invitation from the Obama administration to monitor the 2016 election – reportedly to demonstrate the US commitment to OAS democracy promotion efforts.[55] The OSCE observers stirred up controversy around the 2012 and 2016 US elections: Politicians in Iowa, Texas, and elsewhere voiced loud objections to the invitation and pledged to keep monitors away from their polling stations.[56] Domestic observers – including from the US Department of Justice, political parties, and nonpartisan citizen organizations – make up the bulk of the monitoring effort in the United States.

---

[52] Andrew and Mitrokhin (2020, 243)
[53] Office of the Director of National Intelligence (2017).
[54] Quoted in Milbank (2017).
[55] Friedman (2016).
[56] Keating (2012).

3.3.3 *Georgia*

After Georgia declared its independence from the Soviet Union in 1991, former Soviet official Eduard Shevardnadze took control. According to Steven Levitsky and Lucan Way, "Georgia's competitive authoritarian regime was unstable from the outset," weakened by competition between paramilitaries and by civil conflict in the regions of Abkhazia and South Ossetia.[57] Although Shevardnadze successfully consolidated and maintained power for more than a decade, his regime collapsed in November 2003 during the wave of Color Revolutions that swept through the post-Soviet region. Shevardnadze peacefully resigned after demonstrators, led by Mikheil Saakashvili of the United National Movement (UNM), protested fraudulent parliamentary elections that Shevardnadze's coalition "For a New Georgia!" claimed to have won. Levitsky and Way suggest that the opposition's victory had less to do with the size of the protests – which were, by all accounts, much smaller than those elsewhere, such as Serbia – than with the decision of top Georgian military and police officials to abandon Shevardnadze.[58]

Although Georgia's Rose Revolution caused a change in leadership, it did not result in democratization. Freedom House has rated Georgia as only "partly free" since 2003.[59] Consistent with that designation, citizens' opinions about the quality of the country's elections are mixed. For example, a nationally representative survey in June 2017 asked: "How would you assess the condition of free and fair elections?" On a 5-point scale ranging from "very bad" to "very good," the median response was around 3 ("neither").[60]

After the revolution, Saakashvili became president and used a variety of legal and extralegal tactics – from control of the media to crackdowns on protesters – to keep the UNM in power. A 2008 survey indicated that about one-third (32 percent) of voters believed people had to "vote a certain way to keep their jobs" and a further third (34 percent) believed that that sometimes happened.[61] There was sufficient electoral competition that Saakashvili conceded his party's defeat

---

[57] Levitsky and Way (2010, 222).
[58] Ibid., 222.
[59] See, for example, Freedom House (2021a).
[60] National Democratic Institute (2017).
[61] Driscoll and Hidalgo (2014, 2).

by the Georgian Dream (GD) coalition in the 2012 parliamentary elections. GD won again in the 2016 and 2020 parliamentary elections; the latter was met with protests and, in the second round, a boycott by the UNM as well as opposition party European Georgia. The opposition parties later renounced their seats in parliament. Reflecting Georgia's status as a partial democracy, the headline of the OSCE monitoring mission for this election reported, "Fundamental freedoms respected in competitive Georgian elections, but allegations of pressure and blurring of line between party and state reduced confidence."[62]

GD-supported presidents have been in power since 2013: first Giorgi Margvelashvili and then Salome Zourabichvili since 2018. Similar to the UNM, the GD party is also known for its authoritarian tendencies.[63] At the time of our surveys, Georgia was a semi-presidential republic that held regular elections for both president and a unicameral parliament. However, a 2017 constitutional amendment abolished direct elections for the president; the 2018 elections that we study were the last scheduled direct election for president. In 2020, the GD party secured a significant majority in parliament.

Foreign actors have intervened in Georgia in a variety of ways, both to support democracy and to support specific candidates and parties. Although the Rose Revolution has often been hailed as a victory for democracy promotion, Lincoln Mitchell, the director of the Georgia office of a US nongovernmental organization (NGO) (the National Democratic Institute, NDI) between 2002 and 2004, paints a more complicated picture. On the one hand, high-level US and European diplomats maintained positive relationships with Shevardnadze and viewed him as an important ally in the "war on terror." On the other hand, these governments were funding grassroots efforts by the NDI and other foreign and domestic organizations that were directly supporting Shevardnadze's opponents.[64] Indeed, US electoral assistance grew by 172 percent during the 2 years prior to the pivotal 2003 election and revolution.[65] Meanwhile, the Soros Foundation provided crucial support that sent Georgian civil society activists to Belgrade, Serbia, where they met with activists from the well-known

---

[62] OSCE Parliamentary Assembly (2020).
[63] Fumagalli (2014, 397).
[64] Mitchell (2004, 345–346).
[65] Bunce and Wolchik (2007, 65).

Serbian NGO Otpor who inspired them to create a similar group called Kmara ("Enough") back home.[66] According to most accounts, these international actions played a significant role in Saakashvili's eventual victory.[67]

After the revolution, Western governments continued to engage in democracy promotion in Georgia. Reflecting international interest in the country's democratic development, 65 international organizations – a remarkably large number that brought in a total of 1,241 monitors – registered to monitor the 2013 presidential election.[68] Yet the effectiveness of democracy promotion in Georgia has been questioned.[69] According to Mitchell, the United States turned a blind eye to Saakashvili's antidemocratic tendencies, preferring to claim Georgia as a success story.[70] Even some well-intentioned democracy assistance activities there have had negative unintended consequences. For instance, a civic education campaign in 2008 ended up depressing voter turnout, seemingly because citizens feared that it indicated they were being surveilled by the regime.[71] Given the mixed record of democracy promotion in Georgia, there are reasons to wonder whether the presence of international observers contributes to individual trust in elections or suspicion and nationalist resentment – an important counterargument that we seek to test, as described in Chapter 2.

Unlike other post-Soviet countries, Georgia has not experienced large-scale Russian "black knight" challenges to democracy that have reinforced authoritarian rulers. Instead, Russian hostility has been a feature of post-independence Georgian life.[72] Since the 2008 war over the Russia-backed territories of South Ossetia and Abkhazia, the Russian government has attempted to support pro-Russia groups within Georgia by providing aid to media and NGOs and through information campaigns.[73] Within this context, Saakashvili attempted to use nationalist rhetoric to maintain power, accusing Bidzina (Boris)

---

[66] Beissinger (2007, 262).
[67] Mitchell (2004); Beissinger (2007); Bunce and Wolchik (2007).
[68] Office for Democratic Institutions and Human Rights (2014, 19).
[69] See also Jawad (2008); Bader (2010).
[70] Mitchell (2006, 670).
[71] Driscoll and Hidalgo (2014).
[72] Levitsky and Way (2010, 221).
[73] Bugajski (2012).

Ivanishvili – a billionaire who made his fortune in Russia and founded the GD party – of being pro-Russia.[74] Fears of Russian influence and allegations of ties between GD and the Kremlin continue and were a key motivator during the 2019 wave of protests against the Georgian government.[75]

3.4 Conclusion

We developed a theory of how citizens respond to foreign influences in Chapter 2, and testing that theory requires a citizen-level research strategy. This chapter has explained our approach, the core of which involves analyzing original surveys we conducted in Tunisia, the United States, and Georgia. Various facets of these surveys – including their composition, timing, and questionnaires – were designed to shed light on how (and when) foreign interventions on elections shape citizens' perceptions of election credibility.

In Chapters 4 and 5, we use empirical evidence collected by both observational and experimental methods in all three country cases to test the observable implications outlined in Table 2.1. To empirically test the *average effects* of election monitoring on election credibility, we use experiments that randomly inform participants in our surveys about the presence of monitors at the election under study, and, in separate experiments, about their positive or negative evaluations of the election. We use a simple comparison of means to determine how this information affects election credibility relative to control groups that received no such information. Similarly, to empirically test the average effects of election meddling on election credibility, we compare average levels of credibility in a control group to those of treatment groups exposed to information about election meddling at the election under study. We combine this experimental evidence with other observational data in our surveys, including examining the correlation between self-reported perceptions of foreign influence and perceptions of election credibility, as well as self-reported knowledge of monitoring and meddling at an election and perceptions of election credibility. These tests provide mixed evidence for the conventional wisdom about monitors and meddlers.

---

[74] Mitchell (2009, 149–153); Radnitz (2012, 3–4).
[75] Kakachia and Lebanidze (2019).

In Chapters 6 and 7, we test the conditional effects of foreign actors' identities, individuals' vote choices, and the uncertainty of the electoral context. To do so, we once again use observational and experimental data collected through our surveys in all three countries. In all the survey experiments, we randomized the identity and characteristics of foreign actors to examine whether those perceived or described as more capable (and more neutral in the case of monitors) would have stronger effects on election credibility. We tested this hypothesis by comparing average levels of election credibility in our treatment and control groups. While we could randomize the identity and characteristics of foreign actors in the information we provided participants, we could not randomize who our participants supported in elections. Thus, our empirical approach to testing the conditioning effects of vote choice requires measuring vote choice in our surveys and interacting this measure with indicators for our experimental treatment groups. We do this by measuring individuals' intended vote choice in our pre-election surveys and self-reported vote choice in our post-election surveys. Finally, in each empirical chapter, we discuss how our results vary across country cases. As noted above, Tunisia is an example of an uncertain transitional election context in which foreign actors might be expected to have a greater influence than the more certain contexts of a long-running consolidated democracy (the United States) and a country categorized as a partial democracy over the last several years (Georgia). Our results demonstrate that the effects of foreign electoral interventions are conditional on the characteristics of foreign actors, individual vote choice, and the electoral context. In the chapters that follow, we find little evidence of a nationalist backlash.

Our empirical strategy has at least two limitations. First, while we argue that the credibility of elections is an important dependent variable, measuring perceptions of elections may be subject to error. Individuals may report negative or positive feelings about an election based on their true beliefs about it, or because of unrelated attitudes or emotions. Although this may threaten the external validity of the measure, we believe any measurement error should not be correlated with treatment assignment in our experiments; thus, the internal validity of our study is protected. Future work could explore different approaches to measuring perceptions of elections, including perceptions of election credibility and the effects of information about foreign interventions over time in the weeks and months after an election, as well as measuring behaviors and attitudes that ought to be associated with election credibility.

Second, similar to the measurement of our dependent variable, our approach to the experimental interventions and our independent variables also has limitations. Of greatest concern is that we are unable to randomize the foreign intervention itself. Ideally, to test the effects of foreign electoral interventions, we could randomly assign some countries to receive election monitoring and others to receive election meddling. Like many important questions in international relations, however, random assignment at the country level is impossible. Therefore, the main threat to inference with respect to our independent variables is that individuals have already been exposed to monitoring and meddling when they receive the information in our surveys. This phenomenon would contaminate the control group and potentially lead to less updating among the treatment groups if individuals were already aware that an intervention had occurred. We thus believe that the effects we identify are likely to underestimate the true effects of foreign interventions in practice.[76] However, our results may also be thought of as capturing the effects of encountering an additional piece of information about foreign electoral interventions in the news, which is also an outcome of interest.

We now turn to Chapters 4 through 7, which empirically test our theory. We organize our material thematically rather than by country to highlight the ways in which foreign actors shape trust in elections in common ways, despite variations in regime types. We start with Chapter 4, which discusses monitors, and then proceed to Chapter 5, which analyzes meddlers.

---

[76] Although the effects we identify may be underestimates, we believe the null results in our studies are not the result of these research design choices. Recall that our three country cases included a very likely case to find significant results (Tunisia) and two cases we suspected could be more difficult. By implementing the same survey experiment in all three countries and basing some of the experimental design on previous work by Tomz and Weeks (2020) that did find significant results, we are more confident that the null results we identify are true nulls. Moreover, we conducted power analyses and preregistered our design in Georgia, one of the cases least likely to deliver significant results.

4 | *Monitors' Effects*

High-quality international election monitors seek to advance democracy by observing elections and reporting on what they see. But do they generally achieve this goal? Eric Bjornlund, who has led observation missions in such diverse locations as Afghanistan, Cambodia, Egypt, El Salvador, Hong Kong, Indonesia, Kenya, and Pakistan, first with the National Democratic Institute (NDI) and then with Democracy International, offered a mixed assessment in 2001: "I have seen outside monitors contribute to public confidence in the integrity of elections, provide invaluable moral support to democratic activists facing authoritarian regimes, and deter fraud. But I have also seen them stumble – and do great harm to many of the world's fragile democracies."[1]

This chapter explores whether international monitors do, to use Bjornlund's phrase, contribute to public confidence in election integrity. It examines monitors' *overall* effects on trust: whether they increase perceptions of election credibility when they (1) observe elections and/or (2) endorse elections. Drawing on evidence from our original surveys, as well as some previous ones, we find that election observers (EOs) do not always have the expected effects. We find little evidence that monitors' *presence* increases trust in elections, but we discover that monitors' *reports* have some modest effects in our three cases. We identify the clearest positive effects of positive EO reports in Tunisia (our "most-likely" case) and the United States (one of our two "less-likely" cases). We do not find, however, that positive reports shaped perceptions of election credibility in Georgia (our other "less-likely" case) in the way that the conventional wisdom would anticipate; instead, they had a somewhat negative effect. Taken together, these findings suggest that the conventional wisdom may have overstated the overall effects of international monitors on citizens' perceptions of election credibility.

---

[1] Bjornlund (2001, 19–20).

Before delving into these findings, we set the stage by describing who international monitors are and what they do. Using descriptive statistics on monitoring trends over time, we illustrate the growth of international election observation and the ambiguous relationship between monitors and the public's trust in elections globally. Next, we present the research design that we use to better identify the relationship between international monitors' actions and perceptions of election credibility in Tunisia, the United States, and Georgia. We then consider the effects of monitors' presence and reports in the third and fourth sections, respectively.

4.1 About Monitoring

International monitors have become very common features of elections around the world, and a substantial literature has emerged to analyze them. Much of the research on this topic has focused on how monitors affect election integrity and, more broadly, democracy.

Such studies frequently posit that international *monitors' presence* at elections reduces the amount of fraud committed by incumbents and therefore changes citizens' expectations about the level of fraud and their overall perceptions of election integrity. Berman et al. found experimental support for these claims in their analysis of an Afghan monitoring initiative that caused citizens in polling areas where less fraud occurred to view the country as more democratic.[2] By contrast, multiple studies have found that critical *monitor reports* encourage post-election protests, which can then spur election-related violence.[3] Yet as we discussed in Chapter 3, although previous studies document patterns of post-election protest and violence that are consistent with these arguments, they lack sufficient data to directly examine *whether international monitors change individuals' trust in elections.* This chapter does just that.

---

[2] Berman et al. (2019). In this study, the international researchers informed a randomly selected group of local polling centers at the 2010 Wolesi Jirga elections that they would be taking pictures of the officially reported election results. This monitoring intervention significantly reduced fraud at the selected polling centers according to several measures, and voters at these centers reported having higher levels of confidence in Afghanistan's democracy.

[3] Beissinger (2007); Bunce and Wolchik (2007); Tucker (2007); Daxecker (2012); Little (2012); Donno (2013); Hyde and Marinov (2014); von Borzyskowski (2019a).

First, however, it is important to understand what exactly monitors do, and how they have become such a pervasive feature of elections. This insight helps us understand why many people, including the monitors themselves, assume they shape individuals' perceptions of election credibility.

4.1.1 What Monitors Do

There are two ideal types of international monitors: (1) high-quality monitors, who strive to make the electoral playing field fairer and (2) zombie monitors, who seek to legitimize an unfair electoral playing field. We refer to them as ideal types because even monitors that are generally considered to be high quality sometimes display political biases.[4] We consider both here, although most of our experiments pertain to the former.

High-Quality Monitors

High-quality international monitors observe and report on events before, during, and after election day. Examples include nongovernmental organizations (NGOs) such as the Carter Center as well as intergovernmental organizations (IGOs) such as the Organization of American States (OAS) and the Organization for Security and Co-operation in Europe (OSCE).[5] Their presence and reports make it more difficult for incumbents to steal an election by exposing fraud and increasing the costs of cheating.[6] For example, Susan Hyde exploited the as-if random assignment of international EOs in Armenia's 2003 presidential election and found that monitored polling stations had lower vote shares for the incumbent, indicating that the presence of observers reduced fraud.[7] Elsewhere in the post-Soviet region, monitors from the OSCE and other international organizations are thought to have played an important role in the early 2000s during the Color Revolutions; in these revolutions, citizens organized large-scale protests in competitive authoritarian regimes including Georgia and

---

[4] Kelley (2009a); Dodsworth (2019); Kavakli and Kuhn (2020).
[5] See Simpser and Donno (2012, 505–506) for this type of classification of monitors.
[6] Hyde (2011); Kelley (2012b).
[7] Hyde (2007).

Ukraine after elections provided a focal point for mobilization and monitors exposed the extent of incumbents' cheating.[8]

Why do monitors have these effects? Before and during elections, observers attempt to deter and detect fraud through their presence, training, and support. They send long-term missions to evaluate the electoral environment in depth, drawing on evidence they collect throughout the country. They observe the electoral management body, monitor political parties' campaigns, meet with political elites, examine the media environment, and evaluate the ballot counting process and any claims of misconduct. To effectively assess election quality despite incumbents' efforts to evade detection, high-quality international monitors have gradually sent longer and more comprehensive missions and developed professional standards.[9] These costly efforts allow them to render a judgment not only about the level of fraud but also about the extent to which an election meets broader international standards.[10]

High-quality monitors believe their actions shape ordinary citizens' perceptions of election credibility. This belief is illustrated by the Declaration of Principles for International Election Observation, an international agreement currently endorsed by fifty-five NGOs and IGOs, in which monitors have committed to a series of principles designed to promote accurate and credible observation missions. As we noted in the introduction, this document states:

International election observation has the potential to enhance the integrity of election processes, by deterring and exposing irregularities and fraud and by providing recommendations for improving electoral processes. *It can promote public confidence*, as warranted, promote electoral participation and mitigate the potential for election-related conflict.[11]

Reinforcing the content of this declaration, monitors' actions indicate that they believe their presence can legitimize an election to citizens. That is one reason why such observers often decline to – or at

---

[8] Fawn (2006, 1139–1140); Beissinger (2007, 261).
[9] Hyde (2012).
[10] Norris (2013b, 23–24).
[11] Emphasis added. *Declaration of Principles for International Election Observation* (2005, 2).

least debate whether to – accept invitations to monitor elections that they know will entail considerable malpractice. For example, although observers from the European Union (EU), OSCE, United Nations, and the United States had monitored flawed Algerian elections in 1999 and 2004, they declined invitations to do so for the 2009 election in which Abdelaziz Bouteflika, who served as president from 1999 to 2019, secured reelection.[12] Similar issues were part of the debate about whether international monitors should be present at the 2014 election in Egypt that President Abdel Fattah el-Sisi won with 97 percent of the votes. Some observers attempted a compromise solution, with the Carter Center present but only sending what it described as a "small expert mission" and US NGO Democracy International withdrawing its teams as planned when the Egyptian government decided to extend voting by an additional day to boost turnout.[13]

High-quality monitors' reports provide evidence that they believe their actions can influence public attitudes; the reports tend to be more forgiving of malpractice committed by countries facing threats of violence because they do not want to incite the public. For example, a range of EOs refrained from condemning the highly flawed 2000 elections in Zimbabwe in an attempt to avoid encouraging the mounting political violence.[14] Such actions are rooted in EOs' understanding that public perceptions of election credibility are essential for democratization and security. As Patrick Merloe, the director of electoral programs at NDI, explained, "genuine stability, like democracy, is about much more than elections, but both depend on elections being credible."[15]

Zombie Monitors

Organizations such as the Commonwealth of Independent States (CIS), the Russia-led IGO, send zombie EOs to undermine the democratic process.[16] They monitor highly flawed elections in authoritarian

---

[12] Boubekeur (2009).
[13] El Sheikh (2014); Hassan and King (2014); Hendawi (2014).
[14] The groups included the African Union and the Southern African Development Community; an EU representative stated that the election "was by and large satisfactory," despite its obvious flaws. Quoted in Kelley (2010, 161). See also Laakso (2002).
[15] Merloe (2015, 92).
[16] Walker and Cooley (2013).

countries with the goal of strengthening the position of the incumbent nondemocratic government with their presence and then issuing and publicizing positive reports. Nondemocratic governments share those reports to reinforce their victories' legitimacy. According to one analysis of the noncompetitive 2006 presidential election in Belarus, for example, the state-run media gave "extensive coverage" to CIS observers and their glowing assessments of the election.[17]

Like their high-quality counterparts, zombie observers are deeply concerned with how they shape public perceptions of election credibility. For example, while the United States, EU, and Japan did not send observers to the 2018 Cambodian general election, zombie monitors were present, including from the Shanghai Cooperation Organization (SCO), a regional IGO led by China, and lesser known organizations such as the Centrist Asia Pacific Democrats and International Conference of Asian Political Parties.[18] These groups attempted to lend domestic (and perhaps regional) credibility to an election that the EU declared was "not representative of the democratic will of the Cambodian electorate."[19] By overlooking fraud and declaring the election free and fair, zombie observers attempt to tilt the playing field to the benefit of incumbents and distract the public's attention from the efforts of more credible observers.

4.1.2 Monitoring over Time

It is now an international norm for countries that are not long-consolidated democracies to invite international monitors to their elections. The end of the Cold War and the associated "third wave of democratization,"[20] generated both a growing demand for election monitoring (from states that wanted to demonstrate their commitment to democracy) and a growing supply of it (among states and IGOs that sought to engage in democracy promotion).[21]

---

[17] Fawn (2006, 1145).
[18] Morgenbesser (2018).
[19] Khemara (2018).
[20] This wave of democratization refers to the democratic transitions that occurred from the mid-1970s through to the early 1990s in Europe, Latin America, and Asia. See Huntington (1991).
[21] Hyde (2011); Kelley (2012b).

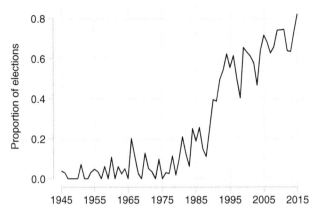

Figure 4.1 Proportion of national elections with international monitors, 1945–2015
Note: The data are from NELDA version 5.0 (Hyde and Marinov 2012).

Data from the National Elections Across Democracy and Autocracy (NELDA) dataset shed light on these trends.[22] NELDA covers all national elections in countries with populations of at least 500,000 between 1945 and 2015. Figure 4.1 illustrates that the proportion of national elections monitored by international EOs increased significantly during the second half of the twentieth century and especially during the late 1980s and early 1990s.[23] International groups monitor around 80 percent of elections globally in the most recent years for which we have reliable data.[24]

In addition to the increase in the number of elections being monitored, there has also been a rise in the number of monitors. Multiple international monitors often observe a single election.[25] A range of actors including IGOs, international NGOs, and states now send teams to monitor the same elections around the world. Prominent IGOs in this field include the African Union (AU), EU, OAS, and OSCE, while prominent international NGOs include the Carter Center, International Republican Institute (IRI), and NDI. For example, 520 international observers monitored the 2019 Mozambican election,

[22] Hyde and Marinov (2012).
[23] Data come from NELDA variable 45 ("Were international monitors present?").
[24] Hyde (2011, 8).
[25] Kelley (2009b).

including invited observers from the AU, EU, and the Commonwealth, some of whom issued quite critical assessments.[26] Finally, and as noted earlier, many autocratic governments or autocratic-led IGOs, such as the CIS and SCO, have become active in election monitoring. The diffusion of the practice of election monitoring to IGOs that are not committed to democracy is evidence of the norm's power in contemporary world politics.

Kelley's Data on International Election Monitoring (DIEM) gathered information about the activities of multiple international election monitors between 1978 and 2004.[27] Although DIEM collected information on a maximum of three international monitoring missions per election, this dataset can be used to explore trends in multiple monitors, though it almost certainly understates the increased presence of multiple international monitoring missions at elections since the end of the Cold War. As Figure 4.2 shows, for elections at which international EOs were present, the average total number of missions observing an election has increased over time.

The growing acceptance of the norm of international monitors can be observed in public attitudes, as well as states' decisions to invite EOs. To assess public acceptance, we examined the results of a unique survey conducted on representative samples of the public in nineteen countries or territories in 2009. The survey respondents were asked, "Do you think that [Country] would or would not benefit from having international observers monitor elections here?"[28] As Figure 4.3 illustrates, support for inviting EOs varied considerably across the surveyed countries, from 40 percent of Indonesian respondents to 86 percent of Kenyans indicating that their country would benefit.[29] Nevertheless, most respondents, and especially the majority of those from outside long-consolidated democracies such as France, Great Britain, and the United States, believed their elections would benefit from having international observers.

---

[26] European Union Election Observation Mission (2019, 19).
[27] Kelley (2012b). These data come from the supplementary election dataset, which contains information about whether twenty-one international EO organizations were present.
[28] Data come from question "dem7" in WorldPublicOpinion.org (2009).
[29] The strong support for international monitors in Kenya is intriguing, given the controversies there surrounding EOs, as noted at the start of Chapter 2.

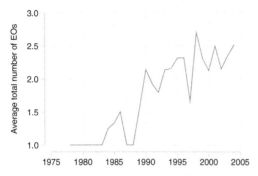

Figure 4.2 Average total number of international EO missions present at elections, 1978–2004
Note: The data are from DIEM (Kelley 2012b). The maximum number of observer missions recorded per election in DIEM is 3.

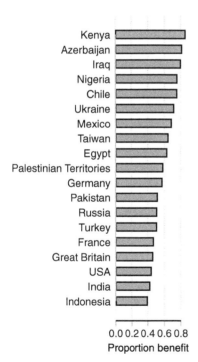

Figure 4.3 Proportion of citizens who think their elections would benefit from having international observers, 2009
Note: The data are from WorldPublicOpinion.org (2009).

Public support for inviting international observers across a variety of settings offers some prima facie evidence to discredit the argument that any form of foreign influence would undermine citizens' perceptions of election credibility because it will be considered a type of unwelcome interference. Later in the chapter, we provide further evidence from our original surveys that fails to support this alternative perspective about the potential for nationalist backlash to foreign interventions in elections.

4.2 Research Design

To understand how EOs influence people in the countries that they monitor, an obvious first step is to examine the relationship between monitors' actions and citizens' perceptions of elections using previously collected data on both. In Chapter 3, we discussed two reasons why performing such an analysis is complicated. First, most surveys that ask about perceptions of election credibility are not conducted around elections. Second, monitors' actions – their decisions about whether to monitor and how to report on elections – are not randomly distributed across elections, which makes it difficult to identify their causal effects.

We begin our research on monitors' individual-level effects by examining relevant correlational data, which include data from surveys conducted by other organizations and from our own surveys. These analyses do not provide evidence that monitors influence individuals' perceptions of election credibility. But given their shortcomings, we propose an experimental research design that can more convincingly test the conventional wisdom about monitors' effects.

4.2.1 Correlational Tests

We first combine the NELDA data on international election monitoring used earlier with existing surveys on citizens' perceptions of election credibility. We draw on nationally representative surveys conducted in Africa, Latin America, and the Middle East and North Africa through the Global Barometers project from 2012 to 2014. All of these surveys were conducted using high-quality and nationally representative samples and contained a similar question about how credible the respondent thought the last national election was.[30] Not all of the surveyed countries held elections between 2012 and 2014, but we can use the NELDA data to see if people in the countries that did believe their elections were more credible when high-quality international monitors were present and less credible when those monitors issued critical reports.[31]

Figure 4.4 shows that there is not a clear relationship in these data between perceptions of election credibility and Western monitors' presence and reports. Contrary to the conventional wisdom, inviting election monitors does not seem to legitimize elections by increasing citizens' trust. Similarly, when Western monitors condemn elections outright (which Figure 4.4 shows is quite uncommon), it does not seem to diminish citizens' trust. Statistical tests further confirm the lack of a significant relationship between monitors' actions and citizens' attitudes.[32] Of course, the lack of a significant relationship could simply reflect some of the limitations of this analysis, which we noted previously.

For that reason, we conducted original surveys that contained a variety of questions about individuals' political beliefs and experiences regarding elections in Tunisia (in 2014), the United States (in 2016, 2018, and 2020), and Georgia (in 2018). As detailed in Chapter 3, we chose these cases in part because they represent a diverse set of regime

---

[30] In the Afrobarometer (2015), the question (Q28) was: "On the whole, how would you rate the freeness and fairness of the last national election, held in [20xx]?" In the Arab Barometer (2015), the question (q303) was: "In general, how would you evaluate the last parliamentary elections that were held on (date)?" The response options ranged from "they were completely free and fair" to "they were not free and fair." In the Latinobarómetro (2014), the question (Q25STGBS) was: "Thinking of the last national election in (country), how fair was it regarding the opportunities of the candidates and parties to campaign?" The first two surveys relied on a 4-point scale; the third relied on a 5-point scale, which we rescaled to a 4-point scale for comparability. For the small number of countries surveyed in both the Afrobarometer and Arab Barometer, we used the data from the Arab Barometer.

[31] The NELDA data come from variables 46 ("Were Western monitors present?") and 47 ("Were there allegations by Western monitors of significant vote-fraud?"). Although not all high-quality monitors are Western, this variable offers the closest approximation of that concept within NELDA.

[32] In two-sample t-tests with equal variances, the *p*-values are 0.908 and 0.460, respectively, for the comparisons involving monitors' presence and negative reports.

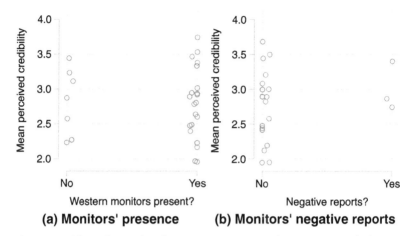

(a) Monitors' presence   **(b) Monitors' negative reports**

Figure 4.4 The relationship between monitors and perceptions of election credibility in existing surveys, by country, 2012–2014
Note: The data on monitors are from NELDA version 5.0 (Hyde and Marinov 2012). The data on perceptions of election credibility are from Afrobarometer (2015); Arab Barometer (2015); and Latinobarómetro (2014). Perceived credibility is measured on a 4-point scale in which 4 represents the most credibility.

types: transitional democracy (Tunisia), consolidated democracy (the United States), and partial democracy (Georgia). These different environments allow us to examine how international monitors influence perceptions of election credibility when individuals have more vs. less certainty about the electoral playing field.

Multiple international EO groups were present at all three countries' elections.[33] Citizens' reported awareness of observers varied widely: A majority of Tunisian respondents (just over 60 percent after both elections) told us that they had heard about monitors in the news, perhaps reflecting both the salience of that country's elections and the importance of EOs in transitional settings.[34] By contrast, minorities of respondents in our surveys in the United States and Georgia reported hearing about EOs in the news – as few as 17 percent of

---

[33] The third section in this chapter provides more details about their missions.
[34] It is likely that there is some measurement error that results from respondents inaccurately reporting whether they had heard about monitors (e.g., people may overstate the extent to which they are knowledgeable about this topic). This concern is a further reason why it is useful to complement the observational data with an experimental design that provides information about monitors to some respondents.

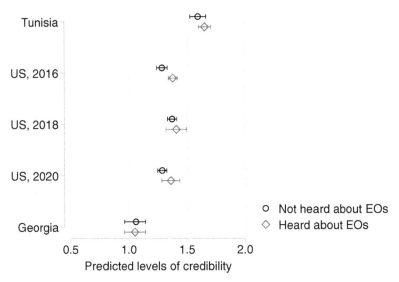

Figure 4.5 The relationship between awareness of monitors and perceived credibility, Tunisia, United States (2016, 2018, and 2020), and Georgia
Note: This figure shows point estimates with 95 percent confidence intervals. All predictions are based on ordinary least squares (OLS) models without control variables. The outcome variable, perceived credibility, uses the standardized measure, which ranges from 0 to 2. The Tunisia data are from both the post-legislative (heard about EOs) and post-presidential surveys (credibility); the US data are from the post-election surveys in 2016, 2018, and 2020 for all variables; and the Georgia data are from the pre-first-round (heard about EOs) and post-second round (credibility) surveys. $N = 1,024$ (Tunisia), 1,340 (US, 2016), 1,289 (US, 2018), 1,455 (US, 2020), and 1,046 (Georgia).

US respondents in 2018. Even in Tunisia, where reported knowledge about monitors was the highest, only about one-third of respondents indicated that they had heard about monitors' reports after both the parliamentary and presidential elections.

Figure 4.5 presents correlational evidence from our surveys on the relationship between reported knowledge about monitors and trust. Perceived credibility is measured here by averaging responses to questions about trust in the election results and belief that the election represented the will of the people. We use this approach throughout this chapter and all the other empirical chapters; Chapter 3 contains a fuller discussion of our measurement approach for this variable, which is scaled from 0 (least credible) to 2 (most credible). Figure 4.5 illustrates that respondents in Tunisia reported the most trust in their elections, followed by those in the United States and Georgia.

Like we observed in Figure 4.4, it is not clear from our original surveys that having heard about observers in the news was associated with more trust in elections. Figure 4.5 does not display a significant difference between people who said they had previously heard about monitors and those who said they had not, with the exception of the survey of Americans in 2016.[35] Even in that survey, however, the relationship does not appear to be very robust, as it loses statistical significance when we control for other variables that are plausibly related to both respondents' likelihood to report that they had heard about monitors and their perceptions of election credibility.[36] Thus, we again find limited correlational evidence that monitors' overall activities shape the public's trust in elections.

4.2.2 Experimental Tests

Since the preceding analyses cannot conclusively test the relationship between awareness of international monitors and perceptions of election credibility, we also adopted an experimental approach. Our surveys provided information to randomly selected respondents in the treatment groups about EOs' presence and reports. Respondents in the control groups did not receive such information. This type of experimental research design enables us to identify the effect of information about EOs on perceptions of election credibility.

Our research entailed four decisions designed to maximize both internal validity (i.e., our confidence about the causal relationship between EOs and credibility) and external validity (i.e., the generalizability of our findings to other countries), while also maintaining high ethical standards. These decisions related to the surveys' question

---

[35] The measures of having heard about monitors in Tunisia and Georgia come from the first-wave surveys, whereas the responses about credibility come from the second-wave surveys, which is an attempt to capture the hypothesized theoretical relationship between these variables. In the United States, the questions about having heard about monitors were only asked in the second-wave surveys.

[36] We include measures of party identification, political interest, political knowledge, age, gender, educational attainment, employment status, and race in an OLS regression. The coefficient estimate for having heard about EOs is 0.004 ($p = 0.886$).

order, the content of the experimental treatments, our approach to debriefing, and the surveys' timing.[37]

In our first decision, unless otherwise noted, the experiments described in this chapter were the first such experiments in the surveys in which they appeared. We avoided repeating experiments in the same survey to prevent our results from being contaminated by earlier treatments.[38]

Second, we considered how best to provide individuals in our surveys with information about international election monitors. In practice, most citizens learn about EOs' presence and reports through the media. Since most international monitoring missions are relatively small,[39] few voters personally witness observers at their polling stations. The observers take a number of steps to promote coverage of their activities, such as holding press conferences (such as the one in Tunisia that we attended, as pictured in Figure 4.6), issuing press releases, and including high-profile individuals in their missions. For instance, the former US President Jimmy Carter participates in some Carter Center missions, and Abdulkarim al-Eryani, the former prime minister of Yemen, was the co-leader of the Carter Center mission to Tunisia in 2014.

Our experiments provided information to respondents about monitors that distilled key points that they *could have* learned from the news in a real-life scenario.[40] The treatments provided general information (e.g., that observers were present or that they generally endorsed or criticized the election) as well as specific information and examples (e.g., that observers had evaluated the legal foundation and thought it was strong in Tunisia). This mix of general and specific information was designed to reflect how EOs are represented in the media and to ensure that all respondents had the same level of information about

---

[37] Chapter 3 contains a discussion of other general issues related to the surveys, including their samples, modes, randomization methods, and ethics.

[38] Gaines, Kuklinski, and Quirk (2007, 9–12). Where contamination is a possibility despite the independent randomization of each experiment, we examine spillover effects in the online appendix (www.cambridge.org/bushprather).

[39] For example, the Carter Center has observed more than 100 elections around the world, and its observation missions often include fewer than 100 individuals. See Hyde (2011, 145).

[40] The English translations of the exact information provided are listed later in the chapter in the research design section for each country.

Figure 4.6 Carter Center press conference to release the initial monitoring report on the 2014 parliamentary election in Tunisia
Note: Authors' photo taken in Tunis, October 2014. Abdulkarim al-Eryani (pictured center) was the co-leader of the mission.

them. To check that respondents grasped the salient aspects of the scenarios, we asked questions after the experiments to probe whether they remembered key aspects of the information about the observers (e.g., their identity) and found that they did.[41]

Third, from an ethical standpoint, it was important to convey truthful information about the activities of international EOs to avoid misleading the respondents.[42] We therefore provided information about observers that were present at the elections we studied and highlighted issues mentioned in their reports.[43] At the end of our surveys, we

---

[41] The results of these tests are reported in the attention check section of the online appendix (www.cambridge.org/bushprather).

[42] The rest of this chapter contains information about EOs' activities and reports in each case to substantiate our claims about the treatments' truthfulness.

[43] Since observers would not endorse *and* criticize the same features of an election, the positive and negative reports described in our treatments were not completely symmetrical. To address this imbalance, we ensured that the positive and negative treatments contained similar types of information (e.g., about the competitiveness of the pre-election environment).

debriefed all respondents about the complete content of observers' reports to ensure they were not given an inaccurate impression that was overly positive or negative.

Fourth, the time period that is most theoretically relevant for our study is immediately prior to and after elections, when citizens form beliefs about election credibility and decide whether to act on those beliefs, such as by engaging in protests. Therefore, our surveys were all administered during this period in each of the three countries. The experiments concerning observer presence could take place prior to elections based on observers' acceptances of invitations to monitor the elections, whereas those about observers' reports were conducted afterwards to incorporate actual content from these reports.

Although many citizens had not yet heard about EOs' endorsements or criticisms given the timing of our surveys, some politically knowledgeable respondents did know about them. Consequently, our treatments in some cases *reminded* people about monitors as opposed to *informing* them for the first time. As described earlier, we asked questions designed to measure preexisting knowledge about observers. But even in Tunisia, where respondents demonstrated the most such knowledge, only 34 percent of respondents reported having heard about EOs' reports after the parliamentary election. In other words, it was still possible to provide many respondents with new information. As expected given the treatments' random assignment, the experimental groups were statistically indistinguishable in their levels of preexisting knowledge about EOs in most cases.[44] Thus, it was possible to experimentally identify the effect of providing new information about observers: Any effect of EOs on trust cannot be explained by preexisting differences in familiarity with observers.

Later in the chapter, we present our findings about monitors' effects in all three countries. Each uses a common experimental approach in which information about observers was randomly assigned to respondents. After the experiments, respondents were asked the common questions, noted previously, designed to determine how credible they perceived the election to be. The design of each survey builds

---

[44] In any analyses where balance tests indicate that there were significant differences across the experimental groups in their preexisting knowledge of EOs or political knowledge more generally, as would be expected to occur occasionally due to chance, we show in the online appendix (www.cambridge .org/bushprather) that our results are robust to controlling for these variables.

on the findings of the previous survey, enabling us to test additional observable implications of our theory. Our basic empirical approach detailed later involves using OLS regressions of the outcome (perceived credibility) on indicators for treatment assignment. Since we randomly assigned respondents to their experimental conditions, we do not include any control variables in this analysis.[45]

4.3 The Effects of Monitors' Presence

In Chapter 2, we theorized that EOs' monitoring activities cause people to believe elections are more credible. The logic, which helps specify the mechanisms underpinning the conventional wisdom about monitors' effects, is twofold. First, the act of inviting international monitors suggests to the public that the government does not intend to cheat. Given the uncertainty about whether political leaders are true democrats or pseudo-democrats, individuals may be reassured when elected officials open themselves up to international scrutiny. Second, and relatedly, high-quality monitors make it more difficult for politicians to steal an election. The public may therefore be more confident that an election has integrity when international monitors have accepted an invitation to observe it.

We contrasted this argument with an alternative one that emphasizes nationalism in individuals' responses to international influences on their elections. This logic implies that the presence of foreign actors, including election monitors, will diminish citizens' trust in their elections. Our surveys can test both the conventional wisdom and this alternative argument.

4.3.1 What Monitors Did

We begin by reviewing monitors' activities at elections in our three case studies. This information is important for both how we designed our surveys and how to interpret citizens' answers to our questions.

Tunisia's 2014 parliamentary and presidential elections were its first democratic elections after the 2011 revolution and thus the first to be

---

[45] The online appendix (www.cambridge.org/bushprather) contains balance tests and regression models that control for demographic variables found to be out of balance. Our results are robust to including these control variables.

observed by international monitors. Given the country's history, the survey participants had limited preconceived notions of EOs, which was useful for our research. Yet, EOs were poised to play a major role since both local and international audiences questioned whether the election would bolster or undermine Tunisia's tentative democratic progress. On the eve of the elections, scholar Noah Feldman mused, "The complex politics of these elections will tell us a lot about whether Tunisia is going to mature into a functioning democracy – or revert to dictatorship like Egypt."[46]

Many observers accepted the Tunisian government's invitation to monitor the 2014 elections, as is often the case for transitional elections. The international groups included three American NGOs – the Carter Center, IRI, and NDI – and four IGOs – the AU, Arab League, EU, and Francophonie.[47] The capabilities and biases of these international EOs varied, so we anticipated that the public was likely to perceive them in different ways, which allows us to examine the importance of observer identity in Chapter 6. Although none of the main international monitors were true zombie EOs, the Arab League came closest as it is primarily comprised of nondemocratic states and tends not to send high-quality monitoring missions.[48] Tunisia's electoral management body, the Independent High Authority for Elections, accredited a total of 1,036 international monitors; organizations such as the EU and American monitoring NGOs oversaw both long- and short-term observation missions.[49]

Turning to the United States, the 2016 and 2018 US elections were more routine in the sense that the United States is a consolidated democracy, while the 2020 US election was more uncertain due to the COVID-19 pandemic. In terms of public opinion, Americans' confidence in their elections is declining.[50] Flaws in US federal elections were revealed with the *Bush vs. Gore* election in 2000, and politicians have stoked Americans' fears since then.[51] For example, during the

---

[46] Feldman (2014).
[47] Several Tunisian political parties and NGOs also served as domestic observers. We compare the effects of international and domestic monitors in Chapter 6.
[48] Boubakri (2012).
[49] Instance Supérieure Indépendante pour les Élections (Tunisia) (2014a).
[50] Alvarez, Hall, and Llewellyn (2008); Gerber et al. (2013); Norris, Cameron, and Wynter (2018, 10).
[51] Beaulieu (2014b).

2016 campaign, then-presidential candidate Donald Trump emphasized the possibility of election fraud, saying during a speech, "Get out
and vote. But they even want to try and rig the election at the polling
booths where so many cities are corrupt. And you see that. And voter
fraud is all too common."[52] Therefore, the 2016 election was actually
likely less certain than would be expected in a long-standing democracy. More recently, changes to electoral institutions necessitated by
the pandemic combined with continued discussions of electoral malpractice by US political actors made 2020 more uncertain in the minds
of Americans as well.

Although the United States is primarily known as a supporter
of EOs in other countries, it also hosts them at its own elections.
US voters are not widely aware of monitors' presence, although
they have occasionally generated local controversy such as in 2012,
when the Iowa and Texas state governments announced that OSCE
observers "would not be welcome."[53] Nevertheless, the US government has hosted OSCE observers since 2004 and observers from the
OAS since 2016 as part of its obligations as a member of these
IGOs. In 2016, for example, the OSCE team included twenty-six
long-term observers and 295 short-term observers present on election
day.[54]

Legal access for nonpartisan – including international – observers
varies greatly across US states, as do de facto norms and practices.[55]
In addition to international observers and nonpartisan citizen groups,
the US elections are also observed by partisan citizen groups and
government observers from the Department of Justice (DOJ), who
monitor states' compliance with federal laws, especially the Voting
Rights Act of 1965.[56] Within this context, we sought to understand
what role monitors might play in shaping public confidence in elections
given that they are present, but not widely recognized, at US elections. Similar to Tunisia then, though for different reasons, the United
States was a relatively blank slate in terms of experience with international observers. Given the low salience of international observers

---

[52] As quoted in Norris, Cameron, and Wynter (2018, 6).
[53] Vanka, Davis-Roberts, and Carroll (2018, 135–136).
[54] Office for Democratic Institutions and Human Rights (2016, 4).
[55] Vanka, Davis-Roberts, and Carroll (2018).
[56] The DOJ EOs are therefore a fairly unusual type of monitors in that they are
explicitly government observers.

in the United States, it was possible that informing Americans about
their presence could cause them to lose confidence in the election by
prompting questions about why EOs needed to be present, as well as
a more nationalistic backlash.

Similar to the 2014 election in Tunisia, Georgia's 2018 presidential
election occurred in an environment that Freedom House characterized as "partly free."[57] Yet, this partially democratic status was not
new in Georgia, contributing to a political environment that was not
especially uncertain. Instead, the presidential election took place in
what one analyst described as "a society with a sense of unfairness
and apathy."[58] Given the country's fairly stable electoral environment,
Georgia was a "less-likely" case for finding that observers' presence
significantly increases trust in elections.

Unlike our other cases, Georgia has a lengthy – and controversial –
history with international monitors. For instance, consider the 2012
parliamentary election, in which the opposition Georgian Dream (GD)
coalition won a surprising victory over President Mikheil Saakashvili's
United National Movement (UNM), which had been in power since
the 2003 Rose Revolution. Ahead of the election, IRI- and NDI-
funded pre-election polls suggested that the UNM was ahead by at
least 20 percentage points.[59] When GD won the election, aided in part
due to a late-breaking UNM prison abuse scandal, Western organizations were "blindsided."[60] Their overestimation of popular support
for UNM contributed to a perception that international monitors from
these organizations (and the West more generally) were biased in favor
of UNM,[61] especially given that the United States and the EU were
strong supporters of the pro-Western Saakashvili.[62] Our interviews
with EO representatives in October 2018 indicate that the allegations of observer bias continued to pose challenges for organizations
six years later, including domestic monitors that cooperate with international partners.[63] Indeed, in a nationally representative survey in

---

[57] Freedom House (2014, 2019).
[58] Melikishvili (2018).
[59] Cecire (2013, 239).
[60] Kirchick (2012).
[61] Cecire (2013, 247).
[62] Mitchell (2006).
[63] Interviews with executive directors and program managers at domestic and
    international NGOs, October 15–17, 2018.

June 2017, only 44 percent of Georgians reported that they "fully trusted" or "trusted" international EOs.[64]

Georgian politicians have played an important role in discrediting monitors. Officials from the ruling GD party attempted to undermine Transparency International (TI) Georgia, for example, by accusing it in October 2018 of being a political party and fascist, as well as long-standing accusations that TI represents foreign interests.[65] Kakha Kaladze, the GD mayor of Tbilisi, similarly accused observers before the runoff election we study of "spread[ing] UNM's narrative."[66] Nevertheless, TI Georgia mobilized 350 monitors for the presidential election.

Given the international community's continued interest in Georgian democracy, the international monitoring presence was substantial at the 2018 presidential election: 1,163 observers from fifty-eight international organizations were accredited.[67] Among the more prominent organizations were numerous international NGOs – including IFES (formerly the International Foundation for Electoral Systems), IRI, and NDI – as well as several IGOs – including the Council of Europe, European Parliament, and OSCE. The large number of international EOs, with their diverse histories and perceptions of capabilities and biases, provided a fertile setting for our research on EO characteristics in Chapter 6.

There was also a substantial domestic monitoring presence, although we did not include a domestic monitors treatment in our experiment in order to preserve statistical power. As usual, the domestic monitoring missions were able to field much larger missions than the international organizations: There were 21,882 observers from sixty-two domestic observer organizations.[68] The largest domestic missions were led by three NGOs: the Analytical International Democratic Institute (2,462 observers), the Civil Alliance for Development (1,034 observers), and the International Society for Free Elections and Democracy (1,030 observers).

---

[64] National Democratic Institute (2017).
[65] Transparency International Georgia (2018).
[66] InterPressNews (2018a).
[67] Central Election Commission (Georgia) (2018a).
[68] Central Election Commission (Georgia) (2018b).

4.3.2 Experimental Design

In all three countries, we embedded experiments in nationally representative surveys to test our argument about monitors' presence. We describe each experiment briefly later.

Our experiments carefully varied the observers' nationalities. We explore the effect of these different nationalities in Chapter 6, where we test our argument about the importance of observers' perceived capabilities and biases. In Tunisia, we gave respondents information about the presence of EOs from different national backgrounds. We then asked them whether they believed the monitors were capable and unbiased. In the United States and Georgia, instead of observing individuals' preexisting beliefs about monitors' capabilities and biases, we gave respondents information about those two characteristics.

Tunisia

We administered our survey in Tunisia after the second-round presidential election in December 2014. There were six experimental groups: a control group that heard no information about EOs and five treatment groups that varied the nationality of the observers (focusing on a selection of domestic and international organizations that were present at the election). Chapter 6 examines variation in EO identity, whereas we pool across the *international* treatment conditions in this chapter to understand the effect of international monitors' presence.

The treatment groups received identical amounts and types of information. The interviewers read out the following text to respondents:

All respondents: Now we would like to ask you some questions about the electoral process and the results of the recent election.

For treatment groups: As you know, voters took to the polls on December 21st to cast their vote for the president. You may not be aware, however, that election observers from [organizations in the United States, the European Union, the Arab League, organizations in Tunisia, the African Union] monitored the election after receiving an invitation from the Tunisian government. The [American, European Union, Arab League, Tunisian, African Union] observers monitored the political situation before and during the election, and they stationed themselves throughout the country to monitor voting and vote counting on Election Day. The [American, European

Union, Arab League, Tunisian, African Union] observers planned to evaluate the elections for compliance with standards for free and fair elections and report on incidences of manipulation, undue partisan interference, voter intimidation, and voter fraud.

The text in brackets was randomly assigned. Given the variety of monitors present in Tunisia and as discussed in Chapter 6, we chose observer groups that we thought would vary in their perceived capabilities and biases, given the variation in resources, experience with democracy, cultural closeness to Tunisia, and history of support for (or opposition to) political Islam.

United States

We fielded two experiments on monitors' presence in the United States – one each in the surveys fielded before the 2016 and 2020 presidential elections. In the 2016 experiment, there were three conditions: a control group that received no information about EOs and two treatment groups that were presented information about monitors' presence and activities, similar to the Tunisia experiment. In addition, two other treatment groups added information about the OSCE monitors that primed the two traits – capability and bias – that we theorized are important for testing our theory about EO identity. We present and analyze their effects in Chapter 6. The text for the 2020 monitoring presence study used the capable and unbiased form of the treatment text from the 2016 experiment, presented later.[69]

In the 2016 study, we included one condition in which the identity of the observers varied, but no information about their capabilities and

---

[69] The 2020 treatment text read: "As you know, voters have already started voting and some will take to the polls on November 3 to cast their vote for president and other offices. You may not be aware, however, that international election observers from the OSCE have been approved by the US government to monitor the election. In the past, the OSCE has been praised for its capable observation teams and for supporting the democratic process regardless of the outcome. The OSCE observers are monitoring the political situation before and during the election, and they will station themselves throughout the country to monitor voting and vote counting on Election Day. The OSCE observers plan to evaluate the elections for compliance with standards for free and fair elections and report on incidences of manipulation, undue partisan interference, voter intimidation, and voter fraud."

biases was provided. The identity treatment included one set of international observers – from the OSCE (the longest-standing international observer of US elections) – and one set of domestic observers – from the DOJ. Again, we focus on the international monitors and compare the international treatment to the control group.

The participants were asked to read the following information about EOs:

All respondents: Now we would like to ask you some questions about what you think the electoral process will be like on November 8.

For treatment groups: As you know, voters will take to the polls on November 8 to cast their vote for the President, Congress, and other offices. You may not be aware, however, that [American, international] election observers from the [US Department of Justice, Organization for Security and Co-operation in Europe (OSCE)] have been approved by the US government to monitor the election. The [Department of Justice, OSCE] observers are monitoring the political situation before and during the election, and they will station themselves throughout the country to monitor voting and vote counting on Election Day. The [Department of Justice, OSCE] observers plan to evaluate the elections for compliance with standards for free and fair elections and report on incidences of manipulation, undue partisan interference, voter intimidation, and voter fraud.

The text in brackets was randomly assigned. Our analysis excludes respondents who proceeded through the survey too quickly to have plausibly read the text.[70]

Georgia
Our Georgia experiment was embedded in the survey fielded immediately prior to the first-round presidential election in October 2018. There were four experimental conditions: a control group that heard no information about EOs, and three treatment groups.

---

[70] Recall from Chapter 3 that the US surveys were the only ones conducted online. Our treatments ranged in length from 137 to 160 words, and our control condition had twenty-five words. Researchers use 300 milliseconds per word to estimate the average reading speed in Internet surveys (Zhang and Conrad 2014, 129). This benchmark implies respondents should have spent 7.5 seconds on average reading the control text and 41.1–48.0 seconds reading the treatment texts. We dropped the 25 percent of respondents who spent less than 3.742 seconds reading the page with the experimental text from our analysis.

Unlike our previous experiments, the treatments did not name specific organizations. Given the controversial history of monitoring in Georgia, we wanted to reduce the likelihood that individuals' prior experiences with EOs would influence how they interpreted the information in our treatments. Moreover, since it is possible that some of our findings from Tunisia and the United States may have hinged in subtle ways on the specific observers that we named in our treatments, we wanted to explore what happened when the observers were not named.

The treatments described international monitors in general and highlighted the specific characteristics emphasized in our theory. Due to statistical power considerations (because this survey also included a separate experiment about meddling), we did not have a treatment that primed monitors' presence without describing their additional characteristics. We described monitors as being capable but biased, incapable but unbiased, or both capable and unbiased. Given the mixed record of international EOs in Georgia (discussed earlier), these treatments were truthful and, we believe, plausible. We also provided additional information to all respondents about observers' activities, similar to our earlier surveys. The precise content of the treatments was:

All respondents: Now we would like to ask you some questions about what you think the electoral process will be like on October 28.

For treatment groups: International election observers have been approved by the Georgian government to observe the election. In the past, international observers have been [praised, criticized] for their [capable, incompetent] observation teams, [but, and] been [praised, criticized] for supporting [some political parties over others, the democratic process no matter who wins]. The international observers are observing the political situation before and during the election, and they will observe voting and vote counting on Election Day. The observers plan to evaluate the elections for compliance with international standards and report on incidences of manipulation, undue partisan interference, and voter intimidation.

Just to remind you, in the past, international observers have been [praised, criticized] for their [capable, incompetent] observation teams, [but, and] been [praised, criticized] for supporting [some political parties over others, the democratic process no matter who wins].

The text in brackets was randomly assigned. For the following analysis, we pool across the treatment conditions; Chapter 6 compares the treatment effects to each other.

It is possible that in all three case studies, our experimental treatments prompted respondents to be more attuned to the potential for flaws in their elections through the descriptions of what election monitors do. This aspect of our research design may explain why our treatments did not have a larger positive effect on average (as discussed later). However, we believe it is a feature of our design, rather than a bug, since it reflects the way that people learn about monitors' activities in the real world. For example, a *USA Today* article on the 2020 US general election said of the OSCE observer team: "Its mission is to assess how well a democratic vote is functioning and to make recommendations for improvements in areas that touch on transparency, accountability and voter pluralism."[71] Given that media reporting on observers highlights that they are assessing election quality, our treatment vignettes mirrored that approach.

4.3.3 The Limited Effects of Monitors' Presence

Across all three cases, we find little evidence that monitors' presence enhanced perceptions of election credibility. This finding contradicts the conventional wisdom outlined in Chapter 2 about how monitors can legitimize elections. It also challenges the nationalist counterargument, which maintains that any foreign intervention in an election is likely to spark a nationalist backlash, which in this case could be observed in terms of perceptions of election credibility.

Figure 4.7 presents our findings across the three cases. It compares the mean level of election credibility for respondents in the control groups (which did not hear information about monitors) vs. those in *any* of the treatment groups that heard information about the presence of international monitors. If international election monitors increase perceptions that elections are credible regardless of whether EOs are perceived to be capable or unbiased, then we would expect respondents in the treated groups to believe elections were significantly more credible than respondents in the control group. They did not.

Although the overall trend is positive, the predicted levels of election credibility did not change significantly in any of the cases when we compare respondents in the control groups to an average across all of the treated respondents; therefore, we cannot be confident that the

---

[71] Hjelmgaard (2020).

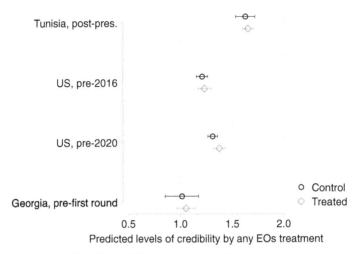

Figure 4.7 The effect of international monitors' presence on perceived credibility, Tunisia, United States (2016 and 2020), and Georgia
Note: This figure shows point estimates with 95 percent confidence intervals. All predictions are based on OLS models without control variables. The outcome variable is perceived credibility and uses the standardized measure, which ranges from 0 to 2. $N = 881$ (Tunisia), 725 (US, 2016), 704 (US, 2020), and 580 (Georgia).

effect is different from zero. Recall that in Tunisia, we randomized the nationality of the international monitors, whereas in Georgia, we gave respondents information about how capable and unbiased the monitors were. When we pool these groups together by country, the mean level of credibility is nearly identical to the control group. On the one hand, learning about monitors does not decrease beliefs that the election was credible. On the other hand, it only slightly increases election credibility. In no case is there a statistically significant difference between the treated and control groups. As outlined in Chapter 3, our multi-country research design helps address one potential explanation for the null effect: the level of prior uncertainty about election credibility. Although citizens in one of our cases (Georgia) were quite confident in their prior beliefs about election credibility, making it a tough test for identifying a significant monitoring effect, those in another case (Tunisia) were a most-likely audience for identifying such an effect given the uncertainty that typically surrounds the first election after a regime transition.

We investigate these null results further in subsequent chapters. In Chapter 6, we look more closely at whether only the presence of monitors that the public perceives as capable and unbiased improves the credibility of elections, as the theory predicts. Furthermore, we examine how perceptions of capability and bias vary according to the national origin of the monitoring groups described in our treatments. To preview the findings, although the presence of monitors has no effect on election credibility on average, when monitors are perceived to be capable and unbiased, they can enhance credibility.

4.4 The Effects of Monitors' Reports

Previously, we established that monitors' presence has no effect on perceptions of election credibility, on average. But what about their reports? The conventional wisdom is that people will have more trust in elections when they hear about positive monitors' reports than when they are given information about negative reports. As explained in Chapter 2, the theoretical logic underpinning this hypothesis is that monitors' reports contain valuable information about election integrity. High-quality monitors gather this information through the sorts of activities described in the previous section.

4.4.1 What Monitors Said

What monitors actually said about the elections we studied influenced our experimental design. We first studied the effects of EO reports on the October 2014 Tunisian parliamentary election. International EOs were united in their overall praise of this election. They agreed that it was transparent and reflected the will of the people. Tunisian politicians cited their reports as evidence of the election's legitimacy, such as when President of the National Constituent Assembly Mustapha Ben Jaafar was reported in the news as saying that "election observation ensures more transparency and credibility to the electoral process and reflects a real image of the positive steps taken toward entrenching freedom and democracy."[72]

Yet, as is typical, the observers also suggested ways that election integrity could be improved. The most-noted criticisms of the election

---

[72] Agence Tunis Afrique Presse (2014b).

related to illegal campaigning outside polling stations and violations of Tunisia's campaign finance rules. Moreover, several groups noted rumors of vote buying, although those reports were unconfirmed. On the whole, observers characterized the infractions as fairly insignificant, since they did not affect the election outcome. For example, NDI's preliminary statement described the election as "a major step forward...There were isolated irregularities and incidents, none of which, however, appeared significant enough to materially affect the outcome of the elections in the districts where they occurred."[73] Since EOs delivered mixed – though undoubtedly positive – reports about the election, this gave us ample opportunity to create treatments about observers' positive and negative reports that reflected their true statements (i.e., that were both ecologically valid and nondeceptive).

Observers at the American and Georgian elections we studied documented a similar combination of positive and negative findings. In the United States, we conducted surveys on this topic immediately following the 2016 and 2020 presidential elections and the 2018 midterm elections. The OSCE issued generally positive reports of these elections, as would be expected for elections in a consolidated democracy. For example, it described the 2016 election as "highly competitive and demonstrated commitment to fundamental freedoms of expression, assembly and association."[74] The United States was not, however, immune to criticism. The negative content most emphasized in the OSCE reports related to "obstacles for voters," especially those from historically marginalized communities, such as some states' voter identification rules and reductions in the number of polling places.[75] The OSCE reported similar issues at the 2018 and 2020 elections.[76]

---

[73] National Democratic Institute (2014, 1).
[74] Office for Democratic Institutions and Human Rights (2016, 1).
[75] Ibid., 1, 4, 10. These concerns are potentially more aligned with Democrats' concerns about voter access than with Republicans' concerns about voter fraud. Chapter 7 analyzes how vote choice conditions EO reports' effects, where we identify stronger treatment effects among Democrats than Republicans in 2016.
[76] Office for Democratic Institutions and Human Rights (2018) and OSCE Parliamentary Assembly (2020).

We administered the Georgia survey in the days following the November 2018 run-off presidential election. The run-off election took place one month after the first-round presidential election, which was the focus of the experiment on observer presence described earlier. EOs assessed the presidential election critically, though they did not condemn it outright. The preliminary NDI report applauded the election for being competitive and largely free of violence, yet criticized it for "aggressive, personalized, and unprecedented attacks by senior state officials against the country's most respected civil society organizations," as well as "[l]ongstanding problems of an uneven playing field and abuse of administrative resources."[77] These criticisms may have helped galvanize post-election discord. UNM leaders – including exiled former president Mikheil Saakashvili and losing presidential candidate Grigol Vashadze – condemned the run-off election result; the latter called it a "stolen election" in a speech in front of thousands of post-election protesters in Tbilisi, although he did not cite observers' reports according to media coverage of his speech.[78]

4.4.2 *Experimental Design*

Our experimental design involved a control group that did not receive information about EOs and two treatment groups that received information about either the positive or negative content of EO reports. We reprint the information provided in each experiment discussed later.

Tunisia

In the post-legislative survey in Tunisia, we randomly varied the content of monitors' reports as well as their identities, referencing both American and Tunisian observers. We chose these groups because we wanted to compare international and domestic observers. We chose American monitors given their prominence in the overall election monitoring field. We focused on American observers in Georgia as well, following a similar rationale. EO identity does not moderate the treatment effect, and we pool across the two nationalities below to focus on

---

[77] National Democratic Institute (2018b, 2).
[78] Radio Free Europe/Radio Liberty (2018).

the main effect of monitors' reports.[79] Interviewers read the following aloud:

All respondents: As you know, voters took to the polls on October 26th to cast their vote for the parliament.

Both treatment groups: You may not be aware, however, that election observers from organizations in [the United States, Tunisia] monitored the election after receiving an invitation from the Tunisian government. The [American, Tunisian] observers monitored the political situation before and during the election, and they stationed themselves throughout the country to monitor voting and vote counting on Election Day. The [American, Tunisian] observers planned to evaluate the elections for compliance with standards for free and fair elections and report on incidences of manipulation, undue partisan interference, voter intimidation, and voter fraud.

Positive reports treatment: After the election, the [American, Tunisian] observers released their preliminary evaluation of the recent election. In their report, the monitors assessed many aspects of the election and cited several areas of success. One of the [American, Tunisian] observers' important findings was that the legal foundation for the election was strong and created a fair and secure environment for competition. Moreover, the [American, Tunisian] observers noted that the election campaigns were clean, transparent, and vibrant.

Negative reports treatment: After the election, the [American, Tunisian] observers released their preliminary evaluation of the recent election. In their report, the monitors assessed many aspects of the election and cited several areas of needed improvements. One of the [American, Tunisian] observers' important findings was that the improper source and use of campaign funds undermined the fairness of the competition. Moreover, the [American,

---

[79] As we discuss in Chapter 6, domestic observers are commonly thought to have advantages over international observers, in terms of both the size of their missions and their local legitimacy. Meanwhile, American observers might be expected to be particularly suspect among international groups given high levels of anti-Americanism in the Arab world linked to US interventions in the region (Jamal 2012; Jamal et al. 2015; Benstead, Kao, and Lust 2020). Yet as we show in Chapter 6, American and Tunisian EOs had similar levels of perceived capability and bias in Tunisia, which likely explains why we did not identify a significant effect of nationality.

Tunisian] observers noted that there have been allegations of vote buying and illegal influence from parties.

Given the fairly long text, the interviewers reinforced the verbal treatments by giving respondents fliers that included the monitor's national flag and a "thumbs up" or "thumbs down" symbol to summarize their assessment.

United States

We used a similar approach in the post-election surveys in 2016, 2018, and 2020 in the United States. All three US experiments had two treatment groups and a control group that did not receive information about EOs. In each survey, respondents were told the US government had invited monitors from the OSCE – the most consistent international observer of American elections – to observe the election. The positive and negative content referenced in our experiment was drawn from the OSCE's preliminary reports on each election. As such, the content varied a bit between the three experiments, although it was generally quite similar. Due to our concerns about respondent speeding and fatigue in the 2016 survey described earlier, we slightly shortened the treatments in the 2018 and 2020 surveys. The 2016 text was as follows:

All respondents: Now we would like to ask you some questions about what you think the electoral process was like on November 8. As you know, voters took to the polls on November 8 to cast their vote for the President, Congress, and other offices.

Both treatment groups: Election observers from the OSCE monitored the election after receiving an invitation from the US government. The observers monitored the political situation before and during the election, and they stationed themselves throughout the country to monitor voting and vote counting on Election Day. The OSCE observers planned to evaluate the elections for compliance with standards for free and fair elections and report on incidences of manipulation, undue partisan interference, voter intimidation, and voter fraud.

Positive reports treatment: After the election, the observers released their preliminary evaluation of the recent election. In their report, the monitors cited several areas of success. One of the observers' important findings was that the election demonstrated commitment to legal freedoms of expression, assembly, and association. Moreover, the elections were administered by competent and committed staff, who enabled the exchange of best practices and provided standards for New Voting Technologies.[80]

Negative reports treatment: After the election, the observers released their preliminary evaluation of the recent election. In their report, the monitors cited several areas of needed improvement. One of the observers' important findings was that recent changes to election laws and decisions on technical aspects of the process were often motivated by partisan interests, causing undue obstacles for voters. Moreover, voting rights are not guaranteed for all citizens, leaving many sections of the population without the right to vote.[81]

As the text shows, we did not randomize EO identity, in part to preserve statistical power.

Georgia

Like the earlier studies, the Georgia experiment informed randomly selected respondents about international monitors' reports, whereas a control group received no such information. It was embedded in the post-election survey after the second round of the presidential election. The treatments described the observers as being from the United States. We did not vary observer nationality in order to preserve statistical power, similar to our decision in the US surveys. The positive treatment highlighted traditional aspects of election integrity, including the election's strong legal foundation, vibrant

---

[80] In 2018 and 2020, the positive reports content read: "In their preliminary evaluation of the election, the OSCE observers cited several areas of success. One of the observers' important findings was that the election demonstrated commitment to legal freedoms of speech, assembly, and association. Moreover, the elections were administered by competent and committed staff, who enabled the exchange of best practices and provided standards for New Voting Technologies. These conclusions were reached after the OSCE observers evaluated the elections for compliance with standards for free and fair elections."

[81] In 2018 and 2020, the negative reports content read: "In their preliminary evaluation of the election, the OSCE observers cited several problem areas. One of the observers' important findings was that the fundamental right to vote was denied to some groups of citizens due to recent changes to election laws and decisions on technical aspects of the electoral process. Moreover, campaign rhetoric was often intensely negative and, at times, intolerant, including on social networks. These conclusions were reached after the OSCE observers evaluated the elections for compliance with standards for free and fair elections."

campaigns, and satisfactory administration. The negative treatment noted the election's problems with campaign finance and allegations of voter intimidation and illegal influence from parties. All of these characteristics were highlighted in real US observers' preliminary reports. The survey interviewers provided the following information:

All respondents: Now we would like to ask you some questions about what you thought the electoral process for the run-off presidential election was like.

Both treatment groups: American election observers were approved by the Georgian government to observe the election. After the election, the American observers released their preliminary evaluation.

Positive treatment: In their report, the American monitors assessed many aspects of the election and cited several areas of success. One of their important findings was that the legal foundation for the election was strong and created a fair and secure environment for competition. Moreover, the American observers noted that the election campaigns were vibrant and that the election administration was transparent and efficient.

Negative treatment: In their report, the monitors assessed many aspects of the election and cited several areas of needed improvements. One of their important findings was that the improper source and use of campaign funds undermined the fairness of the competition. Moreover, the American observers noted that there have been allegations of voter intimidation and illegal influence from parties.

4.4.3 Monitors' Reports Influence Trust

As with the experiments on election monitors' presence, we asked respondents about election credibility immediately following the information about monitors described earlier. Figure 4.8 displays the mean level of election credibility for respondents in the negative and positive treatment conditions in each survey.[82] If EOs' reports provide information to respondents about the fairness of the electoral playing

---

[82] The online appendix (www.cambridge.org/bushprather) includes analyses that compare each of the treatments separately to the control. The positive and negative treatments produced small but statistically insignificant changes in perceived credibility relative to the control group in opposing directions.

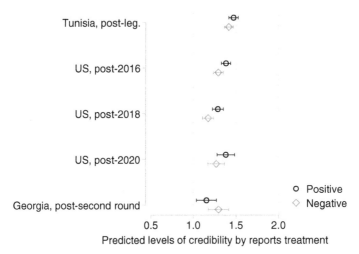

Figure 4.8 The effect of monitors' reports on perceived credibility, Tunisia, United States (2016, 2018, and 2020), and Georgia
Note: This figure shows point estimates with 95 percent confidence intervals. All predictions are based on OLS models without control variables. The outcome variable is perceived credibility and uses the standardized measure, which ranges from 0 to 2. $N = 762$ (Tunisia), 676 (US, 2016), 419 (US, 2018), 360 (US, 2020), and 477 (Georgia).

field and whether local politicians are cheating types, then individuals in the negative reports treatment condition will have lower levels of trust in the election than respondents in the positive reports treatment condition.

As in the elections studied in Figure 4.7, Figure 4.8 demonstrates that Tunisians had the highest levels of trust in the election, followed by Americans. Once again, Georgians had the least trust in elections of the three cases. Americans' electoral trust over time remains between that of Tunisians and Georgians.

Figure 4.8 illustrates that in the Tunisia experiment as well as the 2016 and 2018 US experiments, hearing about positive EO reports caused people to believe the election was more credible than hearing about negative reports. In the 2020 US experiment, there was a similarly sized effect, but the results do not quite reach traditional levels of statistical significance due to the smaller sample size. This effect also misses traditional levels of significance for Tunisia, whereas in the United States in 2016 and 2018, the effect sizes are slightly larger and do reach statistical significance.[83] Further tests indicate that monitors' reports influenced citizens' trust in the results of the election more than their beliefs that the election reflected the will of the people, suggesting that they may be more informative about issues related to electoral fraud than about the broader fairness of the electoral playing field.

In both Tunisia and the United States, the substantive effect of EO reports was fairly modest. For example, there was a 7 percent average increase in our measure of credibility when we compare Americans who heard about negative vs. positive reports after the 2016 election. To put that effect size into context, consider that there was a 55 percent average increase in our measure of credibility when we compare reported Clinton voters to reported Trump voters in that election. Thus, although the effect of EO reports was statistically significant, it was considerably smaller in substantive terms than some other factors that influence perceived credibility.

Unexpectedly, we observe the opposite pattern for Georgia's post-second-round presidential election: Individuals in the positive report treatment group had *lower* levels of trust in the election than those in the negative report treatment group.[84] Similar to the other effects, this treatment effect is fairly modest – a 12 percent decrease in perceived credibility when we compare respondents in the positive treatment group to those in the negative treatment group. This effect could represent either a partisan or a nationalist backlash effect. As we will show in Chapter 7, this effect appears to be driven by election losers, who reacted negatively to the positive information monitors included in EO reports. By contrast, we do not find that an indicator of the respondent's level of nationalism moderates the treatment.[85]

Overall, our surveys suggest that EO reports do affect individuals' perceptions of election credibility in meaningful ways, although they do so in the expected direction in only two of our three cases. As

---

[83] The p-values are 0.147, 0.026, and 0.013, respectively, in two-tailed tests. For a discussion of additional robustness checks in Tunisia related to spatial effects, please see Bush and Prather (2017).

[84] $p = 0.098$ in a two-tailed test.

[85] We create a dichotomous measure of nationalism based on a scale of responses to three questions. Whereas partisanship is a significant moderator of the treatment, as indicated by the interaction between the treatment and party identification ($p = 0.008$), nationalism is not ($p = 0.593$). Moreover, a chi-square test does not reveal a significant partisan difference in reported nationalism ($p = 0.918$).

noted previously, reported knowledge about monitors and their reports was fairly limited among the general public in Georgia and the United States, according to our surveys. The findings from Figure 4.8 suggest, however, that monitors' reports do have the potential to change individuals' minds when people become aware of them. Although the effects are fairly modest in those cases where we identify them, even in the "high uncertainty" (and thus most-likely) case of Tunisia, they shed light on governments' decisions about when to invite monitors (and which one to invite), topics to which we return to in Chapter 8.

4.5 Conclusion

This chapter explored two mechanisms through which international EOs can enhance trust in elections: (1) being present at elections and (2) issuing positive reports (and decreasing trust by issuing negative reports).

Our experiments tested both propositions. The first experiments identified the effect of information about observer presence. The next experiments identified the impact of information about EO reports. Identifying these effects in the real world is difficult because observers are only invited (and accept invitations) to monitor certain elections, which tend to be more credible to begin with. Moreover, after observers arrive, the people who tend to get exposed to information about their activities are different from those who do not. For both reasons, correlations between observers' activities and citizens' perceptions in the real world – though limited, as shown in Figures 4.4 and 4.5 – could be misleading. Our experiments helped address these limitations by comparing across groups of people that received different information about EOs but were otherwise similar.

Overall, international monitors were occasionally a valuable source of information for the public. Yet, their effects have important limits. Their mere presence was not enough to legitimize any of the elections we studied. Western monitors' fears that their presence will have such an effect is a common explanation for why they decline to monitor elections that they anticipate will be undemocratic, such as the EU's decision not to observe the 2010 general elections in Sudan or the OSCE's decision not to observe the 2008 presidential election in Russia.[86] The Declaration of Principles of International Election Observation even states that "an organization should not send an international election observation mission to a country under conditions that make it likely that its presence will be interpreted as giving legitimacy to a clearly undemocratic electoral process."[87] We find no evidence to support this conclusion in the context of public opinion when looking across international monitors *in general*, although even the least democratic elections we studied – Georgia's – were not what most analysts would consider to be fully authoritarian. Our null results regarding the effects of monitors' presence on perceived credibility also challenge the notion that international monitoring – which citizens could perceive as a form of meddling – will generate negative reactions among the public.

Monitors' reports are more informative for the public, but their effects also depend on the context. We found that such reports affected the public's trust in the expected directions in Tunisia and the United States, but not in Georgia. Although we acknowledge that this impact was relatively small in Tunisia and the United States, this makes sense given our relatively modest treatments as well as some of the theoretical reasons we identified in Chapter 2 about why foreign actors' effects may be more limited than previously appreciated. These findings provide some support for previous findings in the literature that critical reports can sometimes help mobilize the public against the regime via protests, whereas sometimes positive reports can have the opposite effect. In Georgia, positive reports caused individuals to perceive the election as *less* credible than negative reports. To unpack this unexpected finding, and others in this chapter, we explore how the effects of monitors vary according to their characteristics (and those of the respondents) in Chapters 6 and 7. In Chapter 5, however, we consider whether meddlers' overall effects also challenge the conventional wisdom.

---

[86] Drennan (2015).
[87] *Declaration of Principles for International Election Observation* (2005).

5 | *Meddlers' Effects*

When Russia meddled in the 2016 US presidential election, scholars, policymakers, and analysts all worried it would cause Americans to lose faith in their elections. In May 2019, as the US Congress considered new legislation to improve election security, one of the authors of the bill, Senator Richard Blumenthal (D-Conn.), framed it in terms of the need to prevent further damage to Americans' political trust: "This is Vladimir Putin's game plan – sow distrust, discord, disillusionment and division... There's a real danger to distrust in the integrity of our election system that has lasting damage."[1]

Yet, Blumenthal's proposed legislation that would require campaigns to report any foreign nationals' offers of support, the Duty to Report Act, failed to win bipartisan support. Related proposals, including the Securing America's Federal Elections Act and the Foreign Influence Reporting in Elections Act, also stalled without sufficient backing from Republicans. The absence of a robust anti-meddling policy response in the United States is surprising, considering that foreign electoral interference represents a clear intervention in countries' domestic affairs and thus seems likely to prompt a nationalist backlash against meddling. Studying how citizens respond to information about foreign electoral interference can shed light on why such a backlash – and a stronger policy response – has not occurred.

Few prior studies have explored how foreign meddling affects citizens' perceptions of elections.[2] Previous research has instead tended to focus on how meddling influences election results or democratic

---

[1] As quoted in Milligan (2019).
[2] Corstange and Marinov (2012); Shulman and Bloom (2012); Marinov (2013); Bush and Prather (2020) examine how meddling affects individual-level public opinion in specific cases, but not perceptions of *election credibility*. In addition, Tomz and Weeks (2020) include trust in elections as one outcome in their study of how meddling affects American attitudes, as discussed in Chapter 3. We build on their study in this chapter.

institutions,[3] or countries' strategic incentives to pursue meddling as a foreign policy.[4] Although these studies represent important steps toward understanding the long-term, macro-level effects of election meddling, they largely overlook its impacts on the average citizen's perceptions of election credibility – even though such effects are widely suspected and may contribute to longer-term outcomes. We address this oversight by examining how meddling affects individuals in target countries on average in this chapter.

To review, in Chapter 2, we developed a framework that grounds the conventional wisdom – that meddling diminishes citizens' perceptions of election credibility on average – within a broader theory of public opinion formation. In this chapter, we test this conventional wisdom. In support, we find that perceptions of foreign meddling are negatively correlated with assessments of election credibility in all three cases: Individuals who think a foreign power has interfered in their country's election tend to believe the election is less credible. Yet, new information about the presence of foreign election meddling did not cause individuals to update their beliefs about the credibility of elections in all of our experiments. In the United States, information about the *absence* of meddling had a positive effect on trust. We find mixed evidence in Georgia that concerns about meddling are linked to lower levels of trust; the clearest effects emerge in the context of a hypothetical election in which respondents were very uncertain about election credibility. In other words, and similar to our findings in Chapter 4, we find that the conventional wisdom has real limits. In Chapters 6 and 7, we test how the effects of meddling depend on the meddler's identity and individuals' vote choice.

5.1 About Meddling

The political science literature contains relatively few studies on election meddling, though it has expanded in response to recent events. An important finding from this literature is that election meddling often succeeds. It usually increases the electoral chances of the supported candidate, holding constant many other variables such as the target country's region, regime type, and economic conditions.[5] For

---

[3] Berger et al. (2013); Levin (2016, 2019b).
[4] Bubeck and Marinov (2017, 2019).
[5] Levin (2016).

example, Dov Levin estimates that the covert Soviet intervention in support of Willy Brandt and the Social Democratic Party in the 1972 West German election – which included bribes to key elected officials in coordination with the *Stasi* to secure their support in a vote of no confidence against Brandt earlier that year – proved decisive in Brandt's re-election as chancellor.[6]

Moreover, meddling can have negative long-term effects on democracy.[7] For example, the US government covertly helped Guyana's incumbent government commit voter registration fraud to win the 1968 election; the government continued to use this fraudulent technique to stay in power for some time, even after it turned toward socialism (and thus away from the United States during the Cold War) in 1969.[8] Therefore, although meddling does not always succeed, it may make the electoral playing significantly less fair, in both the short and long terms.

Given these effects, it is plausible that meddling would affect perceptions of election credibility. Yet as we argued in Chapter 3, knowing whether it does have such an effect requires specific data, which this chapter provides. To inform our approach, we begin by reviewing what previous research can tell us about what meddlers do and to what extent they are a common feature of elections. This discussion helps further motivate our analysis of whether meddling affects individuals' perceptions of election credibility.

5.1.1 What Meddlers Do

Election meddling refers to a foreign actor's deliberate endeavor to undermine the fairness of another country's election by seeking to tilt the electoral playing field to benefit a particular candidate or party. States are the main actors that engage in election meddling, although the nonstate actors (both nongovernmental organizations (NGOs) and intergovernmental organizations) that engage in zombie monitoring are also increasingly relevant meddlers, as we discussed in Chapter 4.

Levin identifies six general types of meddling: campaign funding to a favored side; nonmonetary campaign assistance to a favored side; dirty

---

[6] Ibid., 200.; Shimer (2020, 76–78).
[7] Levin (2019b).
[8] Rabe (2005, 159–160).

tricks against disfavored candidates, such as spreading disinformation about them, physically harming them, or spying on their campaign activities; threats or promises on behalf of the intervening government; giving or accepting foreign economic aid; or other concessions by the intervening government such as supporting a contentious claim over a disputed territory.[9]

Meddling can be either covert or overt. Sometimes states do not bother to conceal their efforts to help a favored side.[10] In December 2018, for example, Russia's interior ministry announced that Moldovan citizens who had overstayed their residence permits in Russia would be allowed to return to Moldova (presumably to vote) between January 1 and February 25, 2019, and return to Russia without penalty.[11] Observers interpreted this announcement as an effort to promote the election chances of the pro-Russian Party of Socialists of the Republic of Moldova, the favored party of Moldovan citizens residing in Russia, in the February 24, 2019, Moldovan parliamentary election. In another, much earlier example of relatively overt election meddling, the United States openly sought to help the Christian Democratic Party defeat the Popular Democratic Front, a Communist–Socialist coalition, in the 1948 Italian general election.[12]

At other times, countries attempt to engage in covert election meddling, but information about their intervention becomes public thanks to efforts of the media, intelligence services, or even election observers (EOs) prior to or immediately following the election. Russia's intervention in the 2016 US election fits this pattern, as does its attempt to influence the French presidential election the following year.[13] In other cases, information is revealed over time, such as US interference in some Latin American elections during the Cold War, including in the Dominican Republic and Nicaragua.[14]

Although the United States and the Soviet Union/Russia are the best-known election meddlers, other regional powers – or would-be regional powers – are also active. Under Hugo Chávez, for example,

---

[9] Levin (2019a).

[10] Levin estimates that one-third of great power interventions are overt. See Levin (2019a, 96).

[11] Rusnac (2018).

[12] Miller (1983, 37). This influence also included a substantial covert element.

[13] Vilmer (2018).

[14] Robinson (1996, Ch. 5); O'Rourke (2018, Ch. 8).

Venezuela took an active interest in elections held in nearby countries. According to *New York Times* reporting on Peru's 2006 presidential campaign, Chávez called candidate Alan García "'shameless, a thief,' and warned that if he were elected 'by some work of the devil,' Venezuela would withdraw its ambassador."[15] Ultimately, this disagreement led to the mutual withdrawal of the Venezuelan and Peruvian ambassadors amid accusations of Venezuelan meddling. Meanwhile, in advance of the 2006 presidential election in Nicaragua, Chávez supported Sandinista leader Daniel Ortega's return to office by signing an energy cooperation agreement with him and selling discounted oil to Sandinista-led municipalities during the country's energy crisis.[16] Similarly, Iran is an important intervener in the Muslim world, including as a major funder of Hizballah, the Shia political party and militant group in Lebanon.[17]

Like monitors, at least some meddlers explicitly seek to influence citizens' faith in democracy. Although it is difficult to determine meddlers' true motives, affecting citizens' electoral trust is likely a common goal. For example, US government reports have posited that Russia's interference in the 2016 US election sought to undermine Americans' trust in their electoral institutions, perhaps to delegitimize an anticipated victory by Hillary Clinton, the candidate perceived as the greater Russia hawk.[18] Yet even in the event of a Trump victory, Russian meddling could have a desired effect by causing long-term effects on Americans' trust in their institutions.

Eurasia experts Lucan Way and Adam Casey similarly concluded that the wave of Russian electoral interventions since 2015 has been "clearly aimed at undermining democratic governance."[19] Indeed, the current chief of Russia's armed forces, Valery Gerasimov, has outlined the principles of subversion. In 2013, he stated in a speech that was later printed as an article: "The information space opens wide asymmetrical possibilities for reducing the fighting potential of the enemy."[20] In this speech, he advocated using information warfare to sow chaos in enemy states, as he argued Western states had done

[15] Forero (2006, A1).
[16] Ibid., A1; Rogers (2006, 1).
[17] Corstange and Marinov (2012, 658).
[18] Fandos and Wines (2018); Jamieson (2020, 215).
[19] Way and Casey (2018, 1).
[20] Gerasimov (2016, 27).

during the Color Revolutions and the Arab Spring. The Gerasimov doctrine suggests that Russia's recent electoral interventions in the United States and Europe seek to increase the electoral chances of pro-Russia candidates and parties *and* to cause citizens to question the legitimacy of their democratic systems. In other words, election meddling seeks to influence not only how fair the electoral playing field *is* but also how fair citizens *perceive it to be.*

5.1.2 Meddling over Time

It is difficult to determine exactly how often meddling takes place, since it is often covert and may never be uncovered. Nevertheless, some reliable cross-national data sources have attempted to do just that. These data suggest that, in contrast to the clear increase in monitoring over time documented in Chapter 4, foreign meddling has been a more consistent feature of world politics and has perhaps declined over time. Moreover, far fewer elections have experienced meddling compared to monitoring.

Figure 5.1 is based on data from the National Elections Across Democracy and Autocracy (NELDA) dataset, which draws on historical sources to identify attempts by foreign actors to meddle in national elections between 1945 and 2015. These data show that the number of national elections affected by foreign meddling has remained fairly constant over time; an average of 6 percent of elections experienced meddling during this period.[21] Though the NELDA data on election meddling may be incomplete, given that states seek to keep information about it secret, the trends suggested in Figure 5.1 are broadly consistent with those found in other data sources, such as the Partisan Electoral Interventions by the Great Powers dataset.[22]

---

[21] Data on meddling come from NELDA variable 58 ("Did an outside actor attempt to influence the outcome of the election by making threats to withhold, or by withholding, something of value to the country?"). NELDA codes this variable based on sources such as Lexis-Nexis Academic, Pro-Quest Historical Newspaper Databases, and histories of specific countries.

[22] Levin (2019a, 2). Information about covert interventions sometimes becomes public as time passes, which is why Levin ceases data collection in 2000. According to his calculations, "Between 1946 and 2000, the US and the Soviet Union/Russia have intervened in about one of every nine competitive national-level executive elections." See O'Rourke (2018) for data on covert attempts at regime change, including during elections.

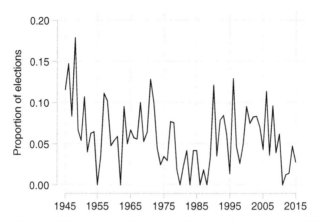

Figure 5.1 Proportion of national elections that experienced foreign meddling, 1945–2015
Note: The data are from NELDA version 5.0 (Hyde and Marinov 2012).

Election meddling was a well-known feature of the Cold War, though it may have become less frequent toward the end, as Figure 5.1 suggests. Yet, the figure illustrates that these types of interventions continued afterwards. More recent well-known examples include US opposition to Chavismo in Venezuela since 1999 and Russia's support for incumbent Prime Minister Viktor Yanukovych during Ukraine's 2004 presidential election.[23]

Although election meddling has not become more frequent over time, advances in communications technologies have enabled new forms of meddling related to disinformation. For example, social media platforms such as Facebook allow foreign meddlers to deceive users and spread conspiracy theories, including by engaging in targeted advertisements and other messages. New forms of electronic voting technology may also create opportunities for foreign meddling, such as when pro-Russia hackers tampered with the computer system of Ukraine's electoral commission during the latter's 2014 presidential election, attempting to alter the vote tallies of the candidates just 40 minutes before the results were due to be reported on national television.[24]

[23] McFaul (2007, 68); Gill (2018).
[24] Clayton (2014).

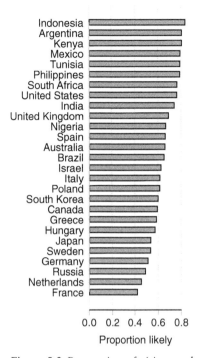

Figure 5.2 Proportion of citizens who think their elections will face cyberattacks, 2018
Note: The data are from Pew Research Center (2018). This figure shows the proportion of respondents who said a cyberattack on a future election was "very likely" or "somewhat likely."

Even if the *number* of meddling incidents has not risen, if the *salience* of these episodes increases, fears of meddling may still have growing consequences for electoral trust and democracy. Such fears may have become especially salient in democratic countries due to events in the 2010s. Indeed, a majority of those surveyed by the Pew Global Attitudes Project in twenty-seven countries in 2018 believe cyberattacks were "very likely" or "somewhat likely" (Figure 5.2).[25]

---

[25] Q48c of this survey asked, "How likely or unlikely do you think it is that, in the future, a cyberattack will result in the following situation? Elections in [country] will be tampered with." See Pew Research Center (2018). Although cyberattacks could also be domestic in origin, since this question was asked within the context of other questions about "cyberattacks from other countries," we think it primarily captures public concerns about foreign meddling.

5.2 Research Design

To understand how meddling influences people in the countries where it occurs, ideally we could compare the relationship between instances of meddling and citizens' trust in elections. However, it is not straightforward to study how foreign actors affect perceptions of election credibility using existing data for two reasons, as we explain in Chapter 3: (1) we lack appropriate survey data on citizens' trust from around election day and (2) the problem of selection bias, since foreign actors do not intervene at random. Nevertheless, in Chapter 4, we use existing survey data to shed light on correlations between monitors and trust on a global sample of countries. Unfortunately, we cannot use that method to assess meddlers, since meddling is not common enough for us to be able to match data on its occurrence with enough relevant survey data to draw inferences.

In this chapter, we use correlational evidence from all three of our case studies. This approach allows us to examine whether individuals who believe foreign actors are meddling in an election have less faith in the credibility of the election. We find that they generally are. However, as we elaborate later in this chapter, we are not confident that the relationship is truly causal. Thus, we also outline an experimental research design that can more credibly examine that causal relationship.

5.2.1 Correlational Tests

With the exception of the post-election survey in Georgia, all of our surveys contained the same questions about foreign influence. This approach provides a comparable measure of perceptions of foreign influence around elections that we can use over time and across countries to examine whether individuals who perceived negative foreign influence at an election were less likely to think the election was credible. First, we asked, "To what extent do you think other countries will/did influence the results of the [description] election?" The response options were "a lot," "some," "not too much," and "not at all." For respondents who said they perceived at least some influence, we then asked, "Do you think this influence will be/was primarily positive, negative, or both positive and negative?" We use the responses to these questions to examine whether individuals who believed foreign actors negatively influenced the election also thought it was less credible.

Table 5.1 presents the proportion of respondents who perceived at least some foreign influence in each survey in which this question was asked, as well as the proportion of respondents who viewed that foreign influence as negative, positive, or both. For every election we studied, *most* respondents thought there was at least some foreign influence. The US data reveal a particularly interesting pattern. Whereas most of the post-election questions about foreign influence were asked immediately after the election we studied, the 2018 pre-election survey also asked respondents about the extent to which they believed the *2016* election had been influenced by foreign actors. In 2018, 83 percent of respondents thought the 2016 election had been subject to at least some foreign influence, up from 72 percent immediately after the 2016 election. This pattern makes sense, as further credible information about Russian meddling had been made public and covered extensively in the media during the two years following the election. Table 5.1 illustrates that more than half of the individuals surveyed in all three countries perceived a significant amount of foreign influence.

Overall, respondents perceived the nature of foreign influence as more negative than positive. The largest disparity between perceived positive and negative influence was observed in the 2018 pre-election survey of Americans that asked respondents about the 2016 election. Among individuals surveyed in 2018 who perceived at least some foreign influence at the 2016 US election, respondents were more than three times as likely to say that influence was negative (57 percent) as they were to describe it as positive (16 percent). In Tunisia and Georgia, perceptions of the nature of foreign influence were more balanced between negative and positive. In fact, more respondents in Georgia considered foreign influence to be positive than negative. These ambivalent responses about the effects of foreign influence contradict the alternative perspective outlined in Chapter 2, which is that individuals will view *all* forms of foreign influence on elections negatively as violations of sovereignty.

There are at least three reasons why Americans may have viewed foreign influence more negatively than Tunisians and Georgians in our surveys. The first and most obvious explanation is that widespread foreign election meddling did not occur (or at least was not reported by credible sources) in either Tunisia or Georgia. The second reason could be that in both of those countries, high-quality international election

Table 5.1 *Perceptions of foreign influence in elections*

Country	Year	Election	Survey Timing	Any Foreign Influence	Percent Perceiving Negative Influence	Positive Influence	Both Types
Tunisia	2014	Legislative	Post-election	63	45	41	14
Tunisia	2014	Presidential	Post-election	59	45	34	21
US	2016	Presidential	Pre-election	78	34	36	31
US	2016	Presidential	Post-election	72	44	19	37
US	2016	Presidential	Asked in 2018	83	57	16	27
US	2018	Legislative	Pre-election	76	39	26	35
US	2018	Legislative	Post-election	62	36	19	44
US	2020	Presidential	Pre-election	84	54	17	29
US	2020	Presidential	Post-election	75	42	18	39
Georgia	2018	Presidential	Pre-election	78	29	41	31

Note: Responses about whether foreign influence was positive, negative, or both include all respondents who said there was at least "some" foreign influence. Only respondents from the control groups in the monitoring or meddling experiments are included.

monitoring and other forms of democracy promotion – types of foreign influence that citizens may perceive more positively since they generally seek to promote a fair electoral playing field – are more commonplace than in the United States because Tunisia and Georgia are not consolidated democracies.[26] Consequently, Tunisians and Georgians may appreciate the positive roles that foreign actors can play around elections. The fact that international monitoring is more limited and less recognized in the United States may make Americans less familiar with some of the potentially beneficial aspects of foreign influence. Finally, it is possible that for historical reasons, Tunisians and Georgians are less shocked by – and are therefore perhaps more tolerant of – foreign influence in their elections.[27]

Given that most respondents perceived some degree of foreign influence, and that there is substantial variation in their views about the nature of that influence, we next examine how perceptions of foreign influence are related to perceptions of election credibility. Our theory predicts that meddling diminishes electoral trust, so we expected individuals to be less likely to think an election was credible if they believed foreign actors had a negative influence. Perceived negative foreign influence is not a precise measure of perceived meddling, since people may view meddling that benefits their favored candidate or party as a positive influence. Nevertheless, we believe it is a plausible indicator, and respondents' answers to an open-ended question about the countries that were the likeliest negative influences (such as Russia in both the United States and Georgia) map onto what we know are the likeliest foreign meddlers. Thus, we regress our measure of election credibility from each relevant survey on a variable indicating whether the respondent perceived foreign actors' influence to be positive, negative, or both, and on a set of control variables. Recall from Chapter 3 that election credibility, as we define it, indicates whether the respondent trusts the election results and believes the election reflects the will of the people (0 = least perceived credibility, 2 = greatest perceived credibility).

---

[26] Although recall from Chapter 4 that we found limited evidence that international monitors' presence, in general, increased perceptions of election credibility.

[27] For a related argument about Lebanon, see Corstange and Marinov (2012, 667).

This analysis is correlational since we cannot rule out the possibility that respondents' beliefs about election credibility influenced what they reported about their perceptions of foreign influence – or that some other factor influenced both their beliefs about election credibility and their perceptions of foreign influence. We therefore control for multiple potential confounders that could influence perceptions of both election credibility *and* foreign influence, including whether the respondent voted (and for whom), age, educational attainment, employment status, political interest, political knowledge, reported knowledge about EOs, and sex. In the United States and Georgia, the controls also included the respondent's race or ethnicity, whereas in Tunisia (a more ethnically homogenous society), they instead included geographic location. In Chapter 7, we more closely examine the role of one very important factor – individual vote choice – that shapes perceptions of negative foreign influence.

Figure 5.3 presents the results of our analysis, which support the conventional wisdom that perceptions of foreign meddling, as measured by perceptions of negative foreign influence, undermine credibility. In every survey, the people who believed foreign actors had a negative influence on the election were less likely – and in most cases, significantly less likely – to believe the election was credible than those who reported that foreign actors had a positive (or both positive and negative) influence. The results also shed light on how beliefs about foreign actors' more positive influences on elections, such as high-quality election monitoring and democracy promotion, can enhance credibility in some cases. Relative to the baseline response of "both positive and negative," respondents who believed foreign actors had a positive influence on the election were more likely – again in most cases, significantly so – to believe the election was credible.[28]

Again, and contrary to assumptions that individuals will respond negatively to any form of foreign influence, different types of foreign influence were associated with different trends in perceptions of election credibility. The effects in opposite directions presented in Figure 5.3 indicate that if we compare respondents who said foreign actors had a positive influence with those who said they

---

[28] The online appendix (www.cambridge.org/bushprather) contains tables that
    show comparisons of the "negative influence" and "positive influence"
    categories to the "both positive and negative" category.

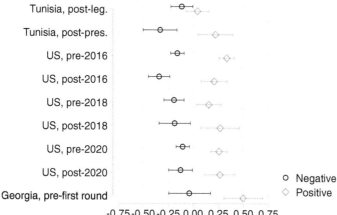

Figure 5.3 The correlation between perceptions of foreign influence and credibility
Note: This figure displays point estimates with 95 percent confidence intervals. All predictions are based on ordinary least squares (OLS) models that contain control variables (see discussion in main text), including for any experiments on election monitoring and meddling that were part of the survey. "Both positive and negative" is the reference category for perceived foreign influence. The outcome variable is perceived credibility and uses the standardized measure, which ranges from 0 to 2. $N = 641$ (Tunisia, post-leg.), 424 (Tunisia, post-pres.), 1,079 (US, pre-2016), 507 (US, post-2016), 834 (US, pre-2018), 390 (US, post-2018), 1,069 (US, pre-2020), and 453 (US, post-2020), 453 (Georgia, pre-first round).

had a negative influence, in nearly every model we find statistically significant differences in perceptions of election credibility. These patterns support the conventional wisdom outlined in Chapter 2: that meddling decreases trust, whereas other interventions like election monitoring increase it. Yet, it remains difficult to determine whether they reflect a true causal relationship or a mere correlation, given that an omitted variable could explain perceptions of foreign influence *and* perceptions of election credibility. Thus, we now investigate the results of our election meddling experiments in the United States and Georgia, which are designed to identify the causal relationship between beliefs about meddling and perceptions of election credibility.

5.2.2 Experimental Tests

It was more straightforward to implement an experimental research design using information on election monitoring, which is public in nature, than it was to conduct an experiment on meddling, which is often more covert, especially in the cases we study. Monitoring's overt nature makes it possible to provide straightforward information to citizens about the presence and reports of various monitoring groups at a given election. By contrast, it is frequently not certain whether election meddling has taken place. Our three cases vary in the extent of known meddling. There was speculation about foreign influence in Tunisia and Georgia, but there was no credible evidence at the time of the elections (or at the time of writing) that foreign actors had tried to directly influence the results in a partisan way.[29] In the United States, significant Russian interference in the 2016 presidential election was widely acknowledged, but the extent of meddling in the 2018 midterm elections and 2020 presidential election was less certain, although intelligence reports suggest that some countries engaged in influence attempts. Even when meddling is known to have occurred, it is difficult to determine whether it altered an election's results.

Given these ambiguities, we used multiple strategies to assess how information about meddling affects election credibility. Our experiments were embedded in our 2018 and 2020 surveys (both pre- and post-election) in the United States and our 2018 surveys in Georgia. They built on our correlational findings and current events in each context. The experiments allowed us to isolate the causal effects of meddling on individual beliefs about election credibility by priming respondents with information about meddling (or its absence). Unless otherwise noted, in both countries, the meddling experiments were administered at the beginning of the surveys to ensure that other experimental treatments did not contaminate our results. Our standard questions about election credibility (noted earlier) were always asked directly after the experiment. In some cases, we randomly divided

---

[29] This is not to say that foreign countries do not take sides in Tunisian and Georgian politics. In Tunisia, for example, Saudi Arabia and the United Arab Emirates have offered targeted economic support to the secularist party Nidaa Tounes, whereas Qatar is believed to do the same for Islamist party Ennahda. The distinction is that this general support has been ongoing since the Tunisian revolution in 2011 and is not a targeted partisan electoral intervention. See Cherif (2014, 2017); Bush and Prather (2020).

the respondents from the same survey between two experiments – a monitoring experiment (as described in Chapter 4) and a meddling experiment – in order to study each topic separately. We briefly describe the experimental designs here; Chapter 3 discusses more general issues related to the survey samples, modes, randomization methods, and ethics. Our general approach to the analysis involves OLS regressions of perceived credibility on the respondent's experimental group. Control variables are not needed in these models since the experimental groups were randomly assigned.[30]

As with our experiments on election monitoring, we only supplied truthful information about meddling to avoid changing people's opinions about the credibility of their country's elections based on false information or otherwise contributing to general distrust. Therefore, before evaluating the results of the experiments, we discuss what was known at the time of the surveys about meddling in the United States in 2018 and 2020 and in Georgia in 2018.

Background: United States

In the United States, prior to both the 2018 and 2020 elections, media and government agencies had uncovered credible information that other countries were attempting to influence the electoral playing field. For example, US national security agencies issued a joint statement in October 2018 warning:

We are concerned about ongoing campaigns by Russia, China and other foreign actors, including Iran, to undermine confidence in democratic institutions and influence public sentiment and government policies. These activities also may seek to influence voter perceptions and decision making in the 2018 and 2020 US elections.[31]

Similar warnings were issued before the 2020 election. An August 7, 2020, press release from the Office of the Director of National Intelligence stated:

Ahead of the 2020 US elections, foreign states will continue to use covert and overt influence measures in their attempts to sway US voters' preferences

---

[30] Our results are robust to including such controls. The online appendix (www
.cambridge.org/bushprather) reports the results of balance tests and regression
models that include control variables.
[31] Director of National Intelligence (2018).

and perspectives, shift US policies, increase discord in the United States, and undermine the American people's confidence in our democratic process. They may also seek to compromise our election infrastructure for a range of possible purposes, such as interfering with the voting process, stealing sensitive data, or calling into question the validity of the election results. However, it would be difficult for our adversaries to interfere with or manipulate voting results at scale. Many foreign actors have a preference for who wins the election, which they express through a range of overt and private statements; covert influence efforts are rarer. We are primarily concerned about the ongoing and potential activity by China, Russia, and Iran.[32]

Similar to our monitoring experiments described in Chapter 4, our US experiments included the information contained in these press releases and news reports about meddling; the control group did not hear information about meddling.

Background: Georgia

As we described in Chapter 3, Georgia has experienced substantial foreign interventions in its elections since the Rose Revolution in 2003 – including from Western actors attempting to promote democracy as well as (perceptions of) pervasive Russian influence in Georgian politics. The backdrop for those perceptions is the 2008 Russo–Georgian War, in which Russia supported the separatist regions of South Ossetia and Abkhazia and bombed and occupied parts of undisputed Georgia; it was also part of the Soviet empire. While not an example of meddling *per se*, both of Georgia's main presidential candidates, Salome Zourabichvili and Grigol Vashadze, accused the other of being in Russian President Putin's pocket during the 2018 elections we study. We commonly saw posters linking candidates with Russia in Tbilisi during our field research around the election (see Figure 5.4 for one example) – a common tactic to undermine candidates, given Georgians' generally negative attitudes toward Russia.

Although the National Democratic Institute (NDI) expressed concerns about the possibility of Russian influence in its preliminary election report in 2018,[33] to the best of our knowledge, there is no credible evidence of outright partisan interventions during Georgia's 2018 election. In the months before and after the presidential election,

---

[32] Evanina (2020).
[33] National Democratic Institute (2018b, 3).

Figure 5.4 Posters featuring presidential candidate Grigol Vashadze
Note: The poster of Russian President Vladimir Putin holding a child with Vashadze's head reads "Our candidate!" in Russian. Authors' photo taken in Tbilisi, October 2018.

we systematically reviewed Georgian media reports and spoke with Georgian experts about rumors of election meddling and found no concrete reports of meddling. Across three news sources and over a period of 51 days, only eleven articles mentioned accusations of meddling, always by Russia but levied against both candidates; no specific details about the nature of such meddling were provided.[34] For example, a member of parliament from the Georgian Dream (GD) party said of competing UNM candidate Grigol Vashadze: "We will not allow a Russian *matryoshka* to become president."[35] One explanation for the apparent absence of Russian meddling at this election, or more concerns thereof, is that Russia's preferred candidate, the de facto GD

---

[34] With help from a Georgian research assistant, we monitored the media between October 16 and December 15, 2018. The first-round election was held on October 28 and the runoff was held on November 28, so our analysis covered both election periods. We searched for election-related articles from the following sources: the website of InterPressNews, a leading daily news source; the website of Rustavi2, a Georgian television station that is perceived to support the United National Movement (UNM); and hard copies of *Kviris Palitra*, one of the most-circulated weekly newspapers in Georgia.

[35] InterPressNews (2018b).

nominee, Salome Zourabichvili, was already expected to win.[36] In other words, meddling may not have been necessary. Given the lack of credible evidence of foreign meddling, we pursued a different approach in our experiments in Georgia than those we carried out in the United States.

We used two types of experiments in Georgia in our two surveys. The first was a *question-order* experiment. Prior studies have established that the order in which questions are asked in a survey can influence individuals' responses.[37] Questions that immediately precede the question of interest can raise the salience of an issue such that it influences how individuals respond to subsequent questions. For example, if a researcher asks Americans about their views on immigration immediately before a question about whether they approve of Donald Trump's presidency, this should increase the salience of the immigration issue and cause respondents to consider the question about Trump through the immigration lens more than they would have done otherwise. We leveraged this phenomenon to study the relationship between meddling and perceptions of election credibility in Georgia by randomly selecting some respondents to be asked about their perceptions of election meddling before our measures of election credibility.

The second type of experiment was a *hypothetical vignette*: We asked a randomly selected subset of respondents to consider a hypothetical scenario about a future election. Drawing on a pioneering design introduced by Tomz and Weeks in the US context,[38] we randomized details about the existence and nature of election meddling and then asked people how they would judge the credibility of that election. A common concern about hypothetical experiments is that respondents' answers will not translate well to a real-world setting. For example, the election environment, with the emotional highs and lows associated with winning and losing, is difficult to approximate in a hypothetical experiment. Yet, we maintain that Georgia's context – particularly its lack of concrete meddling in 2018 but extensive experience with meddling in the past – made it a good fit for a

---

[36] Another explanation is that the election was initially viewed as low stakes since the Georgian president's role became ceremonial after a constitutional shift in 2017. Nevertheless, the election subsequently came to be "seen as a crucial test for Georgian Dream." See Associated Press (2018).
[37] See, for example, Zaller and Feldman (1992).
[38] Tomz and Weeks (2020).

hypothetical vignette experiment given the challenge of implementing alternative designs. The treatments in this experiment were considerably less subtle than those in the question-order experiment, making them an appropriate complement.

5.3 The Effects of Meddling in the United States

Our experiments on election meddling in the United States took place in 2018 and 2020, two and four years, respectively, after Russia's campaign to influence the 2016 election in favor of then-presidential candidate Donald Trump. The 2016 partisan electoral intervention represented a very large real-world "treatment," as Americans learned more and more about the extent of Russian influence in the months after the election, culminating in the release of the Report on the Investigation Into Russian Interference in the 2016 President Election, known as the Mueller Report, in April 2019.[39]

As would be expected in this context, Americans' trust in their elections declined from 2016 to 2020. When asked to reflect on the credibility of the 2016 election immediately afterwards, the mean response for Americans was 1.5 on our 0–2 scale, indicating a high level of perceived credibility. When asked to anticipate the credibility of the 2018 and 2020 elections immediately beforehand, the mean responses were 1.3 and 1.34, respectively – equivalent to around a 10 percent decrease in perceptions of electoral credibility.[40] Although we cannot attribute this downward trend exclusively to Russian meddling since other forces could have also played a role, the significant decline in Americans' confidence in their elections illustrates that concerns about foreign meddling may negatively and significantly impact citizens' perceptions of election credibility.

In this section, we examine the results of two US experiments – one pre-election and one post-election – designed to identify the effect of additional new information about election meddling in 2018 and 2020. The same two experiments were fielded in 2018 and then replicated in 2020. These experiments were somewhat challenging

---

[39] Mueller (2018).
[40] In Chapter 7, we show that this diminished trust does not affect all Americans equally but is instead correlated with partisanship.

to implement given that Americans had already heard so much about election meddling in the preceding years. In fact, we find that information about the *absence* of meddling had the clearest effect, which *improved* perceptions of election credibility.

5.3.1 Experimental Design

In the pre-election US experiment, we investigated how information about election meddling affected Americans' perceptions of election credibility in the week before the 2018 Congressional election and the 2020 presidential election. Because no concrete proof had emerged before our experiments that actual meddling had occurred during the pre-election periods, we drew on news reports about US intelligence agencies' warnings that foreign actors *could* attempt to influence both elections to create our experimental treatment.[41]

Respondents could have interpreted this information as either bad news or good news about election credibility. On the one hand, news that foreign countries were attempting to influence the elections suggested that the electoral playing field may not have been fair. On the other hand, the fact that the government was gathering information about the potential for meddling before the elections implied that it was attempting to combat foreign interventions and maintain a fair electoral playing field. We call this experimental treatment "no meddling" given the direction of the effect,[42] although respondents could have interpreted it as an indication that there *would be* meddling.

Given the content of the officials' warnings, we truthfully and randomly varied three factors we thought were likely to shape individuals' responses to meddling in our treatment in 2018: the meddler's identity, the meddling tactic,[43] and the source of information about meddling. In 2020, we only varied the meddler's identity because the 2018

---

[41] Fabian (2018); Seldin (2018); Ward (2018).

[42] This label reflects our "ex post" interpretation of the results rather than a strong "ex ante" prediction. It is consistent with the effects of an explicitly and more exclusively "no meddling" treatment in a subsequent US survey that we describe later.

[43] See Tomz and Weeks (2020) on the importance of meddling tactics for citizen responses.

experiment revealed that the tactic and source had little effect on election credibility. Reports about the possible threats to election security in 2018 and 2020 both referenced Russia, China, and Iran.[44] We discuss and analyze the effects of meddler identity in Chapter 6. As noted previously, in 2018, we also varied the meddling tactic. Some tactics, if successful, affect election results more directly than others. We chose one tactic that had less direct effects on election results (spreading misinformation) and one that had more direct effects (hacking voting machines). The meddlers referenced in our vignette have used both tactics.[45] In 2018, we also varied the source of the information about meddling to be either partisan (Republicans) or more neutral (US national security agencies), since both Republicans and national security agencies issued reports about the possibility that these three actors might interfere in the 2018 midterms.[46]

The vignette from the 2018 experiment took the following form. We told respondents that we wanted to give them some information about the midterm elections and to ask them what they thought the electoral process would be like on November 6. The text read:

As you know, voters will take to the polls on November 6 to cast their vote for Congress and other offices. Recently, [Republicans, US national security agencies] said that [Russia, China, Iran] is seeking to influence the results of the November 6 midterm elections. These ongoing foreign campaigns involve a variety of strategies designed to affect the election. In particular,

---

[44] In early 2021, the US intelligence community acknowledged that its pre-election accusations about Chinese meddling were incorrect (National Intelligence Council 2021).

[45] The joint statement by US national security agencies cited earlier specifically referenced the possibility that Russia, China, and Iran would use misinformation, stating, "Elements of these campaigns can take many forms, including... seeding disinformation through sympathetic spokespersons regarding political candidates and disseminating foreign propaganda." See Director of National Intelligence (2018). Though unsuccessful at changing the election results, state-linked Chinese hackers attacked Cambodia's election commission prior to the 2018 general election, and state-linked Russian hackers targeted Ukraine's election commission in 2014, as well as US states in 2016. See Clayton (2014), Associated Press (2017), and Groll (2018). Iran has also been active in launching cyberattacks against American targets. See Volz and Finkle (2016).

[46] Fabian (2018).

[Russia, China, Iran] is said to have the ability to [spread misinformation about the election and candidates, hack voting machines to change the results of the election].

In 2018, all text in brackets was randomly assigned. The 2018 experiment produced a $2 \times 2 \times 3$ experimental design, while the 2020 study simply contained the foreign meddler treatment.[47] The surveys in both years included a control group that received no information about election meddling prior to the questions concerning election credibility. Given our interest in this chapter in the overall effect of meddling, we pool across the different treatments to understand the effects of providing respondents *any* information about meddling. Using difference-in-means tests, we found no significant differences across the various meddling treatment groups in their effects on perceived credibility on average.

After the 2018 and 2020 pre-election surveys, we invited the same respondents to take a post-election survey, which included a new experiment about election meddling that drew on the best information publicly available at the time about the extent of meddling in each election. Because the conclusions about Russia's interference in both elections were very similar, we were able to replicate the 2018 experiment in 2020. Thus, we only reproduce the exact text from the 2018 experiment here.

After the 2018 and 2020 elections, there was evidence that Russia had created fake accounts on several social media websites with the goal of influencing the election.[48] US officials did not, however, believe Russia's efforts were "widespread" or that they had successfully compromised voting systems or other infrastructure.[49] The nature of the intelligence reports allowed us to give some respondents truthful information about Russia's attempts to influence the election and to provide other respondents with truthful information that Russia's influence was not widespread. The conventional wisdom outlined in Chapter 2 suggests that information about Russia's use of the Internet to spread misinformation would reduce the election's

---

[47] In 2020, the source was fixed as "US national security agencies" and respondents simply read that the foreign actor's efforts involved "a variety of strategies designed to affect the outcome of the election."

[48] O'Sullivan (2018).

[49] Volz (2018).

credibility, whereas news that Russia's efforts were not widespread would constitute a "negative" treatment and increase perceptions of election credibility.

Similar to the pre-election survey, these treatments were embedded in vignettes that were randomly assigned to respondents. The control group did not receive a vignette. The exact text that was provided to respondents in 2018 was:

Meddling treatment: Just before the election, US Government Security Officials and several tech companies said that Russia attempted to influence the results of the November 6 midterm elections. In particular, Russia created fake accounts on a number of internet websites. The purpose of these accounts may have been to spread lies about the election and certain candidates. US Security Officials continue to investigate what effect Russia's interference had on the results.

No meddling treatment: Just before the election, US Government Security Officials said that there was no indication of a widespread Russian attempt to influence the results of the November 6 midterm elections. In particular, federal agencies say they have not seen intrusions into voting systems or related election equipment. Additionally, there is no indication of compromise to the nation's election infrastructure that would prevent voting, change vote counts or affect the ability to tally votes. US Security Officials continue to investigate the midterm elections for signs of Russian interference.

In 2020, we continued to provide information about factors such as the meddler's identity, meddling tactics, and source of information about meddling in the vignettes to continue to fix ideas about the scenario in the respondents' minds. However, we did not vary those characteristics in the post-election surveys in part because we did not find significant differences across the traits in the pre-election experiment in 2018.

As we noted in Chapter 4, at the end of the 2018 and 2020 post-election surveys in the United States, we debriefed all respondents, including those who participated in the separate election monitoring experiment and those in the control group. To ensure that study participants were not given an overly positive or overly negative impression of the election, we shared a copy of the interim Organization for Security and Co-operation in Europe report on each election; these reports documented some instances of meddling by foreign sources as well as other irregularities but were generally positive about the integrity of both elections.[50]

5.3.2 The Effects of Meddling's Absence

To analyze how meddling influences individual attitudes, we regress perceived credibility on variables indicating the individual's experimental group. As in our US analysis in Chapter 4, we eliminated respondents who proceeded through the survey too quickly to have read the experimental treatments properly.[51] Each survey also included a question, asked after the questions about perceived credibility, directly related to the meddling treatment that was designed to identify inattentive respondents.[52] We consider respondents who could not accurately remember the country in the vignette to be inattentive. Including inattentive respondents in experimental analysis can lead researchers to underestimate treatment effects and reach other incorrect conclusions, but excluding them is also potentially problematic since attention in surveys is correlated with other relevant traits such as education.[53] In this chapter, we therefore present the treatment effects for *both* the full sample and for the respondents who passed the attention check.

Our experiments significantly affected perceptions of election credibility in 2018, but not 2020 (Figures 5.5 and 5.6). In the 2018 study, when we compare respondents who heard about the absence of foreign meddling – either in the somewhat ambiguous pre-election experimental treatment or in the more explicit post-election experiment's "no meddling" treatment – to those in the control group, we

---

[50] Office for Democratic Institutions and Human Rights (2018, 2–3) and OSCE Parliamentary Assembly (2020, 1).

[51] The vignettes were 69–75 words. Based on average reading times of Internet surveys, respondents should have spent 20.7–22.5 seconds reading them. See Zhang and Conrad (2014). We exclude the 25 percent of respondents who spent less than 3.185 seconds reading the page with the vignettes.

[52] In the pre-election survey, we asked respondents to recall the country mentioned in the vignette. In the post-election survey, we asked respondents to recall whether they were told that US officials said there was no indication of widespread Russian interference in the election or that US officials said that Russia had attempted to interfere.

[53] Berinsky, Margolis, and Sances (2014); Alvarez et al. (2019). The online appendix (www.cambridge.org/bushprather) includes an analysis of the individual determinants of passing the attention check.

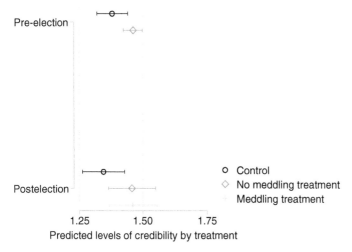

(a) Full sample

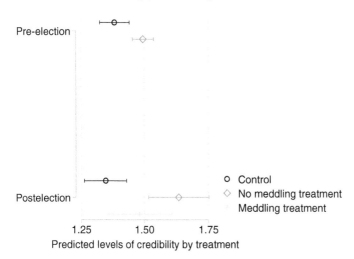

(b) Attentive sample

Figure 5.5 The effect of meddling on perceived credibility in the United States, pre- and post-election, 2018

Note: This figure shows point estimates with 95 percent confidence intervals. All predictions are based on OLS models without control variables. The outcome variable is perceived credibility and uses the standardized measure, which ranges from 0 to 2. $N = 1{,}705$ (pre-election, full sample), 1,411 (pre-election, attentive sample), 629 (post-election, full sample), and 472 (post-election, attentive sample).

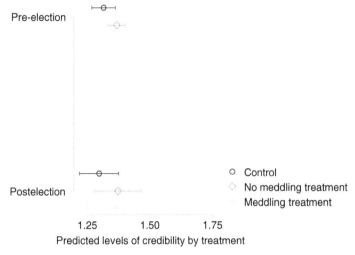

(a) Full sample

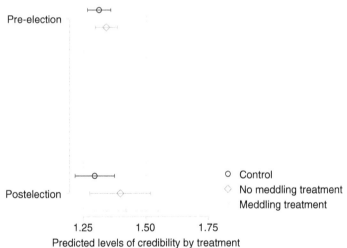

(b) Attentive sample

Figure 5.6 The effect of meddling on perceived credibility in the United States, pre- and post-election, 2020

Note: This figure shows point estimates with 95 percent confidence intervals. All predictions are based on OLS models without control variables. The outcome variable is perceived credibility and uses the standardized measure, which ranges from 0 to 2. $N = 1{,}247$ (pre-election, full sample), 867 (pre-election, attentive sample), 639 (post-election, full sample), and 479 (post-election, attentive sample).

find a significant difference in perceived credibility.[54] In both cases, the treatment caused respondents to perceive the upcoming election as *more* credible. This relationship is especially clear among the attentive respondents in Figure 5.5, who exhibit a 9 percent increase in perceived credibility before and a 21 percent rise after the election.[55] Our finding that providing respondents with information about the absence of foreign meddling reassured them about election credibility is consistent with the conventional wisdom that meddling can diminish credibility. In both 2018 experiments, the "no meddling" treatments enhanced respondents' trust in the election results as well as their belief that the election reflected the will of the people, although the treatment effects were generally larger for individuals' beliefs about the will of the people.[56]

Yet, the same experiments fielded in 2020 had a more limited effect on perceptions of election credibility (Figure 5.6). Although the effects are similar in direction to those uncovered in 2018, none of the treatments produced effects on election credibility that were significantly different from those in the control group. However, we found a small, positive increase in election credibility for respondents who received the meddling warning and no meddling treatments in the pre- and post-election surveys, respectively. It is also clear that the meddling treatment in the post-election survey did not decrease election credibility relative to the control.

We briefly discuss the 2020 results here and then analyze the 2018 results in more detail in the next section. We attribute our finding of more limited effects in 2020 to two reasons. The first is the source of potential meddling in the election. As we discuss in Chapter 3, the primary concerns expressed by US political elites during the 2020 election cycle related to *domestic* threats to election integrity. For example, President Trump and his campaign promoted

---

[54] The online appendix (www.cambridge.org/bushprather) contains a table with these results.

[55] The *p*-values are 0.002 and 0.001 (0.002), respectively; Benjamini–Hochberg corrected *p*-values are in parentheses for the second experiment, which contained two treatments. We use the Benjamini–Hochberg procedure to ensure that the findings that appear statistically significant are robust even though our experiments had multiple treatments, which increases the probability of incorrectly concluding that an observed treatment effect is meaningful.

[56] The online appendix (www.cambridge.org/bushprather) reports these results.

the false narrative that voting by mail would lead to election fraud by the Democratic Party,[57] and then-candidate Joe Biden publicly warned that President Trump would try to steal the election.[58] Thus, Americans in 2020 already had strong signals from political actors about candidates' types (true or pseudo-democrat) and the electoral playing field. Consequently, our experiment's signal that information about foreign meddling sends about candidates' types and the fairness of the electoral playing field may have been less impactful. Second, and relatedly, although officials did warn about potential interference in US elections from abroad, these threats were likely not as salient to Americans or as consequential to their perceptions of election credibility as domestic factors. By contrast, Russian interference in the 2016 presidential election was still quite salient in 2018, partly because the Mueller investigation was ongoing at the time.

In the 2020 post-election survey, the meddling and no meddling treatments also likely interacted with the election results in a different way than in 2018. Specifically, the treatments referenced Russian meddling, which Americans associate with support for the Republican Party and Donald Trump. However, because Joe Biden, the Democratic candidate, won the 2020 election, respondents would be less likely to believe that meddling affected the outcome. As we detail in Chapter 2, meddling is only likely to affect perceptions of election credibility if the meddler is perceived to be capable of changing the results.

Deepening the Analysis: The 2018 US Experiment

We offer two explanations for why respondents seem to have interpreted the pre-election treatments about meddling as "no meddling" rather than "meddling" treatments. First, the survey was fielded after the entire country (including our sample) was "treated" with a considerable amount of information about Russia's electoral intervention in support of Trump. In the two years after the 2016 election, the US government did relatively little to increase election security.[59] In this context, we suspect our vignette reassured respondents that political leaders and institutions were gathering information about (and attempting to prevent) foreign interference in the upcoming election.

---

[57] Saul and Epstein (2020).
[58] Viser (2020).
[59] Milligan (2019).

Our finding that respondents interpreted this information as evidence that the government was attempting to *prevent* meddling makes sense, given that the 2016 Russian intervention was intended to be covert but was detected and revealed by the US government.

The second, related, explanation is that knowing the result of an election can help citizens assess whether meddling occurred and was successful. Yet since the survey was administered *before* the 2018 election, respondents may have been uncertain about whether the meddling the vignette warned about was likely to take place and affect the election outcome.

To support this interpretation, we consider the relationship between perceived foreign influence (i.e., the same question analyzed in Table 5.1) and the treatment in our 2018 pre-election survey in the United States. We can conduct this analysis since the perceived foreign influence question was asked after the experiment, though not immediately. Respondents who were exposed to the warning about meddling treatment were significantly less likely to think other countries would influence the results of the midterm elections in both the full sample (difference = 0.15 on a 4-point scale; $p = 0.003$) and the attentive subsample (difference = 0.20; $p < 0.001$).[60] These patterns seem to confirm that the treatment affected respondents' perceptions of election security: Those who received the treatment warning about election meddling believed foreign influence was less likely.

Figure 5.5 illustrates that the "no meddling" treatment increased trust in the 2018 election compared to the control group. The difference is marginally statistically significant when we examine the full sample and clearly significant in the attentive subsample.[61] This finding is consistent with that of the pre-election experiment, which established that Americans' assessments of election credibility take into account information regarding the potential absence of meddling.

The "meddling" treatment also increased trust compared to the control, although this difference is only marginally statistically significant in both samples and has a smaller substantive effect in the attentive

---

[60] See the online appendix (www.cambridge.org/bushprather). These treatment effects are based on OLS regression analyses that include the controls from the analysis that produced Figure 5.3.

[61] p-values with Benjamini–Hochberg corrected p-values in parentheses are 0.071 (0.071) and 0.001 (0.002), respectively.

subsample.[62] This pattern was unexpected, but the meddling treatment may have had a marginally positive effect in this experiment for some of the same reasons why the ambiguous pre-election experimental treatment increased perceptions of election credibility. Put differently, heightening respondents' knowledge of government efforts to detect meddling in the post-election survey was reassuring, though not as reassuring for attentive respondents as informing them that the meddling was unsuccessful.

Further analysis reveals that the post-election treatment effects, especially for the "no meddling" treatment, are driven by respondents who expressed doubts about election credibility in the pre-election survey.[63] Hearing information that possibly contradicted many respondents' prior beliefs about Russia's potential negative influence on the 2018 midterms significantly enhanced their confidence in the election results. This pattern is consistent with the logic that individuals are motivated by accuracy goals when processing new political information, since it implies that the people for whom the treatments represented good news were the ones who were most likely to update their opinions. The significance of this negative treatment about the absence of meddling further establishes how (the lack of) meddling affects perceptions of election credibility.

This deeper analysis of the 2018 results suggests two important conclusions. First, while awareness of negative foreign influence is associated with more negative perceptions of election credibility, it is complicated to experimentally inform respondents about foreign meddling in a credible way. Our treatments clearly did not cause respondents to believe that meddling affected the electoral playing field in this context. Second, and by contrast, the results from our 2018 pre- and post-election surveys imply that when people are given reassuring information about the absence of foreign meddling, they are more likely to trust the election. Although these findings do not entirely support the conventional wisdom – as we are unable to show that meddling decreases perceptions of election credibility on average – they are

---

[62] The *p*-values are as follows, with Benjamini–Hochberg corrected *p*-values in parentheses: 0.079 (0.080) and 0.080 (0.080).
[63] This analysis is reported in the online appendix (www.cambridge.org/ bushprather) and contains the controls from the analysis that produced Figure 5.3.

consistent with its general theoretical logic given the positive effect of information about the absence of meddling.

5.4 The Effects of Meddling in Georgia

Although Georgia has experienced considerable meddling in its recent elections, in the weeks leading up to the two rounds of the 2018 presidential election, there were no credible reports of systematic meddling, as explained earlier. Since we could not provide respondents with truthful information about meddling, we adapted our experimental design to a context in which there were substantial fears about foreign influence using two types of experiments – question-order experiments and a hypothetical vignette. We discuss each separately later. Although we do not find significant meddling effects in the former, we do in the latter.

5.4.1 Question-Order Experiments

We included question-order experiments in both the first wave of our survey, which took place on the eve of the first-round presidential election, and the second wave, which was administered after the second round. This approach allowed us to raise the salience of the possibility of meddling in the minds of randomly selected respondents just before we asked questions about election credibility. Respondents in the pre-election survey were randomly assigned to participate in (1) this experiment about meddling, (2) the experiment about monitoring described in Chapter 4, or (3) a control group that was only asked the questions measuring election credibility.

Experimental Design
In the pre-first-round election survey, respondents in the meddling experiment were asked two questions about election meddling before the election credibility questions. The first question asked if they had heard about foreign meddling attempts and the second asked whether they thought it was likely that meddling was occurring. The first three treatment groups randomized the identity of the potential meddler – the text within the brackets was randomly assigned – but were otherwise identical:

Some people have talked about [Russian, European, American] attempts to change the results of the upcoming presidential election. How much have you heard about [Russian, European, American] attempts to change the results of the upcoming election?

How likely do you think it is that [Russia, European countries, the United States] [is, are] attempting to change the results of the upcoming presidential election?

We focused on Russia, European countries, and the United States as the potential meddlers since they were all rumored to influence Georgian politics but were plausibly perceived as having distinct capabilities and biases, which are relevant dimensions of our theory. Before the runoff election, for example, opposition groups accused GD in general and Zourabichvili in particular as "acting in Russia's interests."[64] We did not detect equivalent accusations of American or European election meddling in the news in 2018, presumably because the prevailing anti-Russia sentiment in Georgia makes accusations of Russian meddling a more attractive strategy for politicians. Yet, Western countries play a substantial role in Georgian politics; it has pursued EU and North Atlantic Treaty Organization membership as long-term goals since independence. Thus, the United States and European countries were also plausible meddlers within that context.

The fourth treatment group answered slightly different questions. Similar to the Russian treatment questions described earlier, respondents in this group were asked whether they had heard about Russian meddling attempts and if they thought it was likely that Russia was attempting to interfere with the election results. This treatment also included a short (truthful) statement with information that NDI, an American NGO that is prominent in Georgia, had warned about possible Russian attempts to undermine the results of the upcoming election.[65] Given that NDI is a somewhat controversial organization in Georgia due to events surrounding the 2012 election as detailed in Chapter 4, we thought including it as the source of information about meddling was particularly interesting. Respondents in this treatment group were asked the following two questions:

The National Democratic Institute (NDI) has warned about Russian attempts to undermine confidence in the results of the upcoming presidential election. How much have you heard about the National Democratic

---

[64] Rustavi2 (2018b).
[65] National Democratic Institute (2018b).

Institute's warnings about Russian attempts to undermine confidence in the results of the upcoming presidential election?

Based on the National Democratic Institute's warning, how likely do you think it is that Russia is attempting to change who will win the upcoming presidential election?

Similar to our analysis of the US meddling experiments, and because we are interested theoretically in the overall effect of meddling in this chapter, we pool across the different meddling treatments in our main analysis discussed later. This approach allows us to focus on the effect of *information about meddling in general* rather than meddler identity or the information source. There were few differences among the treatment effects.

Since no credible reports of meddling emerged after the pre-first-round election survey, to avoid disseminating false information we repeated the question-order experiment in our post-second-round election survey. Because we anticipated having fewer respondents in this second survey due to attrition, we had only two meddling treatment groups; participants in these treatments were asked the following question about either possible Russian or US meddling:

As you may know, some people have talked about attempts by [Russia, the United States] to change the results of the recent presidential election. How likely do you think it is that [Russia, the United States] attempted to change the results of the presidential election?

As with the pre-first-round election experiment, we pool across the meddling country to examine the overall effect of meddling on perceived credibility.

These treatment questions could have affected beliefs about election credibility in two ways by design. First, they could have primed all respondents with the possibility of foreign meddling. If this were the case, we would expect the questions to reduce reported perceptions of election credibility relative to the control group for all treated respondents. Second, the treatment questions could have primed respondents in a more directional manner: Those who believed foreign meddling was likely might have been primed by these questions to think of the presence of meddling at the election, whereas those who thought foreign meddling was unlikely might have been primed to think of the

absence of meddling.[66] If the questions did indeed affect study participants' perceptions of election credibility, we would expect them to
reduce reported perceptions of election credibility for respondents who
thought meddling was likely and, similar to our findings in the United
States, to enhance perceptions of credibility for those who thought
meddling was unlikely. We explore both possibilities in the analysis
discussed later.

The Modest Negative Effects of Meddling

Figure 5.7 displays the results of our analysis of the relationship
between the meddling primes and perceptions of election credibility
in Georgia.[67] All models compare the treatment respondents to those
in the control group, who were not asked about election meddling
before the questions about election credibility. We begin by examining whether first responding to the questions about meddling caused
a notable decrease in confidence in election credibility relative to the
control in the pre-first-round election experiment. It did not; the estimated treatment effect is negative but does not achieve normal levels
of statistical significance.

We next examine responses to the question about how likely the
named country was to meddle in the election. Across the countries, only 46 percent of Georgian respondents thought meddling was
"somewhat" or "very" likely to occur. This pattern could reason-
ably explain why the meddling treatment did not significantly reduce
people's beliefs about election credibility, on average. If respondents
believed foreign actors were unlikely to try to change the results of the
election, then the question-order experiment may have inadvertently
primed them to think about the *absence* of meddling, rather than its
existence.

---

[66] Because respondents' beliefs about whether meddling was likely or unlikely
were not randomly assigned, we include control variables in our analyses
discussed later that are plausibly correlated with both those beliefs *and*
perceptions of election credibility. Although the treatment itself was randomly
assigned, we include the same control variables for all estimates in Figure 5.7
for consistency's sake.

[67] Unlike the US surveys, which were conducted online, this survey was
conducted in person by trained interviewers as discussed in Chapter 3. We
therefore have fewer concerns about respondents' attention and do not drop
any respondents from the analysis.

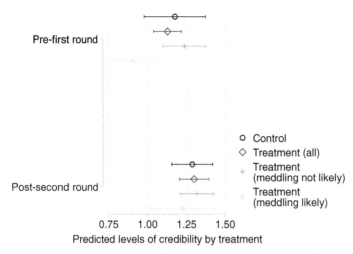

Figure 5.7 The effect of meddling salience on perceived credibility in Georgia
Note: This figure displays point estimates with 95 percent confidence intervals. All predictions are based on OLS models that contain control variables (see discussion in main text). The outcome variable is perceived credibility and uses the standardized measure, which ranges from 0 to 2. $N = 473$ (pre-election) and 532 (post-election).

To explore this possibility, in Figure 5.7, we subset the data based on whether respondents said meddling was unlikely or likely. Because the respondents in the control group were not asked these questions, that group remains the same. Prior to the election, the treatment was associated with weakly positive effects among respondents who thought meddling was *not likely*, and with clearer and marginally statistically significant negative effects among those who thought meddling was *likely*.[68] For those respondents, the meddling treatment was associated with a 21 percent decrease in perceived credibility, on average, compared to the control. This negative effect was slightly clearer for trust in the results of the election than for belief that the election reflected the will of the people. The question about European countries meddling was most clearly associated with a reduction in perceptions of election credibility among respondents who thought meddling was likely, although all the treatment effects tended to be negative.[69]

---

[68] $p = 0.678$ and 0.06, respectively.
[69] The European meddling treatment is associated with a 35 percent decrease in perceived credibility, but its effect is not significantly different from the other meddling treatments.

The post-second-round election experiment examines both the average treatment effect (ATE) and the treatment effect conditional on thinking meddling was likely or unlikely (Figure 5.7). The meddling treatment had weaker effects in this survey than in the pre-election wave, likely because the expected candidate (Salome Zourabichvili) won; thus respondents may have been reassured that foreign interference had not occurred. In the post-election survey, only 21 percent of respondents in the treatment conditions thought meddling was likely.

In no model does answering a question about election meddling cause respondents to significantly change their views about election credibility. This null effect is apparent among the full sample of respondents and in the subsamples of respondents who thought meddling was unlikely vs. likely.

Our theory from Chapter 2 provides a possible explanation why the meddling primes had relatively limited effects on perceptions of election credibility in Georgia: The environment may not have been uncertain enough. We expect people to be more likely to update their beliefs about elections in response to foreign interventions when they are less certain about the election's credibility. In the Georgian runoff election, 75 percent of respondents in the control group had the highest level of certainty in their beliefs about the election (a 4 on a 4-point scale); only 1 percent reported any amount of uncertainty. It is therefore perhaps unsurprising that our meddling primes did not cause individuals to update their views on the election.

5.4.2 Vignette Experiment

Since there were no credible reports of a major foreign campaign to influence the Georgian presidential election, we fielded an additional experiment in our post-second-round survey to examine the effects of meddling on perceptions of election credibility when there is less certainty about the election and more certainty that meddling took place. At the end of the survey, we asked respondents to consider a hypothetical future election with these characteristics.

Our hypothetical vignette was modeled on an experiment conducted by Michael Tomz and Jessica Weeks in the United States.[70] Similar

---

[70] Tomz and Weeks (2020).

to theirs, our experiment concerned a future election in which meddling occurred in the form of a partisan statement, campaign funding, or ballot box stuffing. We pool across these conditions in our main analysis discussed later to estimate the overall effect of meddling on election credibility. Unlike their survey, we manipulated information about the meddler's capacity to influence the election by holding constant the party the foreign actor supported and varying which party won the election.[71] A successful intervention would thus be one in which the party the foreign actor supports wins the election. We analyze this aspect of the experiment in Chapter 6. There was also a control condition that did not mention meddling.

Russia was the meddler in all the meddling tactics mentioned in the experiment, since Russian interference is highly salient in Georgian politics and is thus likely to be relevant in a hypothetical future election. Russian meddling in our vignette always occurred in support of the GD party, the only plausible scenario (even though some GD supporters accuse UNM of being close to Russia, too). For example, the summer 2019 protests that rocked Tbilisi concerned popular perceptions that GD had become too cozy with Russia after a member of the Russian Duma gave a speech and sat in the Georgian parliament.[72] The exact text of the experiment was as follows for the campaign funding condition as an example (randomized text in brackets):[73]

All respondents: Now, imagine that in 2020, there is a hard-fought election for the Georgian parliament.

Control group: In the end, [UNM, GD] wins a majority of the seats in the parliamentary election.

Meddling treatment: In 2020, the government of Russia developed a plan to influence the parliamentary election in Georgia. The plan was designed to help Georgian Dream and hurt UNM. According to the plan, agents from Russia would contribute funding to Georgian Dream candidates' campaigns. Russia carried out its plan to help Georgian Dream and hurt UNM. In the end, [UNM, GD] won a majority of seats in the parliamentary election. Authorities began investigating how Russia's actions might have affected the results of the election.

---

[71] In addition, we did not randomize which side the meddler supports.
[72] Kakachia and Lebanidze (2019).
[73] For the other treatment wordings, see the online appendix (www.cambridge .org/bushprather).

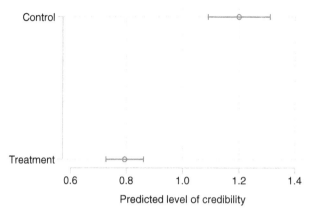

Figure 5.8 The effect of meddling on perceived credibility in Georgia, hypothetical election
Note: This figure shows point estimates with 95 percent confidence intervals. All predictions are based on OLS models without control variables. The outcome variable is perceived credibility and uses the standardized measure, which ranges from 0 to 2. The data come from the post-second-round election survey. $N = 1,024$.

The conventional wisdom predicts that respondents in the meddling treatments would perceive the 2020 elections as less credible than those in the control group because Russian actions could signal that the electoral playing field was unfair.

Given the hypothetical nature of the experiment, we expected respondents to be relatively uncertain about the election's credibility, and that was indeed the case. One way of examining the level of uncertainty is to look at how many respondents said they did not know how credible the election was. In the hypothetical vignette, 21 percent of respondents said they "didn't know" whether they trusted the results of the election or believed that it reflected the will of the people. By contrast, only 3 percent of respondents answered "don't know" to both of those questions about the credibility of the actual 2018 presidential runoff election. According to our theory in Chapter 2, being more uncertain about the election in the hypothetical vignette should make meddling more likely to significantly decrease trust.

Figure 5.8 illustrates that in the hypothetical vignette, respondents were more likely to think the election was credible when they were not given any information about meddling. When we pool across the meddling tactic, the decrease in credibility associated with hearing about foreign meddling is substantial – around 34 percent. The significant ATE is clear for both components of credibility: trust in the election results and belief that the election reflects the will of the people. Consistent with what Tomz and Weeks find, our respondents were more likely to believe an election was credible when they learned that Russia simply made a statement compared to hearing about more aggressive meddling actions such as providing funding to a campaign or stuffing ballot boxes; the latter comparison reaches statistical significance at conventional levels.[74]

5.5 Conclusion

In this chapter, we tested a common belief about election meddling that is thought to motivate recent examples of partisan electoral interventions – that it decreases citizens' trust in elections – and find only modest support.

First, we showed that outside interference is salient to publics around the world, and that in Tunisia, the United States, and Georgia, people perceived a considerable amount of foreign influence on elections. Contrary to assumptions that all foreign interventions will be perceived as an unwelcome form of outside interference, however, citizens in these countries sometimes perceived foreign influences positively or as a mix of positive and negative. In line with the conventional wisdom, when people perceive foreign influence negatively, as tends to be the case with election meddling, they also had considerably less trust in elections than they do when they perceive foreign influence more positively.

Second, we drew on experimental evidence from the United States in 2018 and 2020 and Georgia in 2018 to more precisely estimate *how* meddling affects trust in elections. The picture here was also mixed. In the United States, when respondents were given information both before and after the 2018 election that meddling was *not* occurring, they were more likely to perceive the election as credible. We were unable to identify significant negative effects of informational treatments about meddling in the United States in 2018. It is possible that this is because meddling does not have the effects hypothesized

---

[74] The *p*-value for the ballot vs. statement comparison is 0.001, or 0.002 with the Benjamini–Hochberg correction to reflect the three treatments.

by many, although it could also be because Americans had already been exposed to so much information about meddling in the preceding years. We also found little evidence that meddling affected perceptions of election credibility in 2020.

In Georgia, it was also fairly difficult to change respondents' views about real-world election credibility through our design of making meddling more salient. Nevertheless, when asked to consider a hypothetical future election in 2018, respondents' perceptions changed markedly when they believed that meddling occurred and was successful. The difference seems to be that Georgian respondents were much less certain about the credibility of the hypothetical election than they were about past elections. This insight about uncertainty surrounding hypothetical elections is important to keep in mind since much of our previous knowledge about how meddling affects citizens' attitudes has been generated through studies of such elections.[75]

When combined with our findings about monitors' effects in Chapter 4, these results suggest that caution is required when assuming that various types of foreign interventions will affect individuals' perceptions of election credibility. In the next two chapters, we argue that the reason why monitors and meddlers do not necessarily have the anticipated overall effects is that they only provide valuable information about candidates' types and the electoral playing field when two conditions are met: (1) the foreign actors are perceived as able and willing to affect the electoral playing field and (2) individuals are receptive to new information. Chapter 6 considers the first dynamic, while Chapter 7 considers the second.

---

[75] Tomz and Weeks (2020).

6 | *Intervener Identity*

Chapters 4 and 5 considered whether monitors and meddlers affect citizens' perceptions of election credibility on average, and found fairly limited effects. Yet, foreign actors are not all the same. For example, the Latin American Council of Electoral Experts (CEELA) – a monitoring institution that "lacks an official website and an organizational charter" – is quite different from the European Union (EU) and the Organization of American States, which are highly professional and capable monitors.[1] And whereas CEELA has repeatedly issued positive reports about flawed elections in Venezuela, these other more credible international observer groups have declined to monitor Venezuelan elections due to concerns about electoral integrity.[2] It is therefore plausible that these different monitors would affect the electoral playing field, and citizens' perceptions thereof, differently.

Intervening countries also vary considerably in their ability to meddle in a foreign election. Russia is well known for using sophisticated disinformation campaigns, such as the messages it sent prior to the 2016 US presidential election targeting specific politically salient groups, including immigration hawks, African Americans, and veterans. By contrast, Iranian disinformation campaigns in the United States and elsewhere have historically been less complex, "with messaging typically on a single side of an issue in line with government policy goals" such as "countering Israel." Yet, Iran's meddling capabilities have improved since 2016, which suggests that the gap with Russia may be closing.[3]

Given these differences in foreign actors' intentions and capabilities, in this chapter, we explore how the identity of the intervener shapes the effects that foreign actors have on local trust in elections. For each

[1] Global Americans (2018).
[2] Sabatini (2018).
[3] Timberg and Romm (2019).

type of foreign intervention – monitoring and meddling – we examine the significance of intervener identity in two ways.

First, we show how citizens' perceptions of foreign actors vary. Given our theoretical emphasis on how foreign actors shape the electoral playing field, we focus on citizens' perceptions of whether foreign actors are willing and able to influence how fair that playing field is. In both case studies in which we asked respondents specific questions about monitors and meddlers (Tunisia and the United States), citizens perceived foreign actors in notably distinct ways. The foreign actors that Tunisian respondents perceived as most capable were unexpected, which illustrates the subjective elements of evaluating foreign actors. We compare perceptions of domestic and international election monitors and find that it is not *foreignness* that causes observation groups to be perceived as either trustworthy or (as the nationalism counter-argument might have it) lacking in trust.

Second, we demonstrate that foreign actors' effects on perceptions of election credibility depend on their characteristics. When people perceive monitors as being capable and unbiased, their presence is more likely to increase election credibility. Conversely, when people perceive meddlers as capable, their activities are more likely to diminish trust. These findings offer important nuance to the findings presented in Chapters 4 and 5. Although monitors' and meddlers' overall effects on perceptions of election credibility may be limited in important ways, *some* foreign actors do significantly affect those perceptions.

Finally, we conclude the chapter by considering the sources of individuals' beliefs about foreign actors. Given their limited information about many monitors and meddlers, ordinary citizens use foreign actors' nationality as a heuristic to indicate their likely capabilities and biases. Individual characteristics such as vote choice also shape the likelihood that people will believe foreign actors are affecting the electoral playing field – an issue we explore in Chapter 7.

6.1 Intervener Identity and Election Monitoring

As documented in Chapter 4, many different intergovernmental organizations (IGOs), nongovernmental organizations (NGOs), and other actors are active in international election monitoring, making it what some scholars have described as a "complex regime."[4] Moreover, the number and type of monitors that observe elections have grown in recent years. We know from previous research that these monitors differ in their real-world effects on the electoral playing field.[5] Do they also differ in their effects on citizens' *perceptions* of the electoral playing field?

6.1.1 How Perceptions of Election Monitors Vary

Our theory, described in Chapter 2, posits that observers' perceived capabilities and biases are key factors that shape whether they will affect perceptions of election credibility. We begin by exploring how individuals' perceptions of monitors along these dimensions vary depending on the monitor's nationality. One of our main interests is how citizen and elite perceptions of foreign monitors may diverge.

The existence of zombie observers (international monitors from undemocratic countries and international organizations) hints at the possibility of such a divergence. In addition to well-known zombie groups such as from the Commonwealth of Independent States (CIS) or the Shanghai Cooperation Organization, zombie monitors also include groups such as the "obscure, Oklahoma-based Independent American Center of Political Monitoring" that featured heavily on state media after the fraudulent 2013 presidential election in Azerbaijan.[6] These monitors lack "an audience back in the West" and suggest to many international audiences that a country's leaders are pseudo-democrats faking a commitment to democracy.[7] Inviting zombie monitors is thought to be a policy "largely meant for domestic consumption" because domestic audiences are more likely than international audiences to view such monitors favorably.[8]

To understand citizens' perceptions of election monitors, we draw on data from a survey we conducted after Tunisia's second-round presidential election in December 2014. Our monitoring experiment (described in detail in Chapter 4) provided information to respondents about the presence of election observers (EOs); the nationality of the

---

[4] Kelley (2009b); Pratt (2018).
[5] Kelley (2012b); Pratt (2020).
[6] Walker and Cooley (2013).
[7] Michel (2015).
[8] Ibid.

monitors was randomized.[9] We then asked questions designed to measure how individuals' perceptions of EOs' characteristics varied across the different EO groups.

Since many EO groups were present at the Tunisian election, we were able to highlight five types of observers. Our experiment included monitoring groups from four different nationalities or regions: monitors from American organizations,[10] the African Union (AU), Arab League, EU, and Tunisian NGOs. As described in Chapter 4, all four types of international EOs were present at the election. Since their true capabilities and biases varied, we anticipated that the public was likely to perceive them in different ways as well, which enables us to examine the importance of observer identity in this setting.

As is typical, there were many more domestic than international monitors. The most prominent groups were Tunisian NGOs, including Mourakiboun (5,898 observers), Civil Pole for Development and Human Rights (5,174 observers), and ATIDE, the Tunisian Association for Electoral Integrity and Democracy (4,555 observers).[11]

All the monitoring groups in our experiment praised the election overall, even as they cited various areas for improvement. For example, an IRI report commended Tunisia for having "met international standards for freedom, credibility, and transparency."[12] Given the common evaluations across the diverse monitoring groups, as well as the fact that our experiment provided the same information to respondents

---

[9] The experiments conducted in the United States and Georgia randomized information about international monitors' capabilities and biases instead of observing real-world variation in those traits. We analyze these experiments later in the chapter.

[10] We did not provide the names of specific American or Tunisian groups because we believed Tunisians did not know enough about EOs to distinguish, for example, between different American NGOs such as the Carter Center, International Republican Institute (IRI), and National Democratic Institute (NDI). As shown in the online appendix (www.cambridge.org/bushprather), when EOs are discussed in the media, their nationalities are often referenced. Our treatments thus matched common usage in Tunisia. That said, some caution is needed when comparing the effects associated with the named vs. unnamed EOs. It is possible that specific American or Tunisian EOs would have been perceived as more capable, less biased, or both.

[11] Instance Supérieure Indépendante pour les Élections (Tunisia) (2014b).

[12] International Republican Institute (2015, 2). For a full summary of the international EOs present at the elections and their conclusions, please see the online appendix (www.cambridge.org/bushprather).

about the functions of monitors, any differences in perceptions of those groups should reflect differences in beliefs about the monitors themselves.

After asking respondents in the treatment groups (who had heard information about EOs' presence) about their perceptions of election credibility, we asked them a standard pair of questions about their perceptions of the monitors' capabilities and biases. Specifically, we asked how capable respondents thought observers were of detecting fraud during the election. We group responses of "very capable" and "somewhat capable" into a "capable" category, and consider "not too capable" and "not capable at all" to be assessments of "not capable."[13] To measure perceptions of monitors' biases, we asked whether the respondent thought the observers preferred one political party over another or supported the democratic process, whatever the outcome of the election.[14] If the respondent thought the observers would support the democratic process regardless of the election outcome, we consider the monitors to be perceived as unbiased, whereas if the respondent thought they supported a particular party, we consider the monitors to be perceived as biased.

Using responses to those questions, we created a measure of Tunisians' overall perceptions of election monitors. This measure is coded 2 if respondents viewed the observers as both capable and unbiased and 1 if they perceived the observers as *either* capable or unbiased; 0 indicates respondents believed observers were *neither* capable nor unbiased.

Tunisians generally had a positive view of monitors: The majority of respondents in our survey reported that the monitors we asked them about were capable and unbiased. More than three-quarters (79 percent) of respondents judged observers overall as "somewhat capable" or "very capable." Similarly, 78 percent of respondents thought that the observers would support the democratic process regardless of the election's outcome. Together, 66 percent of participants assessed monitors as both capable and unbiased. Yet, these

---

[13] We transformed the responses into a dichotomous variable in our main analysis to make it comparable to our dichotomous measure of perceived bias. However, our results are robust to using the original 4-point coding. See the online appendix (www.cambridge.org/bushprather).

[14] This question was based on research on electoral interventions by Daniel Corstange and Nikolay Marinov. See Corstange and Marinov (2012).

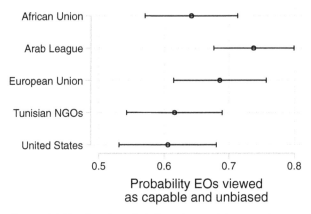

Figure 6.1 Predicted probability of perceiving monitors as both capable and unbiased, Tunisia, 2014, post-presidential election survey
Note: This figure shows point estimates with 95 percent confidence intervals. All predictions are based on ordered-logit models that include control variables (see discussion in main text) and robust standard errors. The outcome variable is a measure of perceptions of EOs' capability and bias, which ranges from 0 to 2. $N = 744$.

overall tendencies mask considerable variation across monitoring groups of different nationalities. Citizens and international elites appear to differ in their beliefs about monitors.

Figure 6.1 illustrates the predicted probability that respondents in our post-presidential survey would perceive observers as both capable and unbiased. To increase precision, our estimates are based on an ordered logistic regression that controls for variables that are plausibly related to Tunisians' perceptions of monitors.[15] Figure 6.1 shows that the Arab League EOs were significantly more likely to be seen as both capable and unbiased than monitors from the AU, Tunisian organizations, or the United States. Although the Arab League EOs were more likely to be perceived as capable and unbiased than EU monitors, as well, the difference is not significant at traditional levels.[16] Because Arab League EOs were perceived as relatively capable and unbiased,

---

[15] Specifically, we control for the respondent's vote choice in the presidential runoff election, age, sex, employment status, political interest, and political knowledge.

[16] $p = 0.276$. This pattern is likely why we see the smallest (though still significant) difference in the treatment effect on election credibility between the Arab League and EU EOs in our analysis discussed later.

we expected them to have the clearest credibility-enhancing effect in Tunisia, and later in this chapter, we show that they did.

In studies with multiple treatment groups (such as ours), there may be a higher risk of incorrectly concluding that an observed treatment effect is meaningful. Researchers have designed several methods to address this problem, known as the false discovery rate. As in Chapter 5, we use the Benjamini–Hochberg procedure to address this issue; it allows us to establish that the significant difference in perceived capability and bias between Arab League monitors and other monitors is robust.[17]

Tunisians associated the Arab League monitors with *both* of the positive qualities we measure. Respondents were significantly more likely to view the Arab League observers as capable than they were to report that their counterparts from the AU, Tunisia, or the United States were capable. Only observers from the EU had a roughly similar level of perceived capability.[18] The survey respondents also perceived Arab League observers as significantly less biased than those from the United States and less biased (though not significantly so) than all other groups except the AU.[19]

Tunisians' positive assessments of Arab League EOs are in many ways surprising. The Arab League first began monitoring elections in Algeria in 1995; its efforts since then have focused on regional elections and are considered "modest."[20] Although the Arab League is not a "zombie" group that falls into the same category as CEELA or the Russia-led CIS, scholars do not consider it to be one of the more

---

[17] The difference is statistically significant at the $p < 0.05$ level for three of the four comparisons. The p-values are as follows, with the Benjamini–Hochberg corrected p-values in parentheses: Arab League vs. AU = 0.044 (0.059), Arab League vs. EU = 0.276 (0.276), Arab League vs. Tunisian NGOs = 0.014 (0.028), and Arab League vs. United States = 0.008 (0.028).

[18] The online appendix (www.cambridge.org/bushprather) reports these results. The p-values are as follows, with the Benjamini–Hochberg corrected p-values in parentheses: Arab League vs. United States = 0.012 (0.016), Arab League vs. EU = 0.404 (0.404), Arab League vs. Tunisia = 0.004 (0.008), and Arab League vs. AU = 0.001 (0.004).

[19] The online appendix (www.cambridge.org/bushprather) reports these results. The p-values are as follows, with the Benjamini–Hochberg corrected p-values in parentheses: Arab League vs. United States = 0.068 (0.272), Arab League vs. EU = 0.251 (0.385), Arab League vs. Tunisia = 0.289 (0.385), and Arab League vs. AU = 0.626 (0.626).

[20] Boubakri (2012, 81).

effective international monitors.[21] A study of Arab League observation missions noted a number of general limitations, all of which applied to the specific mission in Tunisia that we study: The missions typically have no legal framework, use "ad hoc" methods, base their assessments on short missions of only a few days, and send small teams.[22] Although the League did voice support for the Tunisian revolution, it is hardly a democracy-promoting organization given the composition of its members, which include Saudi Arabia. At the second-round presidential elections in Tunisia that we study, the League's mission included observers from nondemocratic states such as Algeria, Iraq, Kuwait, Morocco, and Yemen.[23]

Given these member states, what explains Tunisians' positive perception of the Arab League monitors? As we detail in Section 3, it is plausible that Tunisians inferred information about EOs' capabilities and biases based on what they knew about their sponsoring countries and the types of capabilities they valued. For example, respondents might have assumed the Arab League and EU observers had relatively good knowledge about Tunisia due to its cultural, historical, and linguistic ties with other Arab states as well as European countries (especially France). Although Tunisian EOs would also have had a firm understanding of the local political context, they may have been perceived as having fewer financial resources than the international groups. These factors help us understand why Tunisians may perceive Arab League EOs as relatively capable.

Tunisian respondents also perceived Arab League EOs as being relatively unbiased. As Chapter 3 explained, debates about the appropriate role of Islam in politics have been central to Tunisia's political transition. Survey respondents in the Arab world are apt to perceive monitors from the United States and European countries as biased due to these countries' histories of supporting secular leaders and parties in the region, such as in Algeria and Egypt.[24] Indeed, news coverage of American observers (specifically, NDI) in Tunisia around the 2014 elections often references the organization's reliance on US government funding – implying that it might not be politically independent (a claim

[21] Simpser and Donno (2012, 505–506); Kelley (2011, 1546).
[22] Boubakri (2012, 82, 85, 88).
[23] Agence Tunis Afrique Presse (2014a).
[24] Jamal (2012).

that the NDI resident director has disputed in the media).[25] By contrast, the Arab League has no clear partisan bias. Its members have
taken competing political stances in the region and within Tunisia in
secularist–Islamist debates; given that League decisions require majority support, it struggled to coordinate on the major regional issues
of the 2010s, such as the wars in Syria and Yemen. Whereas some
Arab member states (such as Saudi Arabia and the United Arab Emirates) support secularists, others (such as Qatar) support Islamists,
and yet others have no clear pattern of intervention (e.g., Kuwait and
Oman).[26] The heterogeneity of its member states contributes to the
organization's overall reputation for disunity.[27] Similar to the Arab
League, the AU has not taken sides in Arab regional politics, though
it may be perceived to be lacking in financial resources in comparison
given African states' relatively low levels of wealth.

We also highlight the comparison between the Arab League and
Tunisian NGO observers. Prior studies have hypothesized that local
audiences might find domestic observers more effective and legitimate
since they can mobilize more monitors and are native to the area.[28]
For this reason, many foreign governments and international nongovernmental organizations provide considerable support to domestic
monitoring initiatives as part of a broader trend toward "localization"
in foreign aid. Consistent with the general expectations, there were far
more domestic than international monitors (28,675 vs. 1,036).[29] However, our Tunisian respondents perceived domestic observers as both
relatively incapable and biased. Even nonpartisan domestic observers
may be perceived as having a stake in an election outcome, which can
contribute to perceptions of bias. Thus, although domestic observers
may have advantages, they do not necessarily have a better reputation at home than international observers. This finding provides some
evidence that contradicts the expectations of the nationalism counterargument, which, as described in Chapter 2, anticipates that the public
will be skeptical of foreign interventions in their elections, even from
purportedly neutral EO organizations.

---

[25] Szakal (2014).
[26] Worth (2013).
[27] Masters and Aly Sergie (2010).
[28] Carothers (1997, 26). See Bush (2016, 367–368) for arguments about the
importance of local actors in general in democracy promotion.
[29] Instance Supérieure Indépendante pour les Élections (Tunisia) (2014b).

However, other countries might view their own domestic observers more positively. In the US monitoring experiment conducted prior to the 2016 election, we told respondents about the presence of two types of observers: international monitors from the Organization for Security and Co-operation in Europe (OSCE) and federal domestic observers from the Department of Justice (DOJ) (see Chapter 4 for more detail). After recording respondents' perceptions of election credibility, we asked the same questions about the monitors' capabilities and biases as in the Tunisia survey. US respondents perceived the OSCE monitors as less capable and more biased than the DOJ observers, although the difference was not statistically significant.[30] Since Tunisians do not seem to be more nationalistic than Americans, on average, as we discussed in Chapter 3, we suspect that their more skeptical view of domestic monitors has more to do with the two countries' histories of democracy and monitoring.

This section presented clear evidence that individual perceptions of monitors can vary depending on the nationality of the organization. We observed this in Tunisia by varying the nationality of election monitors and then asking questions to measure respondents' perceptions of how capable and unbiased the monitors are. In the following section, we examine whether perceptions of monitors' capabilities and biases affect respondents' assessments of election credibility using data from all three case studies.

6.1.2 The Conditional Effects of Monitor Identity on Trust

The previous section established that there is variation in individuals' perceptions of foreign actors' ability and willingness to influence the electoral playing field. Our theory predicts that when foreign actors are perceived to be willing and able to influence a country's election in this way, they will be more likely to affect perceptions of election credibility. Since international monitors are a potentially trust-enhancing type of foreign intervention, we expect that when people perceive them to be capable and unbiased, their presence is more likely to increase perceptions of election credibility. In Section 6.2, we test that prediction.

---

[30] Based on a two-sample t-test; $p = 0.358$.

Research Design and Main Results

We test these empirical expectations using evidence from each of our surveys. Each survey design was slightly different. In the post-presidential election survey in Tunisia, the first country in which we studied perceptions of election credibility, we informed respondents about the presence and activities of a randomly assigned monitoring group and then asked questions to determine whether they believed the election was credible. Chapter 4 described this experiment in detail and demonstrated that providing information about *any* monitors did not significantly increase trust compared to the control condition of providing no information about monitors. After measuring perceived credibility, we asked the questions we analyzed in the previous section about perceptions of monitors' capabilities and biases. Given the results shown in Figure 6.1, we expected Arab League EOs to be the most likely to increase perceptions of credibility.

In the United States before the 2016 presidential election and in Georgia in advance of the 2018 first-round presidential election, our experimental design (detailed in Chapter 4) built on what we had learned from Tunisia. These later surveys experimentally primed respondents not only with information about the presence and activities of international monitors (as in the Tunisia experiment) but also with information about monitors' capabilities and (lack of) biases. This design improved on the Tunisia experiment since it enabled us to experimentally vary the traits of monitors that our theory specifies ought to matter, rather than simply observing peoples' beliefs about them. This increases our confidence that we are accurately measuring the causal effect of monitors' perceived capabilities and biases on perceptions of election credibility.

The US survey stated that the international observers were from the OSCE and provided general information about EOs and specific information about observers' capabilities and biases.[31] The relevant text in

---

[31] In an additional treatment, we provided information about observers' presence without providing any details about their capabilities and biases. The OSCE observers in the United States did not enhance trust in our experiment without having their positive traits primed, as shown in Chapter 4. The DOJ observers also failed to increase perceptions of election credibility relative to the control according to conventional levels of statistical significance, although they came closer to having a positive effect, as would be expected since they were also viewed relatively positively, as discussed earlier. The average treatment effect

our treatment, with the randomized information in brackets, read as follows: "In the past, the OSCE has been [praised, criticized] for its [capable, incompetent] observation teams, [but, and] been [criticized, praised] for supporting [one political party over others, the democratic process regardless of the outcome]." We referenced OSCE observers since the US government has hosted them since 2004 as part of its membership obligations. Given that the OSCE is a credible monitoring organization that has exhibited (and has been criticized for) some biases,[32] all combinations of traits in our treatments were both plausible and truthful. As described in Chapter 4, OSCE monitors are not widely known in the United States, although US media outlets have mentioned them in the context of political controversies.

In Georgia, our experiment did not specify a particular monitoring country or organization. Instead, the text in our treatment about monitors' capabilities and biases, which was otherwise identical to that used in the United States, simply referenced "international election observers." As explained in Chapter 4, we did not name the observers in Georgia in part because of the country's controversial history of monitoring, which we feared could influence how respondents interpreted the information in our treatments.

Figure 6.2 displays the effect of informing respondents about capable and unbiased international monitors on perceived election credibility in all three cases. In Tunisia, we compare Arab League EOs – the monitors that we identified earlier as being perceived as unusually capable and unbiased – to the control. In the United States and Georgia, we compare respondents in the capable and unbiased treatment to those in the control groups. We use ordinary least squares (OLS) regressions for each comparison; the outcome variable is our standard measure of election credibility, measured on a scale from 0 (least

---

for the DOJ treatment is 0.06 ($p = 0.125$). To preserve statistical power, none of our experimental treatments provided information to respondents about the DOJ monitors' capabilities and biases.

[32] See, for example, the discussion in Kelley (2012b, 62–63) about OSCE monitors' reports on the 1996 election in Bosnia and Herzegovina. Although the OSCE noted "numerous serious election irregularities... [t]he message for the world was that the OSCE and the UN accepted the outcome of Bosnia's 1996 election, leading some to accuse the OSCE of spin." Nevertheless, OSCE monitors are considered high quality in Simpser and Donno (2012, 506) and Kelley (2011, 1546).

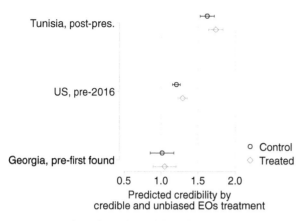

Figure 6.2 The effect of capable and unbiased monitors on perceived credibility, Tunisia, United States (2016), and Georgia
Note: This figure shows point estimates with 95 percent confidence intervals. All predictions are based on OLS models without control variables. The outcome variable is perceived credibility and uses the standardized measure, which ranges from 0 to 2. $N = 1,045$ (Tunisia), 1,313 (US, 2016), and 580 (Georgia).

perceived election credibility) to 2 (most perceived election credibility) as described in Chapter 3.

The figure illustrates that in both Tunisia and the United States, informing respondents about the presence of capable and unbiased monitors increased their trust in the election. Perceived credibility increased by about 7 percent in each case – a modest but meaningful improvement. In Tunisia, the positive effect of the Arab League treatment on perceived credibility is also visible when we compare it to several other monitoring groups in our study rather than the control group: the AU, EU, Tunisian NGOs, and the United States.[33] The positive Arab League EO treatment effect suggests that Tunisian politicians were not wrong to cite observers' presence as evidence of the election's legitimacy, as we noted they did in Chapter 4. The key insight from Figure 6.2 is that monitors that were perceived as unusually capable and unbiased enhanced respondents' perceptions of credibility.

---

[33] The *p*-values for each comparison are as follows, with the Benjamini–Hochberg corrected *p*-values in parentheses: Arab League vs. control = 0.092 (0.073), Arab League vs. AU = 0.017 (0.020), Arab League vs. EU = 0.134 (0.073), Arab League vs. Tunisian organizations = 0.045 (0.073), and Arab League vs. US organizations = 0.194 (0.048).

In the United States in 2016, the prime about capable and unbiased monitors increased trust relative to the control group, which did not hear any information about monitors. It also increased trust relative to the other treatments; the difference from the unbiased-only monitors treatment was marginally statistically significant.[34] As in Chapter 4, we note that despite the United States' status as a democracy, informing individuals about EOs' presence did *not* decrease perceptions of election credibility in any of the conditions. Such a treatment could have prompted a nationalist backlash. Moreover, in a consolidated democracy, awareness of EOs' presence could prompt citizens to ask why a fair election needs to be monitored – and decrease trust and undermine election credibility as a result. In the United States, that was not the case. Instead, international observers that were described as capable and neutral enhanced trust. The finding suggests that election monitoring could have a greater impact on US public attitudes, as long as the monitors are perceived to be credible sources of information about the electoral playing field.

The results from Tunisia and the United States therefore support our hypothesis that monitors will enhance perceptions of election credibility when they are perceived to be both capable and unbiased. Given their different regime types, the similar findings in both countries suggest that the results may be generalizable to diverse settings. Yet in Georgia, we did not find that the capable and unbiased EOs treatment increased trust in the election relative to the control. This could be because Georgians were too confident in their beliefs about election credibility to revise their opinions based on the information contained in our experimental treatment; the country has a relatively certain electoral context given that it has been a partial democracy for some time. Our theory, outlined in Chapter 2, identifies individual certainty as a potentially important conditioning variable, and we are able to test this observable implication.

Prior to our experiment in Georgia in the pre-first-round presidential election survey, we asked respondents how credible they thought the election would be and how certain they were in their answer. This

---

[34] The *p*-values for each comparison are as follows, with the Benjamini–Hochberg corrected *p*-values in parentheses: capable and unbiased vs. control = 0.045 (0.073), capable and unbiased vs. capable but biased = 0.281 (0.020), and capable and unbiased vs. incapable but unbiased = 0.086 (0.048).

is the only survey for which we have a measure of both individuals' preexisting beliefs about election credibility and their certainty in those beliefs. Although Georgian respondents were relatively evenly split in their assessments on the eve of the election – 49 percent anticipated distrusting the election vs. 51 percent anticipated trusting it, and 44 percent anticipated the result would not reflect the will of the people while 56 percent expected it would – they tended to be quite certain in their evaluations. Indeed, two-thirds (67 percent) were "somewhat" or "very" certain in their responses about election credibility. People who already believed the election was likely to be credible were no more or less likely to be certain than people who believed it was not likely to be credible.[35]

When we restrict the sample to Georgian respondents who were previously uncertain about their beliefs about election integrity, information that monitors were capable and unbiased had the expected positive and statistically significant effect.[36] The effect is substantively quite large: Perceived election credibility increased by 46 percent when we compare the treatment respondents to the control group. The treatment informing uncertain respondents about the presence of capable and unbiased monitors increased perceived credibility relative not only to the control but also to the other two treatments (i.e., about capable but biased EOs and incapable but unbiased EOs), although those differences are not significant at traditional levels.[37] By contrast, information about capable and unbiased international EOs had no effect on respondents who were already certain about their beliefs about election integrity.[38]

These patterns are consistent with a logic whereby people seek to hold accurate beliefs about the electoral playing field. According to such a logic, we would expect people to respond to credible new information about elections, including when it comes from foreign actors. Our finding that such information affects respondents who

---

[35] Based on a two-sample t-test; $p = 0.436$.

[36] The online appendix (www.cambridge.org/bushprather) reports the results.

[37] The p-values for each comparison are as follows, with the Benjamini–Hochberg corrected p-values in parentheses: capable and unbiased vs. control = 0.024 (0.073), capable and unbiased vs. capable but biased = 0.334 (0.020), and capable and unbiased vs. incapable but unbiased = 0.274 (0.048).

[38] $p = 0.470$. The online appendix (www.cambridge.org/bushprather) reports these results.

were previously uncertain about the election, but not those who were already firm in their beliefs, makes sense: It suggests that people who thought they might not already hold correct beliefs about the election were most receptive to the experimental treatments.

An alternative explanation for why the capable and unbiased treatment did not increase perceptions of election credibility in Georgia on average is that we did not name a specific EO group in our treatment, as we did in Tunisia and the United States. This design feature raises the question of whether respondents believed the monitors in our treatments were from particular countries. Such a belief could represent a form of confounding, in which respondents infer additional traits beyond what is mentioned in an experimental vignette, and it is *those* traits that caused them to update their beliefs about election credibility.[39] To address this possibility, much later in the same survey we asked respondents in the treatment conditions where they thought the referenced observers were from. Most respondents (59 percent) did not know or declined to say, but 32 percent thought they were from the United States and 26 percent believed they were from Europe.[40] Treatment assignment did not predict the likelihood of a respondent guessing the monitors were from Europe. Those who were told the monitors were capable and unbiased were less likely to say they were from the United States than those who were told the observers were capable but biased.[41] This pattern reinforces our finding from Tunisia that American election monitors face relatively negative stereotypes about their political biases all over the world (recall Figure 6.1).

The relatively negative perception of American EOs' political biases may also reflect the legacy of American NGOs in Georgia. For example, US NGOs that are involved in both election monitoring and democracy promotion supported the controversial election polls in 2012, as discussed in Chapter 3.[42] This history also includes Georgian politicians who have played a role in discrediting international and domestic monitors. As we noted in Chapter 4, officials from the ruling GD party have criticized monitors for being biased and too

[39] Dafoe, Zhang, and Caughey (2018).
[40] The question was open ended, and respondents could name multiple countries.
[41] $p = 0.08$. The online appendix (www.cambridge.org/bushprather) reports the results of this test.
[42] See also Kirchick (2012) and Cecire (2013).

sympathetic to their opponents in the UNM party.[43] Our interviews with EO representatives in Georgia in October 2018 indicate that allegations of observer bias continued to pose challenges for US organizations at that time, as well as for domestic monitors that cooperate with international partners.[44] The head of an international monitoring mission interviewed for this study described strategies for improving the mission's reputation in Georgia, including "rel[ying] on the methodology and reliability of [our] work...and emphasiz[ing] [our] neutrality."[45] This assessment highlights the importance of both perceived capabilities and perceived biases, the two key characteristics emphasized in our theory.

To sum up, in two of the three cases we found that informing respondents about the presence and activities of capable and unbiased international observers caused them to perceive the election as more credible. In the third case, Georgia, informing respondents about such observers did not enhance trust, but this null effect seems to be driven by the fact that most Georgians had strong prior beliefs about the level of election credibility. Informing respondents about capable and unbiased observers had a large positive effect in the subsample of Georgians who were not already certain about election credibility. Overall, these patterns support a theoretical logic in which individuals respond to information about election credibility in a way that reflects accuracy goals.

Deepening the Analysis: The Arab League Effect in Tunisia
Our finding that the Arab League observers were most likely to enhance Tunisians' perceptions of the presidential election's credibility is controversial from a normative and policy perspective since these monitors have significant limitations. In particular, it suggests that domestic audiences may be vulnerable to the influence of noncredible international monitors. Given the significance of this finding, in this section we examine it in more detail.

---

[43] Transparency International Georgia (2018); InterPressNews (2018a).
[44] Interviews with executive directors and program managers at domestic and international NGOs, October 15–17, 2018.
[45] Interview with executive director at an international NGO, October 17, 2018.

One important feature of the Tunisia analysis is that we *observed* respondents' beliefs about EO capability and bias as opposed to experimentally manipulating those beliefs as part of our research design. If our argument about observer identity is correct, then the Arab League EOs' effect on credibility should have been driven by the group's perceived capabilities and political neutrality. To further test the theory, we employ a nonparametric mediation model to estimate the average causal mediation effect (ACME) of the Arab League EO treatment – in other words, to determine how much of the treatment effect is mediated by our joint measure of perceived capability and bias.[46] This estimate examines whether respondents' perceptions of EOs as capable and unbiased was the mechanism through which the Arab League treatment affected the perceived credibility of the election. To estimate the ACME, we created a variable coded 1 if respondents were in the Arab League EO treatment group, and 0 if they were in any other treatment group.

As expected given the results displayed in Figure 6.1, the Arab League treatment is significantly and positively associated with the joint measure of capability and bias. Furthermore, and now consistent with the results displayed in Figure 6.2, respondents in the Arab League EO group viewed the election as significantly more credible than those in the other treatment groups. However, when we control for the hypothesized mediating variable, that is, perceiving monitors as both capable and unbiased, the Arab League effect loses significance, whereas the mediator is highly correlated with credibility. In other words, people who believed the Arab League EOs were capable and unbiased viewed the election as significantly more credible. We would expect to see this pattern if perceptions of EO capability and bias are mediating the Arab League's effect on trust. Furthermore, the estimated ACME is positive and statistically significant.

We also consider two potential alternative explanations for our finding that the Arab League observers significantly enhanced trust relative to the control group. The first relates to respondents' general favorability toward the monitoring groups. We begin by noting that several observers were perceived relatively favorably on only one dimension

---

[46] Imai et al. (2011). This analysis should be understood as correlational since the mediators were not randomly assigned. The results are reported in the online appendix (www.cambridge.org/bushprather).

highlighted by our theory (e.g., the AU EOs were perceived as relatively unbiased but not particularly capable). This pattern is inconsistent with the idea that responses about EOs' traits only reflected individuals' favorability toward the sponsoring country or organization. To further test this alternative explanation, we use answers to a question that probed respondents' attitudes toward various countries and organizations. Contrary to the observable implications of the alternative explanation, Tunisians reported feeling most favorably toward the EU (80 percent) and Tunisian NGOs (72 percent), and somewhat less favorably toward Arab states (63 percent) and the United States (62 percent).[47] We introduced a dichotomous variable indicating whether the respondent felt favorably toward the sponsoring country or organization and its interaction with an indicator for the relevant treatment variable. There were no significant interactions between the treatment and favorability.[48]

A second potential alternative explanation relates to respondents' identification with EOs from particular countries or cultures. Yet, Tunisian observers – with whom the public presumably would have identified the most – were not perceived as particularly capable or unbiased (see Figure 6.1), and they did not improve perceptions of election credibility relative to the control. Moreover, many Tunisians do not strongly identify as Arab, reflecting the country's proximity to Europe and its history as a French colony.[49] A nationally representative panel survey of Tunisians in 2013 and 2015 found that only 5 percent identified as citizens of the Arab community when asked how they related to the world. Similarly, only 5 percent of respondents in

---

[47] We acknowledge that this analysis has a limitation. We asked about favorability toward "Arab states" rather than the Arab League. It is possible that Tunisians felt more positively toward the Arab League organization than toward Arab states in general. However, responses to a question in a nationally representative survey conducted in Tunisia in 2013 indicate that this is unlikely. When asked about their level of confidence in the Arab League, only 19 percent of Tunisian respondents indicated that they had "a great deal" or "quite a lot" of confidence. This analysis draws on the responses to question 125–15 in the World Values Survey Wave 6. See Haerpfer et al. (2014).

[48] These results are reported in the online appendix (www.cambridge.org/bushprather).

[49] Since people often feel favorably toward countries with which they identify, this observation is consistent with respondents' more muted favorability toward Arab states. See Katzenstein and Keohane (2007, 28–29).

that survey agreed with the statement "Above all, I am an Arab."[50] Thus, we conclude that our theorized mechanism of individual beliefs about monitors' biases and capabilities best explains the observed patterns in Tunisia.

6.2 Intervener Identity and Election Meddling

In this section, we examine how intervener identity conditions the effect of election meddling on perceptions of election credibility. As discussed in Chapter 2, perceived bias is not relevant here because election meddling, by definition, aims to enhance the chances of one side in an election. Thus, we seek to learn whether perceptions of capabilities vary across election meddlers and are associated with beliefs about election credibility.

As documented in Chapter 5, partisan electoral interventions are not as common as election monitoring, and fewer types of actors engage in it. Nevertheless, a variety of countries engage in meddling, and some of them are better at altering the electoral playing field than others. As such, we anticipated that individual perceptions of meddlers' capabilities would vary.

6.2.1 How Perceptions of Election Meddlers Vary

In Chapter 5, we presented the results from our experiments on meddlers' effects in the United States (in surveys conducted before and after the 2018 and 2020 elections) and Georgia (in surveys conducted before the first round and after the second round of the 2018 election), which identified limited negative effects apart from the hypothetical context in Georgia.[51] To examine variation in perceived capabilities across meddlers, we use our pre-election surveys in the United States that randomized information about the potential for meddling at the 2018 Congressional election and 2020 presidential election. Unfortunately,

---

[50] Other response options were citizens of the world (6 percent), Tunisia (50 percent), the Islamic umma (or worldwide Christian/Jewish community, 39 percent), or the Berber community (0.3 percent). Data from Moaddel (2015).

[51] Recall that we did not include a meddling experiment in the Tunisia survey, but we did find, as reported in Chapter 5, that when individuals believed foreign actors had a negative influence on elections (i.e., were capable of influencing the election), Tunisians trusted the election results less.

we cannot examine variation in perceptions of potential meddlers in Georgia, as we did not ask respondents about the perceived capabilities of meddlers in our question-order experiments. Instead, we varied information about Russia's capability in the hypothetical experiment about election meddling so that we could experimentally identify its effect.

Our surveys administered prior to the 2018 and 2020 US elections asked respondents about the capabilities of the three countries that US intelligence officials had warned were attempting to meddle in the elections: China, Russia, and Iran.[52] Each respondent was asked about only one country, which was randomly assigned as part of the experiment described in Chapter 5.

Since meddlers are politically biased, by definition, the salient theoretical issue is whether individuals perceive them as being able to influence the electoral playing field. To measure those beliefs, we asked respondents how likely they thought it was that these countries would be able to successfully change the results of the midterm election.[53] We created a binary indicator coded 1 if respondents thought it was "somewhat likely" or "very likely" that the foreign country would change the results, and 0 if they thought it was "not too likely" or "not likely at all."[54]

This question about meddlers' capabilities followed a vignette that described a potential meddling scenario at the election based on news reports about attempted meddling in the election by the three countries. Only around 30 percent of respondents thought the meddler they heard about was capable of changing the result of the election. However, as with perceptions of monitors, individual perceptions varied depending on the foreign country that was allegedly attempting to

---

[52] Director of National Intelligence (2018). An interesting extension that would parallel the design of some of our election monitoring studies would be to have a domestic election meddling treatment in which the *type* of election interference is held constant but the actor is domestic rather than foreign.

[53] Similar to the questions about election monitors' capabilities and biases described earlier, only respondents in the treatment groups received this question. It was asked directly after the questions about perceived election credibility.

[54] We created a binary variable to make this measure more comparable with our measure of perceived EO bias in Tunisia. The results are similar if we used the original 4-point coding; these results are available in the online appendix (www.cambridge.org/bushprather).

intervene. We use a logistic regression to estimate the effect of indicators of the meddling country's identity on the probability that the meddler was perceived as capable. To increase the precision of our estimates (and similar to the analysis presented in Figure 6.1), we also control for several variables that could affect individual perceptions of potential meddling countries (respondent's party identification, age, sex, employment status, political interest, and political knowledge).

As Figure 6.3 indicates, in 2018, Americans believed Russia was significantly more capable of changing the election result than China or Iran.[55] The predicted probability of being perceived to have the ability to change the results of the election was about 9 percentage points higher for Russia than for China or Iran. In 2020, respondents again thought Russia was the more capable meddler by about the same margin, but the treatment effect was no longer significant due to the smaller sample size in the 2020 survey. These patterns make sense given Russia's "sweeping and systematic" interference in the 2016 election, as described in the Mueller Report.[56] By contrast, the threat of Chinese or Iranian electoral interference in the 2020 US presidential election was only highlighted in *some* intelligence briefings. Neither country appears to have the sophisticated meddling apparatus or history that Russia does.[57] The US intelligence community later concluded that pre-election accusations about Chinese meddling were incorrect, stating in 2021, "China sought stability in its relationship with the United States, did not view either election outcome as being advantageous enough for China to risk getting caught meddling."[58] Such accusations – generally made by Trump political appointees – reflected the administration's desire to "downplay" pro-Trump Russian electoral interference.[59]

Given that the experiment took place in a powerful country – the United States – and provided respondents with truthful information about the likely meddlers, we might expect the differences in meddlers' perceived capabilities to be larger or smaller depending on the

---

[55] The *p*-values are as follows, with the Benjamini–Hochberg corrected *p*-values in parentheses: Russia vs. China = 0.003 (0.005) and Russia vs. Iran = 0.005 (0.005).
[56] Mueller (2018, 1).
[57] Barnes (2020); Draper (2020).
[58] National Intelligence Council (2021, i).
[59] Seldin (2021).

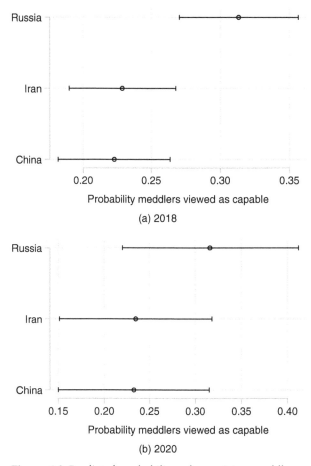

Figure 6.3 Predicted probability of perceiving meddlers as capable, United States, 2018 and 2020, pre-election surveys
Note: This figure shows point estimates with 95 percent confidence intervals. All predictions are based on logit models with control variables (see discussion in main text) and robust standard errors. The outcome variable is a measure of perceptions of meddlers' capability, which is coded 0 (incapable) or 1 (capable). $N = 1,188$ (2018) and 779 (2020).

countries named and the power disparity between the meddler and the target country. For example, American respondents might rate the likely success of a Bolivian attempt to meddle in US elections even lower than China or Iran. Conversely, if we had conducted this experiment in a less powerful country, the perceived differences across meddlers might be smaller as respondents might view many different meddlers as being able to influence the election. Thus, these results make sense for the case and the experiment, but may generalize in different ways depending on the context.

6.2.2 The Conditional Effects of Meddler Identity on Trust

As with monitoring, we expected meddlers' perceived capabilities to affect beliefs about election credibility. If meddlers are not seen as capable of affecting the electoral playing field, then their attempts at meddling may not decrease trust in elections. However, if meddlers are able to successfully alter the electoral playing field – or are perceived to have that ability – then electoral trust may be compromised.

We test these empirical expectations using observational and experimental evidence from our surveys in the United States and Georgia. Again, the survey design varied in each case, this time to reflect the facts on the ground related to foreign interventions.

Main Findings from the United States
Our primary evidence from the United States comes from the survey experiments fielded just before the 2018 midterm elections and replicated in the 2020 pre-election survey. Both experiments truthfully informed randomly selected respondents about an announcement that a foreign country was seeking to influence the results of the upcoming election. The treatment text noted that a randomly assigned country – Russia, China, or Iran – was involved in an ongoing foreign influence campaign. The announcement of this campaign came from either US security agencies or Republican politicians, and the type of meddling involved either a disinformation campaign or attempts to hack voting machines. These features varied at random and independently of the meddling country. This possibility of foreign meddling by China, Russia, or Iran was accurate; we provided it to hold other salient aspects of the situation constant and therefore to minimize the potential for confounding.[60] Chapter 5 provides further detail about this experiment. The results presented later pool across the meddling tactic and source of information about meddling.

---

[60] Dafoe, Zhang, and Caughey (2018).

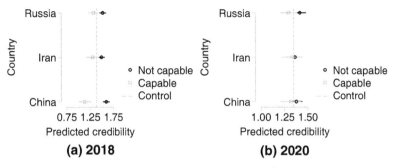

Figure 6.4 The effect of capable and incapable meddling on perceived credibility in the United States, 2018 and 2020, pre-election survey
Note: This figure shows point estimates with 95 percent confidence intervals. All predictions are based on OLS models without control variables. The outcome variable is perceived credibility and uses the standardized measure, which ranges from 0 to 2. $N = 1,240$ (2018) and 830 (2020).

As we described in Chapter 5, the treatment in this experiment *reassured* Americans about election credibility on average. We reasoned that respondents interpreted our treatment as providing good news about election credibility, since the US government had identified the potential for meddling, and therefore was more likely to stop it before the election. In a sense, this warning about the potential for meddling likely conveyed the message that the three meddlers – Russia, China, and Iran – were unlikely to successfully affect the election results. Indeed, as stated earlier in the chapter, only around 30 percent of respondents in both surveys thought any of the meddlers would be capable of doing so. Because we asked respondents how likely they thought it was that the meddler would succeed in its attempts to influence the election, we can compare respondents who believed each country was either capable or not capable to those in the control group who heard no information about election meddling. We emphasize that we *observed* these beliefs (as we did in the EO experiment in Tunisia); we did not experimentally manipulate them.

Figure 6.4 depicts the predicted level of election credibility for each country treatment according to the respondent's view of the meddler's capability. The dashed line represents the predicted level of election credibility for respondents in the control group. The left panel demonstrates that for each meddling country in 2018, respondents reported having more trust in the election results when they viewed the meddler as being less (rather than more) capable of changing them. Moreover, for all three meddling countries, respondents who believed the meddler was not capable of affecting the results had significantly more trust in the election than the control group. Of those who believed the meddling country *was* capable, all respondents had less trust than those in the control group, but only those in the China treatment group had significantly less trust. This analysis provides significant support for our hypothesis that the identity of the meddling country matters, and particularly, that it is *whether respondents believe the meddler is capable of altering the electoral playing field* that is significant.

In the 2020 pre-election survey (results shown in Figure 6.4(b)), the only meddler treatment that had any effect on the perceived credibility of the election was Russia. For Iran and China, there was little difference between the treatment and control regardless of the perceived capabilities of the meddler. This likely reflects the lower salience of foreign meddling in the 2020 US election and heightened concerns of domestic threats to election integrity.

Main Findings from Georgia

As explained in Chapter 5, because there was no credible information about attempts to meddle in Georgia's 2018 election, we were unable to include a truthful experiment with information about meddling in the same way that we did in the United States. Instead, we opted to study the effect of information about meddling using a vignette experiment about a hypothetical future election in our post-second-round presidential election survey. As described in the previous chapter, Russia was depicted in our vignette as meddling in favor of the GD party to promote realism; it was not equally plausible that it would have supported the rival UNM party. Several features of the hypothetical election varied, including the *type of meddling* – a diplomatic statement, providing campaign funds, and ballot box stuffing – and the *success of meddling* – either the GD party won or it lost to the UNM party. The latter characteristic is particularly relevant in this chapter, as it sheds light on Russia's capabilities as a meddler. This design advances beyond that of the US experiment since it randomizes whether the meddling succeeded or did not succeed, rather than only observing respondents' perceptions about whether success was likely.

In our analysis of the experiment in this chapter, we compare people who heard about successful and unsuccessful Russian meddling (i.e.,

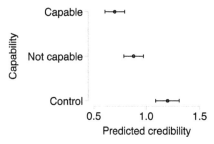

Figure 6.5 The effect of capable and incapable meddling on perceived credibility in Georgia, 2018, post-second-round presidential election survey
Note: This figure shows point estimates with 95 percent confidence intervals. All predictions are based on OLS models without control variables. The outcome variable is perceived credibility and uses the standardized measure, which ranges from 0 to 2. $N = 1,024$.

heard that the GD party won or lost after a Russian intervention to support GD), regardless of the meddling tactic, to people in the control group who heard nothing about Russian meddling. In Chapter 5, we showed that the meddling treatment on average caused Georgians to perceive the election as significantly less credible. In this chapter, we test the theoretical expectation that successful Russian meddling would have a significant negative effect relative to the control of no information about meddling. Our theory does not specifically predict whether reports of unsuccessful meddling will diminish vs. have no effect on electoral trust. On the one hand, unsuccessful meddling may still provide information about whether politicians are committed to democracy, but on the other hand, it may not indicate that the electoral playing field was unfair. At the same time, the results from the United States suggest that meddling that is perceived as unsuccessful may increase trust.

Figure 6.5 illustrates that both treatments – capable meddling and not capable meddling – decreased perceptions of election credibility relative to the control of no information in Georgia.[61] The successful meddling treatment causes quite a large reduction in credibility – about half a point on the 3-point scale relative to the control (equivalent to a 41 percent decrease), which is statistically significant. The unsuccessful

---

[61] $p < 0.001$ for both comparisons, which remain statistically significant even after correcting for the false discovery rate.

meddling treatment also decreases trust, but with half the effect size, though it is still significantly different from the control. One reason why even unsuccessful meddling could decrease perceptions of election credibility is that local politicians may have invited it, which indicates that they are pseudo-democrats. Recall from Chapter 5 that Georgian politicians – including both major candidates in the 2018 presidential election – frequently accuse each other of being stooges of outside powers, especially Russia. The results from Georgia are similar to those from the United States in 2018 in that they demonstrate that capable meddling decreases electoral trust, but contrast with the US results in that even meddling that is not capable decreases trust.[62]

A number of factors could explain this difference between the two cases, including the fact that the experiment in Georgia was hypothetical and the capability of the meddler was randomized rather than observed. The hypothetical vignette also presented a scenario that included the election results. By contrast, the real-world scenario from the United States occurred in a pre-election survey and demonstrated to respondents that the US government was actively investigating foreign meddling before the election. Regardless, these results continue to demonstrate that the characteristics of the intervener matter, given that respondents in the capable treatments had significantly less trust in the election than those in the not capable treatments, and that the same is true for meddlers that are perceived as more and less capable. Thus, and similar to our results about monitor identity discussed earlier in the chapter, the experiments provide support for the theory that the capability of the meddler shapes the effect of meddling on election credibility.

Deepening the Analysis: Comparing the effects of China and Russia in the US 2018 Data

As we did in our evaluation of election monitors, we now seek to deepen our analysis of what we think is one of the most interesting findings about meddler identity. Our experiment prior to the 2018 US election showed that capable meddlers were always associated with

[62] In the United States, when people were informed *before* the election about reports that had uncovered meddling by the foreign country perceived as the most capable meddler, Russia, they trusted the upcoming election more. The increase was modest at around 5 percent and marginally statistically significant ($p = 0.097$). We interpret this effect as being consistent with Americans becoming more reassured that Russian meddling would be prevented.

less electoral trust relative to meddlers viewed as not capable. However, the difference in electoral trust between those who viewed the meddler as capable vs. not capable was largest for China. For China, the difference associated with viewing the meddler as capable was twice as large as the difference for the other two meddlers – Iran and Russia. Why might this be the case?

As noted earlier, in the absence of detailed knowledge about foreign interventions in elections, individuals may use the intervening country as a heuristic for understanding monitors' and meddlers' capabilities and biases. Parallel to what we proposed about monitors, the perceived capabilities of meddlers may have a stronger effect on election credibility if the meddling country exhibits three factors: (1) nondemocracy, (2) inside knowledge of the target country, and (3) history of and perceived resources for meddling.

In our three treatment countries (Russia, China, and Iran), two of these factors are held constant by design as part of our experiment: All three are nondemocracies, and none of them share any cultural or linguistic knowledge of the United States that might make them particularly capable in their meddling attempts. However, the countries do vary on the other factors. In terms of China's history of threats, it has been viewed as an increasingly powerful rival to the United States, and there is reason to think Americans are attuned to the danger posed by rising powers.[63] According to national surveys conducted by Pew, more Americans perceived China as a "major threat" than Russia over the past decade – an increase from 52 percent in 2009 (compared to 38 percent who viewed Russia as a major threat) to 62 percent in 2020 (vs. 56 percent for Russia).[64] Thus, it may be the case that capable meddling by China has such a large negative effect compared to the other two countries because it is viewed as posing the greatest threat and having the most resources.

We can also ask why Russia did not have a larger effect given its history of meddling in the United States. As we discuss later, a country's history of foreign intervention may shape how a subsequent intervention affects election credibility. For example, for monitors, past reports or decisions about whether to accept invitations to monitor may reveal

---

[63] Friedberg (2005); Tingley (2017).
[64] Pew Research Center (2020, 15).

that they are more biased than they claim. Likewise, past interventions can reveal meddlers' capabilities and the direction of their bias.

As we noted in Chapter 5, it is undisputed that Russia attempted to meddle in the 2016 US election. It is unclear, however, whether its meddling affected the election's results. Analysts and ordinary citizens continue to debate whether Donald Trump would have won without the Russian government's support; as former Central Intelligence Agency Director Michael Hayden explained, "It's not just unknown, it's unknowable."[65] Given this uncertainty, it is possible that Russia's meddling did not concretely reveal much about its capabilities. However, its interference in 2016 *did* reveal the direction of its bias: It sought to support Donald Trump's candidacy for president. Thus, it is plausible that in our 2018 experiment, individuals also perceived Russia to be meddling on behalf of Republican candidates (i.e., Trump's fellow partisans). Therefore it may be the case that there was a partisan reaction to our treatment. Although we discuss vote choice as a moderator in more detail in Chapter 7, we briefly examine it here to assess the effect of Russian meddling on beliefs about election credibility.

We replicate Figure 6.4 for individuals who said they voted for either Trump or Clinton in 2016. If past meddling is influencing individuals' responses to the treatment via the mechanism of perceptions of meddlers, then we should see partisan differences in the effects of capable and not capable Russian meddling on election credibility. Figure 6.6 displays the predicted level of election credibility for each country by 2016 vote choice. Note that in the control group, Trump voters had slightly higher levels of trust than Clinton voters.

Figure 6.6 illustrates that while there are relatively few differences between Trump and Clinton voters in how meddlers' capability affects the perceived credibility of the election in the China treatment, we do observe such differences for the Russia treatment. The main difference is that for Clinton voters, capable meddling by Russia significantly decreased trust relative to the control group, whereas incapable meddling significantly increased trust. Although Trump voters who thought

---

[65] Quoted in Mayer (2018). Within the academic literature, for example, Sides, Tesler and Vavrek (2019, 198–200) question the likelihood that Russian interference caused Trump to win instead of Clinton, and Guess, Nagler and Tucker (2019) find that online disinformation was not widely shared. However, Levin (2020, 242) concludes that Clinton would have won absent Russian interference.

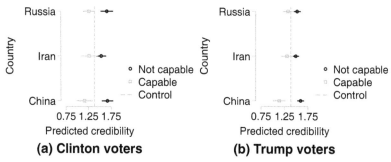

Figure 6.6 The effect of capable and incapable meddling on perceived credibility in the United States in 2018 by 2016 vote choice, pre-election survey
Note: This figure shows point estimates with 95 percent confidence intervals. All predictions are based on OLS models without control variables. The outcome variable is perceived credibility and uses the standardized measure, which ranges from 0 to 2. $N = 451$ (Clinton voters) and 437 (Trump voters).

Russia was not a capable meddler perceived the election as more credible than those who thought it *was* capable, in both cases the treatment effect trends negative. This result is consistent with the idea that past meddling (in 2016) revealed the direction of Russia's bias, and that individuals may be viewing Russia's new meddling attempt (in 2018) through the lens of its previous efforts, such that Democrats question the election's credibility when they believe Russia is capable but are reassured when they think it is not. This finding also suggests that individuals may be motivated by partisan goals as well as accuracy goals when they encounter new information about foreign interventions in elections. We return to this topic in Chapter 7.

6.3 The Sources of Beliefs about Foreign Actors

Our main objective in this book is not to develop and test a theory about the sources of individuals' beliefs about foreign actors. However, in Chapter 2, we suggested that, similar to their perceptions of election credibility, individuals' beliefs about foreign actors can be influenced by both accuracy and directional goals – that is, by a desire to hold beliefs that are both correct *and* consistent with their partisan motivations.

Although the actions of foreign actors do not always receive widespread attention in the media, when they do, this can shape the beliefs of individuals who are motivated by accuracy goals. That is true even for international monitors, which might be regarded as a sufficiently "normal" part of elections not to receive substantial media attention in many countries. For example, a former head of mission for an international NGO engaged in election monitoring told us that he appeared so often on the television news in Georgia that he continued to be recognized in the street by members of the public for years afterwards.[66] As detailed in Chapter 4, monitors take multiple steps, including having prominent individuals participate in their missions and developing media strategies, to draw attention to themselves.

Indeed, foreign actors help shape their own public perceptions. For instance, international monitors attempt to signal that they are capable and unbiased with the composition of their teams, press releases, and branding. To promote a public image of credibility in Georgia, for example, the NDI resident director Laura Thornton appeared on Georgian television before the election to explain the organization's process, which included monitoring during the pre-election period and "a detailed report."[67] This type of outreach was particularly important in Georgia given attempts (described in Chapter 5) by local politicians to undermine international monitors' credibility there. Monitors often heavily use public engagement to shape public perceptions.

Yet, individuals' beliefs about foreign actors may also be rooted in less detailed knowledge, as they can use what they know about the intervening country or organization as a heuristic to evaluate the likely consequences of an attempted intervention. Earlier in this chapter, we hinted at several sources of information about foreign actors that are relevant for citizens, including recent or past actions in elections by the foreign actor in question, as well as their nonelectoral actions. Tunisians, we argued, might have had relatively positive impressions of monitors from the Arab League because those observers came from a diverse set of Arab countries that are culturally proximate to Tunisia but do not have the pro-secularist baggage that European countries might be expected to have. In the United States, the recent history of Russian election meddling helped us understand why Americans viewed Russia as a more capable meddler than China and Iran. And in

---

[66] Interview with former executive director at an international NGO, July 13, 2018.
[67] Rustavi2 (2018a).

Georgia, we noted that the controversial history of American NGOs there was a plausible reason why our survey respondents were more likely to perceive biased international monitors as coming from the United States. Thus, we found patterns in our surveys that are broadly consistent with the accuracy logic.

At the same time, our deeper analysis of the effect of capable Russian meddling on election credibility in the United States showed that individuals may be motivated by more directional goals: Their partisan biases may shape how they perceive foreign actors' capabilities and biases. Beyond the case of the 2018 US election, we might therefore expect election losers – who are motivated to question the credibility of an election – to question the capability of credibility-enhancing election monitors and to trust the capability of credibility-diminishing election meddlers. The best way to explore directionally motivated reasoning is to investigate how perceptions of foreign actors vary by vote choice, which we do in Chapter 7.

6.4 Conclusion

In this chapter, we tested our theory that intervener identity influences how foreign actors shape local trust in elections. Individuals' perceptions of foreign actors vary in ways that reflect those actors' track records, as well as more individual factors. These perceptions in turn shape which foreign actors were most likely to affect individuals' perceptions of election credibility.

International monitors were more likely to enhance credibility when they were perceived to be capable and unbiased. We illustrated this pattern using both observational and experimental evidence from Tunisia and the United States (in 2016). Georgia, as Chapters 4 and 5 also established, was a unique case given respondents' high degree of certainty about election credibility. However, when we restricted the sample to uncertain respondents there, we found similar results about the positive effect of capable and unbiased monitors.

Conversely, meddlers were more likely to diminish credibility when they were perceived as capable. Results from the United States (in 2018) and Georgia supported this conclusion. However, we also note that in the hypothetical experiment in Georgia, even unsuccessful meddling caused respondents to lose trust in the election. At the same time, the negative effect was smaller than the negative effect associated with successful meddling, again reinforcing the ways in which meddlers' capabilities matter.

In addition to shedding light on the determinants of citizens' perceptions of election credibility, these findings provide insights into government behavior. For example, the monitoring effects we identify suggest at least two ways that governments can use international monitors strategically to affect citizens' trust for their own ends. The first is by attempting to discredit critical monitors by questioning their capabilities and biases. The second is by inviting international monitors that may lack credibility internationally but have more credibility domestically in order to legitimize elections.

Similarly, governments may be able to improve trust in elections by publicizing their efforts to combat meddling before election day, which can suggest to the public that meddlers are not capable of swinging the election in favor of their preferred side. At the same time, politicians who have lost elections may be able to discredit their opponents' victories by promoting the idea that powerful outside countries had both the will and the ability to intervene. Finally, since meddling that is perceived as capable undermines trust in elections, political leaders may want to limit disclosures of such meddling to the public. A Department of Homeland Security whistleblower alleged that President Trump suppressed reports on Russian electoral interference in this way, although the White House disputed this accusation.[68] In Chapter 7, we show how differently Republicans and Democrats view such events.

[68] Myre (2020).

7 | *Individual Vote Choice*

When Tom Brady, then the quarterback of the highly successful professional American football team the New England Patriots, was accused of illegally tampering with a football before a playoff game in January 2015, the response was divided. His team's supporters vehemently denied any wrongdoing, while many fans of other teams ganged up in opposition to Brady and the Patriots during the scandal, known as "Deflategate." Those who championed other teams maintained that this was evidence that the Patriots did not win by playing fairly but by manipulating the playing field in their favor. In the absence of a "smoking gun," fans' assessments of the evidence – including a contested scientific report on air pressure – were strongly related to which team they supported.

Backing a political party can be similar to supporting a sports team (albeit with much higher stakes), especially in polarized societies. And in much the same way that fans' emotions are heightened during key matches, partisans' emotions run hottest in the weeks before and after competitive elections.[1] When people support a party – similar to when they back a sports team – it can become a core aspect of their identity. Therefore, they not only want their party to do well, but they also want to believe good things about it, including that it has fairly competed in (and won) elections. Consequently, people who support winning parties may be less receptive than those who support losing parties to news about electoral malpractice. This type of dynamic represents a form of motivated reasoning. As we explained in Chapter 2, individuals' partisan attachments can prompt them to engage in *directionally* motivated reasoning in response to new political information.

Individuals' vote choice can also lead them to process information in partisan ways even when they are driven more by *accuracy* goals. Returning to the Deflategate example, one reason why

---

[1] Flynn, Nyhan, and Reifler (2017, 134).

Patriots fans may not have been persuaded by incriminating information is that they already had a great deal of confidence in their
team's integrity after years of watching it play. A contested scientific report may not have convinced them to reassess the accuracy
of their long-held views. For individuals who may have been uncertain about the team's integrity, the incident created an environment
in which critical news reports caused them to downgrade their opinions of Brady. Extending this logic to elections provides another
explanation for why winning partisans might be less influenced by negative information about election integrity than losing partisans: They
have different pre-existing levels of information and certainty about
elections.

Chapters 4 and 5 explored how individuals updated their beliefs
about election credibility in response to information about monitoring and meddling and found limited overall effects. Then, Chapter
6 demonstrated that the effects of monitors and meddlers depend on
individuals' perceptions of foreign actors' capabilities and biases. This
chapter investigates how individual vote choice – specifically, the distinction between election "winners" and "losers" – conditions foreign
actors' effects on trust.

The chapter first describes how we define and measure winning
and losing in elections. It then illustrates that winning and losing
affect beliefs about election credibility in all three countries studied.
Finally, the central contribution of the chapter is to examine partisan
differences in responses to monitors' reports and meddling.

Across our three case studies and both types of foreign actors (monitors and meddlers), election losers updated their beliefs about election credibility in response to new information about foreign actors'
involvement in elections more often than election winners. In many
cases, the partisan conditional effects we identify could weaken the
foundations of democracy, which requires that supporters of a losing
candidate consent to be governed by the winner. For example, we find
that monitors' positive reports do *not* reassure losers that an election
is credible. Yet, their criticisms can sometimes cause election losers'
confidence in election credibility to plummet even in broadly fair elections. We also find that election losers are more likely than winners to
believe that meddling occurred. Across all cases, election winners have
extremely high levels of trust in elections, which information about
foreign meddling does not undermine.

   Although our finding that citizens respond to foreign actors in partisan ways may seem obvious to those who are familiar with the degree of polarization in American and comparative politics, several relevant strands of international relations (IR) research on the topic do not anticipate these diverging responses. On the one hand, most literature on foreign influences on elections explores their overall – that is, average – effects, including the policy and practitioner literature on foreign influences on elections. Though clearly important, such a focus fails to capture some of the dynamics that our conditional analysis reveals. For example, our finding that election winners do not downgrade their assessments of election credibility in response to information about foreign meddling means that politicians who allow or invite such interference may not be held accountable by their supporters, a point we analyze in more depth in the conclusion.

   On the other hand, a growing concern among IR scholars relates to the way in which citizens resist outside influences on domestic politics, especially in the areas of democracy and human rights. Such studies have found that the public resents external criticism of state policies,[2] which creates a political opportunity for enterprising domestic politicians to engage in repression in order to be seen as defying foreign actors. Our findings demonstrate that foreign interventions – *even blatant meddling in elections* – do not inevitably provoke a public backlash. Only some citizens view such interventions negatively; others tolerate or even welcome them. As we discuss in more detail later, these dynamics have important implications for policymakers' decisions about whether to invite foreign influences – and how to respond to them.

7.1 Defining Election Winners and Losers

Because people who take the time to vote are the most engaged in politics, this chapter focuses on winning and losing *voters* as opposed to nonvoters.[3] We do not expect nonvoters to engage in partisan-motivated reasoning to the same extent because they tend to be less

---

[2] Grossman, Manekin, and Margalit (2018); Gruffydd-Jones (2019); Snyder (2020).

[3] The literature on partisan differences in perceptions of election credibility typically focuses on voters for this reason. See, for example, Alvarez, Hall, and Llewellyn (2008, 756–757); Cantú and García-Ponce (2015, 6).

politically engaged and informed than voters.[4] They are also less likely to have strong prior beliefs about election integrity since they do not follow politics as closely.

For voters, we further distinguish theoretically between the *main* election losers (e.g., Democratic Party voters in the 2016 US presidential election) and other election losers (e.g., voters for third-party candidate Jill Stein in the 2016 US presidential election). Although this distinction departs from some of the literature on this topic,[5] it is both conceptually merited and empirically justified here.

All four presidential elections we study were either de facto or de jure races between two main candidates; it is therefore relatively easy to identify voters associated with the winning and the main losing candidates. Tunisia (2014) and Georgia (2018) both held first-round elections involving numerous candidates and second-round contests between the two leading candidates, who were widely anticipated at the beginning of the election cycles. For the post-presidential surveys in both countries, our analysis focuses on winning and losing voters from the second round. We expect respondents who voted for the winning candidate to report greater trust in the election than those who voted for the losing candidate.

US presidential elections constitute a single round. Hillary Clinton (Democrat) and Donald Trump (Republican) were the main candidates in 2016, while Joe Biden (Democrat) and Donald Trump (Republican) were the main candidates in 2020. The vast majority of voters supported one of these two candidates, although third-party candidates also ran in both elections with no expectation of winning. A losing outcome could be perceived as a victory for third-party candidates if they out-performed expectations or influenced the overall election result. Thus, in the United States, we focus on winning and losing voters from the two main parties.

Deciding how to code winners and losers in legislative elections must take the electoral and party context into account. Our analysis is based on legislative elections in two cases: Tunisia (2014) and the United States (2018).[6] Tunisia's 2014 parliamentary election was

[4] Robertson (2017, 599).
[5] Anderson et al. (2005, 34–35).
[6] The 2016 and 2020 US elections were both presidential and legislative elections. However, since the main focus in a presidential election year is

anticipated to be a contest between Nidaa Tounes, the main secular party, and Ennahda, the country's only Islamist party.[7] Nidaa Tounes won the most seats, which was considered a victory. Ennahda received the second-most seats, but this result was characterized as a loss, as proclaimed in headlines such as "Islamist Party in Tunisia Concedes to Secularists" and "Tunisia's Islamists Down But Not Out After Election Defeat."[8] Other, smaller, losing parties fielded candidates but had not anticipated winning a majority. Ennahda was a realistic contender since it had won a plurality of seats in the Constituent Assembly that governed Tunisia between 2011 and 2014. Thus, the negative emotions associated with losing should have been more evident among Ennahda voters than the smaller parties' voters.

In the 2018 US Congressional election, the Democrats won a majority in the House of Representatives, but the Republicans expanded their Senate majority. Although Democrats taking control of the House was an important shift, the narrative that the election was a "wave" for Democrats only emerged over time as it became clear that the party had won several outstanding races in the House and Senate. Initially, many newspapers emphasized the mixed outcome, with headlines such as "Split Decision" in *The Wall Street Journal* and "Democrats Secure Control of the House; Republicans Build on Majority in Senate" in *The New York Times*.[9] Reflecting this tone, when we asked a subset of respondents in our post-election survey to describe the overall results of the election in an open-ended question, more than three times as many respondents emphasized the mixed result as emphasized the Democrats' victory in the House.[10] Thus, it is not possible to define a winner or loser at the national level. However, people may have experienced the emotions associated with voting for a winning or losing candidate in their district-level (House of Representatives) or state-level (Senate) elections.

---

usually the presidential outcome (and that was certainly the case in 2016 and 2020), we focus on the winner–loser dynamic in those races.

[7] See, for example, Tavana and Russell (2014, 8).

[8] Gall (2014); Markey and Amara (2014).

[9] Graham (2018). Another article written the day after the election began, "It wasn't necessarily the night of either party's dreams." See Cohn (2018).

[10] See the online appendix (www.cambridge.org/bushprather) for more information. As described in Chapter 3, this survey was conducted within seven days of the election.

Unlike the Tunisia survey, the US survey included questions designed to identify local winner–loser dynamics. We asked respondents whether the House and Senate candidates they voted for won or lost. We then coded voters as either winners (both candidates won) or losers (both candidates lost), and drop respondents who voted for one winner and one loser as well as those voting in states with no Senate election that year.[11] We use the resulting variable to assess whether supporting winning or losing local candidates affects beliefs about election credibility in the same way as supporting them nationally does. Almost one-third (29 percent) of the voters in our survey did not know the winner of one or both elections; we do not expect such individuals to be subject to local winner–loser dynamics.[12]

An important characteristic of how we define winning and losing voters is that winning and losing are co-determined with voting for a certain candidate or party, which makes it difficult to determine which dynamic has more influence on perceptions of election credibility. We address this problem in two ways. First, given the panel nature of our surveys, the same people are interviewed before and after the election. If a voter's beliefs about election credibility differ between the pre- and post-election surveys, then this dynamic suggests that winning or losing the election has affected their beliefs about election credibility. Second, we use an experiment with a hypothetical election scenario in Georgia to randomly vary the imagined winner of a future election, as detailed in Chapter 5. Briefly, we asked Georgians in 2018 to imagine the 2020 parliamentary election. We then experimentally varied which party won the most seats. In Chapter 5, we examined how an election meddling treatment decreased trust in elections. In this chapter, we first limit our analysis to the experiment's control group, which received no information about election meddling, but did hear that either the Georgian Dream (GD) or United National Movement (UNM) party won more seats, which allows us to experimentally identify the winner–loser gap. Later, we interact the winner treatment with respondents' partisan affiliation to examine the effect of winning or losing.

---

[11] Since US Senate terms are 6 years, one-third of the seats are contested in each election. Thus, some states would not have had a senator on the ballot in the 2018 election.

[12] To the extent that voters in our survey reported knowing the winner but were incorrect, it should mainly introduce noise into our analysis.

Although these analyses help differentiate between the effects of winning and losing vs. the effects of party identification in some cases, it remains very difficult to differentiate between the dynamics of information processing that reflect accuracy goals vs. directional goals. As discussed in Chapter 2, social scientists who study public opinion generally struggle to distinguish between these two dynamics. After all, it is not possible to directly observe individuals' cognitive processes. Moreover, many responses to new information are consistent with either accuracy or directional goals, depending on the researcher's assumptions about how individuals weigh the probability that different pieces of information are true.[13] For example, a winner–loser gap in perceptions of election credibility could reflect partisans' different assessments due to variation in either (1) their emotional responses to election outcomes or (2) their cool-headed responses to political information. We note instances in which the conditional effects of vote choice suggest a particular mechanism, but we generally do not seek to determine whether an accuracy or directional mechanism better fits the data. Instead, our goal is to understand how individual vote choice conditions the effects of foreign actors on perceptions of election credibility.

7.2 The Winner–Loser Gap in Trust

In this section, we examine evidence of a winner–loser gap in perceptions of election credibility (Table 7.1 summarizes the winners and losers in our three cases). Two noteworthy patterns emerge. First, winners have more confidence in elections than losers across all of our surveys. Although numerous studies have investigated citizens' perceptions of election credibility in the United States[14] and elsewhere,[15] to the best of our knowledge, our study is the first to establish the existence of a winner–loser gap in Georgia and Tunisia. Second, we find that winning or losing an election *changes* individuals' beliefs about election credibility. In the United States, for example, Trump voters were much more distrustful than Clinton voters before the

---

[13] Coppock (2021, Ch. 7).
[14] For example, Alvarez, Hall, and Llewellyn (2008); Beaulieu (2014b); Sances and Stewart (2015); Norris, Cameron, and Wynter (2018).
[15] For example, Anderson et al. (2005); Moehler (2009); Cantú and García-Ponce (2015); Robertson (2017); Wellman, Hyde, and Hall (2017).

Table 7.1 *Summary of election winners and losers in our study*

Country	Year	Election	Winner	Main Loser
Tunisia	2014	Legislative	Nidaa Tounes	Ennahda
Tunisia	2014	Presidential runoff	Beji Caid Essebsi	Moncef Marzouki
United States	2016	Presidential	Donald Trump	Hillary Clinton
United States	2018	Legislative	Ambiguous nationally	Ambiguous nationally
United States	2020	Presidential	Joe Biden	Donald Trump
Georgia	2018	Presidential runoff	Salome Zourabichvili	Grigol Vashadze
Georgia	2020*	Legislative	Assigned randomly	Assigned randomly

Note: The * denotes that this refers to a hypothetical future election in Georgia as described in our experiment in the 2018 post-second-round presidential election survey.

2016 election and much more trusting afterwards. In 2020, Biden and Trump voters had similar levels of confidence in the election before it took place, but afterwards, Biden voters had much more trust in the results than Trump voters. Our observational and experimental data in Georgia exhibit similar patterns.

We begin by examining the winner–loser gap in election credibility in all three cases. We use ordinary least squares (OLS) regression models that regress our standard measure of election credibility (which ranges from 0 to 2, as described in Chapter 3) on an indicator for whether an individual supported the party or candidate that ultimately won or lost the election. These models also include control variables to account for other factors that could influence both vote choice and perceptions of election credibility.[16] We only examine voters in the control group

---

[16] These variables include the respondent's age, educational attainment, employment status, level of political interest, political knowledge, reported knowledge about election observers, and sex. In the United States and Georgia, the controls also included the respondent's race or ethnicity, whereas in Tunisia (a more homogenous society), they also included geographic location. We use this standard set of control variables throughout this chapter. A table containing the full analysis is in the online appendix (www.cambridge.org/bushprather).

in the surveys to avoid including responses about election credibility that may have been influenced by information about monitoring or meddling.

In all of our post-election surveys, we expected voting for the winning candidate or party to be positively correlated with perceptions of election credibility. And indeed, we find a significant winner–loser gap in almost every post-election case (see Figure 7.1). With the exception of the US 2018 survey, which concerned an election for which there was no clear national winner, we find a strong and significant positive association between perceived credibility and voting for the winning candidate or party. This pattern therefore holds across multiple types of elections (legislative and presidential) and in countries with varying regime types (consolidated democracy, transitional democracy, and stable partial democracy). The winner–loser gap is substantial where it exists, ranging from 0.4 to 1.3 points on the 3-point scale. As would be expected, it is generally larger, and in most cases several times larger, than the treatment effects associated with monitoring and meddling that we identified in experiments described in earlier chapters.

Figure 7.1 contains two other notable results. The first is that in the three cases for which we have both pre- and post-election surveys (the United States in 2016 and 2020, and Georgia in 2018), the election triggered dramatic partisan changes in beliefs about election credibility. This change is especially stark for the US 2016 election. In the survey fielded just before the 2016 election, Trump voters (i.e., the eventual election winners) were much *less* likely to think the election would be credible than Clinton voters (i.e., the eventual election losers). After the election, the pattern reversed: Trump voters were *more* likely than Clinton voters to believe the election was credible. One explanation for the pre-election pattern is that Trump consistently warned his supporters of the likelihood of voter fraud during the campaign.[17] Another possible explanation, which is likely related to Trump's pre-election warnings about voter fraud, is that many pre-election polls suggested that Clinton would win, which could have cultivated a pre-election winner–loser mentality. While not as stark, the results from 2020 also show that the election represents an inflection point in partisan differences in electoral trust. Before the election, Trump and Biden voters had similar levels of trust; the winner–loser gap emerged afterwards.

---

[17] Gabriel (2016).

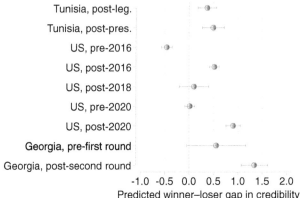

Figure 7.1 The winner–loser gap in perceived credibility
Note: This figure displays point estimates with 95 percent confidence intervals. All predictions are based on OLS models that contain control variables (see discussion in main text). The outcome variable is perceived credibility and uses the standardized measure, which ranges from 0 to 2. The sample size is small in some models because we restrict the sample to voters for the main winning and losing candidates or parties and to the control group in any experiments concerning election meddling or monitoring, which generates fairly large standard errors in some cases. $N = 84$ (Tunisia, post-legislative), 119 (Tunisia, post-presidential), 334 (US, pre-2016), 364 (US, post-2016), 81 (US, post-2018), 342 (US, pre-2020), 189 (US, post-2020), 27 (Georgia, pre-first round), and 95 (Georgia, post-second round).

In Georgia, we also detect a difference in perceptions of election credibility before and after the election. Voters who supported the eventual winner, Salome Zourabichvili, reported more trust than those who supported the main loser, Grigol Vashadze, in both surveys.[18] However, the winner–loser gap is more than twice as large in the post-election survey than in the pre-election survey.[19] Whereas the gap is

---

[18] Though nominally independent, Zourabichvili was supported by the GD party, which held a majority in the Georgian parliament in 2018 and was the party of the outgoing president, Giorgi Margvelashvili. Because GD was the ruling party and had won these previous elections, its voters likely had more faith in the electoral system to begin with.

[19] The precision of our estimate also improves, as the statistical significance shifts from $p = 0.069$ to $p < 0.001$. The sample size for the Georgia pre-election survey is quite small because most people had not made up their minds or would not tell us who they intended to vote for, and because our focus in this

around 0.6 points on our 3-point scale in the pre-election survey, it is around 1.3 points in the post-election survey, which is the largest gap we observe in Figure 7.1. This widening gap is consistent with the emotional highs and lows that would be predicted for supporters of Georgia's two presidential candidates after the election outcome became known, as well as a changing information environment.

The second noteworthy finding reported in Figure 7.1 is that there was not a clear winner–loser gap after the 2018 US midterm election. As noted earlier, this election is a somewhat unusual case in our study because the Democratic Party won a majority in the House of Representatives and the Republican Party expanded its majority in the Senate. To reflect this ambiguity, we define *Winners* in Figure 7.1 with the local-level measure based on whether the respondent's candidates for the House *and* Senate won or lost. The results shown in Figure 7.1 demonstrate that there was no significant relationship between one's candidates winning at the local level and perceptions of election credibility.

As an alternative, we consider the relationship between partisanship and perceptions of election credibility in the United States over the same period (see Figure 7.2).[20] The figure illustrates that prior to the election, Democrats had lower levels of trust in the election than Republicans. Yet afterwards, partisanship was not clearly related to beliefs about election credibility. This post-election pattern is precisely what we would expect to find if individuals' directional goals were mixed due to an ambiguous election result. On the one hand, people would like to believe the election was credible since their party controls one chamber of the legislature. On the other hand, they would also like to believe the election was *not* credible, since their party did not gain control of the other chamber. It is also possible that the pattern shown in Figure 7.2 reveals a more rational form of information updating. Democrats may have been more distrustful than Republicans prior to the election due to their lingering concerns about the integrity

---

analysis is on respondents in the experimental control group. The positive coefficient for *Winners* in the pre-election regression would likely be estimated with a great deal of confidence if we had a larger sample, similar to the post-election regression.

[20] This analysis includes the same variables, measured in the same way, as that reported in Figure 7.1. A table containing this analysis is in the online appendix (www.cambridge.org/bushprather).

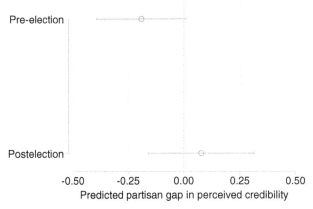

Figure 7.2 Partisanship and perceived credibility in the United States, 2018
Note: This figure shows point estimates with 95 percent confidence intervals.
All predictions are based on OLS models that contain control variables (see
discussion in main text). The outcome variable is perceived credibility and
uses the standardized measure, which ranges from 0 to 2. *Democrat* is coded
1 for voters who identify as Democrat and 0 for voters who identify as Republican, meaning that positive values in this figure indicate that Democrats have
more trust than Republicans. The sample is restricted to the control group
in any experiments concerning election meddling or monitoring. $N = 170$
(pre-election) and 138 (postelection).

of the 2016 election, which we discuss later. If this were the case, then
the ambiguous election outcome in 2018 (which was broadly consistent with our pre-election survey) may have caused accuracy-motivated
Democrats to update their beliefs about election credibility in a positive
direction, indicating that they were reassured that foreign meddling
had not undermined the contest.

The reason why we observe a partisan shift in Figure 7.2 but no
winner–loser gap in the same election (2018) in Figure 7.1 may be
because national-level results matter more to American voters. We
asked people whether they cared more about their party winning the
House (Senate) or winning the election in their district (state). For both
the House and Senate, about twice as many respondents cared more
about the national result than the district or state result.

As discussed earlier, the disadvantage of using observational data to
explore the winner–loser gap is that winning and losing are always co-
determined with party. For example, what if supporters of the winning
party also happen to trust democratic institutions more to begin with?

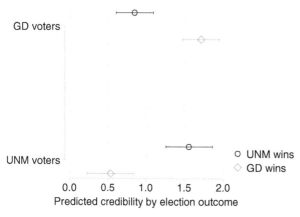

Figure 7.3 The effect of winning on perceived credibility in Georgia, hypothetical election, post-second-round presidential election survey
Note: This figure shows point estimates with 95 percent confidence intervals. All predictions are based on OLS models that contain control variables (see discussion in main text). The outcome variable is perceived credibility and uses the standardized measure, which ranges from 0 to 2. The sample is limited to the control group of the hypothetical meddling experiment. Vote choice is based on reported actual vote choice in the 2018 presidential election. $N = 152$.

There are two ways to overcome this issue. The first is to use observational data over time as winners and losers shift, as we just did in the 2018 US election survey. The second approach is to use a hypothetical scenario and randomly assign respondents to imagine their party winning or losing, as we did in the post-second-round survey in Georgia. This experiment randomized information about whether GD or UNM won the hypothetical 2020 legislative election; it confirms the causal effect of winning or losing on perceptions of election credibility. When we analyze this experiment, we include our standard set of control variables (discussed earlier) to account for the other factors that potentially shape both vote choice and perceptions of election credibility.

Figure 7.3 shows that both GD and UNM voters were significantly more likely to believe the election was credible if their party was described as winning. The gap is substantial: UNM voters had around 1 point more electoral trust on the 3-point scale when their party won. The treatment effect is similar among GD voters. Since voters from both parties reacted to the treatment in the same way, we can be confident that the winner–loser effect is independent of partisanship at least in Georgia.

Yet can foreign actors ever alter individuals' vote choices? For example, can learning negative information about election integrity from monitors and meddlers cause people to change who they vote for? We can test this proposition using our data from Tunisia, since our experiment about election observers' (EOs') reports on the parliamentary election was contained in a survey prior to the presidential election held 2 months later. In this survey, we queried respondents about their intended presidential vote choice after the EO report experiment. Although we found in Chapter 4 that hearing about positive vs. negative reports caused a modest shift in Tunisians' perceptions of election credibility, there is no evidence that doing so caused them to shift their likelihood to vote for Essebsi vs. Marzouki in the presidential election 2 months later.[21]

7.3 Vote Choice and Responses to Monitors' Reports

In all the post-election surveys in which we would expect to find evidence of a winner–loser gap in perceptions of election credibility, we found it. Next, we examine how individuals responded to information from election monitors that could have reinforced or challenged their pre-existing beliefs about the credibility of elections. We focus on monitors' positive and negative reports rather than their presence. The effects of monitors' reports are more likely to be conditional on vote choice given that they can be explicitly positive and/or negative in content.

We re-examine the experiments from Chapter 4 that were fielded in four post-election surveys: Tunisia in 2014, the United States in 2016, the United States in 2020, and Georgia in 2018. These surveys included experiments that randomized whether individuals received information about monitors' positive or negative evaluations of elections. Recall that we found in Chapter 4 that monitors' positive reports significantly increased perceptions of election credibility relative to negative reports in Tunisia and the United States, although the substantive effect was fairly modest. By contrast, if anything, positive reports were associated with *less* trust in Georgia.

---

[21] The estimated difference in probability of voting for Essebsi vs. Marzouki was 3 percent ($p = 0.598$).

Figure 7.4 displays the average treatment effects (ATEs) for winners and losers.[22] The ATEs measure the difference in perceived credibility between respondents in the positive and negative reports treatment groups, respectively, and those in the control group, who did not receive any information about EO reports. Our results are consistent across the three cases: Winners did not update their beliefs about election credibility in response to the information in election monitors' reports in any of the surveys. Losers *did* update, but never in a positive direction. These findings complicate the conventional wisdom about election monitoring, which focuses on observers' overall effects.

We reach these conclusions through regression analysis. To assess the conditional relationship between election monitoring reports, vote choice, and perceptions of election credibility, we use OLS regression models that interact vote choice with indicators for assignment to the monitoring treatments.[23] These models include the same control variables used in our analysis of the effect of vote choice on perceived credibility (as shown in Figure 7.1) since vote choice is observed and not randomly assigned. We focus on the main election winners and losers, since they are the most relevant theoretically, as described earlier; the online appendix (www.cambridge.org/bushprather) contains details about the effects of reports on secondary election losers and nonvoters, which tend to be more limited.

In Tunisia, the main losers of the legislative election were voters for Ennahda, the Islamist party. Ennahda supporters, who had less trust in the election to begin with, did not update their perceptions of election credibility in response to the positive reports in the post-legislative election survey. However, they were more swayed by the negative reports relative to both the control group and the positive reports treatment group. Negative reports were considerably more likely to reduce losers' perceptions of election credibility than positive reports: around 16 percent. These patterns are potentially consistent with motivated

---

[22] Our analysis includes the same set of control variables that we use throughout the chapter; see the discussion around Figure 7.1. In the online appendix (www.cambridge.org/bushprather), we also show the predicted levels of election credibility for election winners and losers in the positive and negative EO reports treatments, as well as tables containing the full analysis.

[23] A table in the online appendix (www.cambridge.org/bushprather) contains the full regression results.

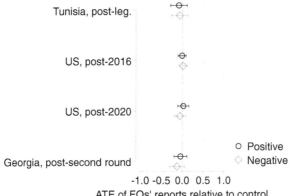

(a) Election winners

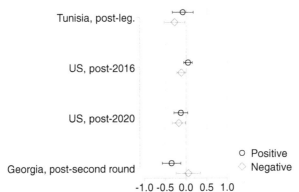

(b) Election losers

Figure 7.4 The effect of monitors' reports on perceived credibility, by vote choice

Note: This figure shows the ATEs for the positive and negative report treatments relative to control with 95 percent confidence intervals. All predictions are based on OLS models that contain control variables (see discussion in main text). The outcome variable is perceived credibility and uses the standardized measure, which ranges from 0 to 2. For definitions of election winners and losers, see Table 7.1. For the EO reports experiments overall, $N = 762$ (Tunisia, post-legislative), 676 (US, post-2016), 298 (US, post-2020), and 477 (Georgia, post-second round).

reasoning, since positive reports could contradict losers' directional goals of questioning the election's integrity, whereas negative reports could reinforce those goals. At the same time, election losers may have had less certain prior beliefs that the election was credible, which would be more consistent with accuracy-driven information updating.

A similar pattern emerged in the United States after the 2016 and 2020 presidential elections.[24] Similar to Tunisia, winners in these elections (i.e., Trump voters (2016) and Biden voters (2020)) had incredibly high levels of confidence in the election afterwards, and EO reports had no effect on their beliefs about election credibility. The main losers (i.e., Clinton voters (2016) and Trump voters (2020)) had significantly less trust in the election. Similar to Tunisia, the positive reports did not improve US respondents' confidence in the election, and in 2020 even slightly diminished it, whereas the negative reports significantly lowered losers' trust relative to the control group.[25] The decrease in perceived credibility for Clinton voters who heard the negative reports instead of the positive reports was meaningful, at about 13 percent. There was little difference between Trump voters in 2020 who heard positive vs. negative reports. Both reports the credibility of the election, but only the negative reports treatment was significantly different from the control.

In the post-second-round election survey in Georgia, as expected and similar to the other cases, voters for the winning candidate, Salome Zourabichvili, had high levels of confidence in the election. They did not update their perceptions of election credibility in response to monitors' reports. Moreover, losers (i.e., supporters of Grigol Vashadze) were not reassured by monitors' positive reports; in fact, their confidence in the election decreased significantly relative to the control when they learned of monitors' positive evaluations. Meanwhile, and unlike the previous two cases, negative reports did *not* reduce losers'

---

[24] Although our 2018 US survey also included an experiment about election monitors (described in Chapter 4), we do not use it to test for conditional effects by vote choice since we showed earlier that Americans had ambiguous directional goals around the 2018 midterm election.

[25] As Chapter 4 noted, the Organization for Security and Co-operation in Europe reports referenced in our negative treatment were somewhat critical of voter access issues in a way that was aligned with Democrats' concerns about election integrity in 2016. It is possible that this content made Clinton voters especially receptive to the information in the negative reports.

confidence in the election – perhaps due to Georgians' general distrust of international monitors, as discussed in Chapter 4.

This pattern may be evidence of a backlash or backfire effect whereby individuals' beliefs become more extreme when they are exposed to contradictory new information, which is not a pattern revealed in the other cases.[26] Prior studies suggest that strong partisans are the most prone to such backlash reactions. Following that logic, we use a pre-treatment question about satisfaction with the UNM party to explore whether UNM voters who were very or somewhat satisfied with the party were more likely to respond negatively to the monitoring treatment. They were not.[27]

What else might explain election losers' negative responses to monitors' positive reports? Chapter 4 provided evidence against a nationalist backlash. Another possibility we consider is that the positive reports caused election losers to question the integrity of international monitors. We find some evidence of this dynamic. Although both GD and UNM voters perceived international monitors as significantly less capable after hearing about their positive reports, the effect size was significantly larger among UNM voters.[28] Thus, we find further support for the idea (which we explore in more depth in Chapter 6) that individuals' perceptions of foreign actors shape their responses to electoral interventions from abroad. We emphasize that this negative partisan response to positive monitor reports only occurred in Georgia, which held the least democratic elections in our study. It is plausible that the negative response to foreign praise of a flawed election – especially among election losers – could apply in other settings.

Overall, the results depicted in Figure 7.4 confirm that individual vote choice is an important moderator of the effects of EO reports. The mechanism driving this pattern is more ambiguous. It could be the case that directionally motivated reasoning shapes how individuals process

---

[26] Nyhan and Reifler (2010).
[27] Nearly one-fifth (19 percent) of Vashadze voters reported that they were very or somewhat unsatisfied with UNM. We find that the reports had a significant treatment effect on both strong ($p = 0.050$) and weak ($p = 0.027$) UNM voters, and the interaction between the treatment and party identification is at least marginally significant in both cases ($p = 0.108$ and $p = 0.032$) despite the reduced sample size.
[28] The p-value for the interaction between vote choice and the positive reports treatment is 0.030.

information from international election monitors. Indeed, the manner in which election losers updated is consistent with directional updating: Positive reports from international monitors did not increase their trust (and in one case, decreased it), while negative reports decreased trust in two of the three cases. Yet, motivated reasoning would also predict that election winners would respond to positive reports since such information is consistent with both their partisan goals and their desire to view election integrity in a good light. In general, however, we did not find that positive reports increased credibility. It is possible that what social scientists term "ceiling effects" were at play: election winners may have already perceived elections to be so credible that there was no room for the EO report treatments to significantly enhance those perceptions. For example, three-quarters (75 percent) of the Tunisian respondents said they had "some" or "a lot" of trust in the parliamentary election results and thought it was "somewhat likely" or "very likely" that they reflected the will of the people.

The patterns we observe could also be consistent with an updating model that assumes individuals are motivated by accuracy – rather than partisan – goals. For example, election losers may have believed the elections we studied were somewhat credible but were not very certain about that. In such a scenario, respondents who voted for a losing party or candidate would be expected to update in response to negative (but not positive) reports.

While we cannot rule out this interpretation, our finding that election losers responded more than election winners to negative reports does not seem to be explained by losers being less certain. We can compare winners' and losers' post-election certainty about election credibility in the 2016 US and 2018 Georgia surveys. We focus on respondents in the control groups, who were not provided any information about monitors or meddlers. In both countries, losers and winners had very high levels of certainty after the elections. In the United States, 91 percent of the main losers (Clinton voters) were "somewhat" or "very" certain of their beliefs about election credibility, compared to 93 percent of the winners (Trump voters). In Georgia, at least 98 percent of both winners and losers were "somewhat" or "very" certain about their beliefs in election credibility after the presidential runoff. Given the high levels of certainty in both cases, we think it is unlikely that the concentration of effects among losers is due to greater uncertainty in their prior beliefs about election credibility.

7.4 Vote Choice and Responses to Meddling

Having established that vote choice conditions how individuals process information from monitors, we now consider how it conditions responses to meddling. We replicate the analysis from Section 7.3 using the meddling experiments included in the 2018 post-election surveys in the United States and Georgia and the 2020 post-election survey in the United States. We find that, contrary to our expectations, vote choice did *not* moderate the effect of meddling on perceived credibility in the United States in either survey, but it did in Georgia. As we discuss later, there are several reasons why the design of our studies in the United States and the electoral context cannot provide conclusive evidence that vote choice does not condition the effect of meddling on perceived credibility.

We then explore other ways in which vote choice may affect responses to foreign meddling and find significant evidence that winning and losing shaped respondents' beliefs about the existence and success of meddling.

7.4.1 Conditioning the Effect of Meddling Treatments

In this section, we re-examine the postelection experiments about meddling from Chapter 5 that were fielded after the 2018 and 2020 US elections and the 2018 Georgian election. Recall from that chapter that information about the *absence* of Russian meddling in these US elections increased electoral trust among Americans, although information about the occurrence of meddling did not have a clear effect. In Georgia, information about meddling in a hypothetical future election significantly decreased trust. Since each country had a slightly different experimental design, we discuss the results separately.

In the United States, since there was no clear national winner in the 2018 election we did not find evidence of a winner–loser gap using the local measure of winning and losing. There were, however, partisan differences in perceptions of election credibility (recall Figure 7.2). In our analyses of vote choice, we therefore examine party identification as the conditioning variable. This measurement choice likely approximates how meddling would have occurred in the 2018 election, as the practice in a legislative election usually targets parties rather than specific candidates in local elections. For the 2020 election, we examine the differences in the effects of meddling across Biden and Trump voters.

Figure 7.5 displays the results from 2018 and plots the predicted levels of election credibility from OLS models that regress election credibility on the treatment indicator, party identification, the interaction between treatment and party identification, and our standard set of control variables introduced in the analysis of Figure 7.1. The results indicate that neither the "meddling" treatment (which told respondents about Russia's efforts to spread misinformation on social media) nor the "no meddling" treatment (which told respondents Russia's efforts were not as widespread as in 2016) clearly affected Democratic and Republican voters' beliefs about the credibility of the election, although the latter treatment effect trends positive for *both* Democrat and Republican voters.[29] This lack of clear directional updating is potentially consistent with the logic of motivated reasoning, since Democratic and Republican voters had ambiguous directional goals vis-á-vis the 2018 election results. Given the lack of a clear winner–loser dynamic, as well as the lower salience of election meddling in 2018, the conditions were arguably not ripe for motivated reasoning in response to our meddling treatment. At the same time, the limited effect of vote choice as a moderator may reflect relatively strong prior beliefs about election credibility and meddling, such that our modest treatments were not sufficient to cause accuracy-driven updating.

The results displayed in Figure 7.6 demonstrate that the treatments have small and insignificant effects on the credibility of the 2020 election for Biden and Trump voters. Biden voters do not update their beliefs about the credibility of the election in response to new information about meddling in either the full sample or the attentive sample. The largest effect is among Trump voters: The meddling treatment did decrease trust in the election somewhat, but the treatment effect is not statistically significant. There are at least two reasons for these null results. The first is that, as we have discussed elsewhere, foreign meddling was not promoted by government intelligence agencies as

---

[29] The p-values are 0.039 and 0.103, respectively, for the attentive sample. Chapter 5 discusses how we define the attentive sample and the advantages and disadvantages of restricting the sample in this way. The online appendix (www .cambridge.org/bushprather) contains the full results.

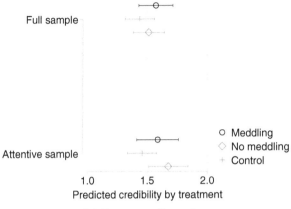

(a) Democratic voters

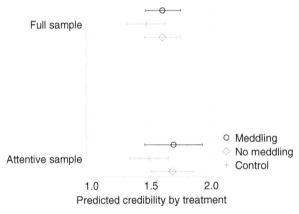

(b) Republican voters

Figure 7.5 Perceived credibility of the 2018 US election, by meddling treatment and vote choice, post-election survey

Note: This figure shows point estimates with 95 percent confidence intervals. All predictions are based on OLS models that contain control variables (see discussion in main text). The outcome variable is perceived credibility and uses the standardized measure, which ranges from 0 to 2. For the meddling experiment overall, $N = 629$ (full sample) and 472 (attentive sample).

a significant concern after the election when this survey was fielded. The primary narrative that emerged was related to fraud by domestic actors. Thus, it is possible that our foreign meddling treatment did not resonate with Trump voters in the way that it might have with Democrats after the 2016 and 2018 elections. A second, related, reason

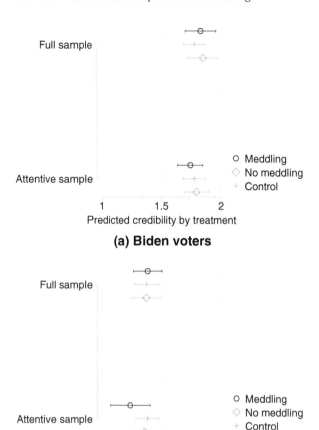

(a) **Biden voters**

(b) **Trump voters**

Figure 7.6 Perceived credibility in the United States, by meddling treatment and vote choice, 2020, post-election survey
Note: This figure shows point estimates with 95 percent confidence intervals. All predictions are based on OLS models that contain control variables (see discussion in main text). The outcome variable is perceived credibility and uses the standardized measure, which ranges from 0 to 2. For the meddling experiment overall, $N = 498$ (full sample) and 370 (attentive sample).

is that the meddling mentioned in our survey was still tied to Russia and still likely believed to benefit Trump voters. Thus, Trump voters may not have reacted as negatively to information about Russian meddling as Biden voters would have (if they had lost), given that Russia appeared to have intervened on Trump's behalf.

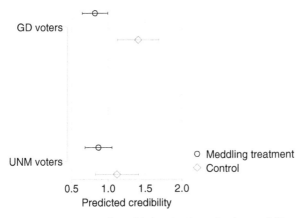

Figure 7.7 Perceived credibility in Georgia, by meddling treatment and vote choice, post-second-round presidential election survey
Note: This figure is based on an OLS model and contains control variables (see discussion in main text). The outcome variable is perceived credibility and uses the standardized measure, which ranges from 0 to 2. For the overall experiment, $N = 317$.

In Georgia, we conducted a hypothetical vignette experiment in the post-second-round presidential election survey in which a foreign country (Russia) meddled on behalf of GD in a future legislative election. As discussed in Chapter 5, the experimental design was based on Tomz and Weeks' experiment on how meddling affects public attitudes in the United States.[30] Our experiment randomized the election winner as either of the country's two leading parties: GD or UNM. In Chapter 5, we found that meddling diminished trust in this hypothetical election and showed earlier in this chapter that supporting the victorious party in this election caused respondents from both parties to have significantly more trust in the election. Now, we consider whether vote choice also moderates the negative effect of the meddling treatment.

First, we regress perceived credibility on vote choice, an indicator of whether the respondent received the meddling treatment, and their interaction, and the same control variables included in the analysis presented in Figure 7.1.[31] As Figure 7.7 shows, the meddling treatment

---

[30] Tomz and Weeks (2020).
[31] The online appendix (www.cambridge.org/bushprather) contains tables with the full results.

tended to decrease trust for both GD and UNM voters. This effect is statistically significant ($p = 0.001$), and we find no evidence of a significant interaction between vote choice and the meddling treatment. Recall, however, that this analysis pools across conditions in which half of the UNM and GD voters are treated with information about their party winning and the other half with information about their party losing. Thus, we next examine the conditional effects of the winning and losing treatments.

For this analysis, we repeat our approach in Figure 7.7 but subset the data according to which party the experiment described as winning. This approach enables us to disentangle partisan vs. winner–loser dynamics in Georgia. Figure 7.8 shows that the meddling treatment's negative effect on election credibility is concentrated among election winners. When GD voters heard that their party won and that meddling had occurred, they were less trusting than when they heard nothing about meddling. The effect is substantial, as GD voters' perceptions of election credibility decreased by around 38 percent on our scale. Similarly, when UNM voters heard that their party won and that meddling had occurred (in favor of the rival party, GD), they also had less trust (about 28 percent less). This pattern is intriguing, since we found that monitors' reports only significantly affected election *losers'* trust; here, meddling affected the *winners'* perceptions of election integrity.

One way of thinking about this finding is that losers' trust was already so low that negative information could not cause it to decline further. Put differently, and in much the same way that ceiling effects may have prevented us from identifying an effect of monitors' positive reports among election winners in Tunisia and the United States, floor effects may have prevented us from identifying an effect of meddling among election losers in Georgia.

This finding also seems to cut against a motivated reasoning interpretation, which suggests that election winners' directional goals would cause them to discount negative information about election credibility, or even double down on their pre-existing belief in response to new information that suggested this original belief was wrong. Instead, accuracy-driven respondents in Georgia who were somewhat uncertain about election credibility may have downgraded their assessments of the election's validity when they learned that meddling had occurred. Accuracy goals may have outweighed directional goals in

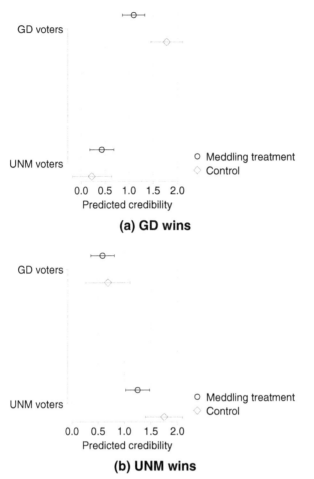

(a) GD wins

(b) UNM wins

Figure 7.8 Perceived credibility in Georgia, by party winner, post-second-round presidential election survey
Note: This figure is based on an OLS model and contains control variables (see discussion in main text). The outcome variable is perceived credibility and uses the standardized measure, which ranges from 0 to 2. $N = 151$ (GD wins) and 166 (UNM wins).

this experiment due to its hypothetical nature.[32] We asked respondents to imagine their opinions if meddling occurred in a future election. Motivated reasoning may be more likely in real elections when emotions are stronger.

[32] Tomz and Weeks (2020), however, found some evidence of directional reasoning when they used a similar design in the United States.

In summary, we found evidence that vote choice conditioned the effect of meddling in one of our cases, Georgia. The negative effects of meddling were clearest in the hypothetical experiment for GD voters when GD was described as winning, although UNM voters also reported a loss in trust in the election when UNM was described as winning. In the United States, we did not find such effects in our 2018 post-election survey, although there are at least two reasons why it might have been quite a difficult case for finding significant effects. First, given the saturation of information about Russian meddling in the two years before the election, Americans' prior beliefs about foreign actors and election credibility may have been relatively firm by the time of our study and thus difficult to alter via our experimental treatments. Second, the 2018 election did not have a clear national winner, which may have discouraged directional updating that can occur based on winner–loser status. The 2020 US election did have a clear winner, but the losers' post-election concerns focused more on domestic sources of election fraud than foreign actors.

7.4.2 *Vote Choice and Perceptions of Meddlers*

Because meddling is often covert and difficult to observe, it is plausible that members of the public will hold divergent views about it. Partisans may view meddlers' capabilities in distinct ways. Moreover, even if meddling is exposed, it may be unclear whether foreign assistance actually affected the election outcome. Chapter 6 established that perceptions of meddlers' capabilities are key to their effects on credibility; here, we consider how vote choice may affect those perceptions.

Winners may be more likely to be exposed to information that minimizes the extent or impact of meddling, and their directional goals may also affect how they react to such information; for instance, it could cause them to perceive foreign interference as inconsequential to the eventual outcome. Public officials' reactions to Russian meddling in the United States in 2016 contain evidence of this dynamic. Whereas Democrats were open to the possibility that Russian meddling swung the election in Trump's favor, Republican Paul Ryan, former speaker of the House of Representatives, acknowledged meddling but said, "It is also clear... it didn't have a material effect on our elections."[33]

---

[33] Economist (2018a, 35).

We use evidence from our surveys in three ways to shed light on this dynamic. First, we examine whether election winners were less likely than losers to believe election meddling had occurred. Second, using data from the United States, we analyze rates of passing an attention check related to our Russian meddling treatment to determine whether individuals were more likely to ignore information about meddling that was incongruent with their partisan commitments. Finally, our surveys explore perceptions of meddlers' capabilities to determine whether winners perceived meddlers as less capable than losers. In general, we find evidence of partisan differences across all three tests.

Beliefs about Negative Foreign Influence

To begin, we explore partisan differences in responses to questions about foreign influences. Recall from Chapter 5 that we asked a common question in all of our surveys about perceptions of foreign influence: "To what extent do you think other countries will/did influence the results of the [description] election?" For respondents who said they perceived at least some influence, we then asked, "Do you think this influence will be/was primarily positive, negative, or both positive and negative?" Although perceived negative influence is an admittedly blunt indicator of election meddling, we consider respondents who perceived at least some negative influence to be the most likely to have perceived at least some foreign meddling.

As explained in Chapter 2, we expect election losers to perceive more foreign meddling than winners. To test that expectation, we create a variable that takes a value of 1 if the respondent perceived as least some negative influence, and 0 otherwise.[34] We regress this variable on the individual's vote choice, operationalized in the same way as described earlier, and use logistic regressions. We also include the same control variables from our earlier analyses in this chapter since they are plausibly related to both vote choice and perceptions of foreign influence. This analysis focuses on the post-election surveys in Tunisia and the United States (in 2016 and 2020, the elections with clear winner–loser dynamics) since we did not ask the question about perceptions of foreign influence in the post-election survey in Georgia.

---

[34] A score of 0 encompasses respondents who did not perceive at least some foreign influence as well as those who perceived some influence but thought it was more positive.

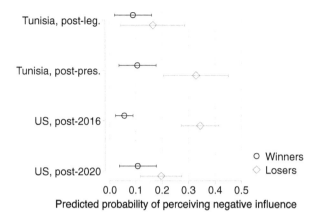

Figure 7.9 Perceived negative foreign influence, winners vs. losers, Tunisia and the United States (2016 and 2020)
Note: This figure shows predicted probabilities with 95 percent confidence intervals. All predictions are based on logit models that contain control variables (see discussion in main text). $N = 86$ (Tunisia, post-legislative), 120 (Tunisia, postpresidential), 364 (US 2016, postpresidential), and 196 (US 2020, post-presidential).

Figure 7.9 presents the results of our analysis, which reveal that election winners perceived less foreign influence than election losers in all four cases; this difference is statistically significant after the presidential elections in both Tunisia and the United States. Essebsi voters (the winners) had only an 11 percent probability of perceiving at least some negative foreign influence in the presidential election, compared to 33 percent of Marzouki voters (the losers). The winner–loser gap in perceptions of meddling is stark after the 2016 US election, but less pronounced after the 2020 election. In 2016, Trump voters had only a 6 percent chance of perceiving at least some negative influence, despite credible reports of Russian meddling. By contrast, Clinton voters had a 34 percent chance of perceiving such influence. While the winner–loser gap in perceptions of negative foreign influence persisted after the 2020 election, it was less than 10 percentage points. Yet in 2020, supporters of the winner (Democrats) perceived less negative influence than the losers (Republicans). In other words, *the winner–loser gap in perceived negative foreign influence held even though the party of the winner flipped from 2016 to 2020.*

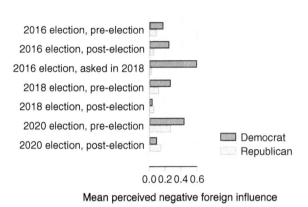

Figure 7.10 American perceptions of negative foreign influence over time
Note: The question about the 2016 election that was asked in 2018 appeared in the pre-election survey. This graph includes the same respondents across all surveys. $N = 129$.

Another interesting way to examine how directionally motivated reasoning shapes perceptions of foreign influence is to consider how Americans' views of meddling changed over the course of the 2016 election cycle. Since we interviewed the same people immediately before and after the 2016 election, we can measure how the election outcome changed their views about meddling. We also invited the 2016 survey participants to take follow-up surveys in 2018 and 2020, which were administered before and after the congressional and presidential elections in those years. As discussed in Chapter 5, the 2018 surveys asked respondents to reflect back on foreign influences in the 2016 election.

Figure 7.10 displays the changing opinions about foreign influences within the same group of Americans over time. It breaks these opinions down by self-identified party affiliation, which is strongly correlated with vote choice during the 2016 and 2020 presidential elections and is more relevant than winner–loser status for dynamics related to the 2018 midterm elections.[35] The figure demonstrates that Republicans and Democrats had similar views on election meddling on the eve of the 2016 election. In the days immediately following Trump's victory,

---

[35] We replicate Figure 7.10 in the online appendix (www.cambridge.org/bushprather) using Trump and Clinton voters and the differences are even starker.

however, these views became highly partisan: A large gap emerged between Democrats and Republicans with Democrats expressing significantly greater concerns about negative foreign influences. Polarization on this topic became even more intense over the next two years. When asked in 2018 to reflect back on the 2016 election, almost 60 percent of Democrats reported that at least some negative foreign influences occurred in 2016; the percentage of Republicans that believed that remained negligible.

Once again, our findings related to the 2018 midterm elections demonstrate that the split election results did not create an environment conducive to partisan differences on the topic of meddling. Whereas perceptions that foreign meddling had occurred in the 2018 election were still somewhat polarized, they were considerably less polarized than they were after the 2016 election. Although Democrats' serious concerns about foreign meddling persisted up until the 2018 election, they were largely allayed after the election, which did not have a clear national winner but did involve substantial Democratic gains. Interestingly, Republicans' concerns about foreign influence remained extremely low around the 2018 election, and much lower than in the period leading up to the 2016 election.

Concerns about negative foreign influence increased again around the 2020 election; Democrats were again more concerned about foreign meddling than Republicans. However, Republicans expressed more concern about meddling in 2020 than at any time in the previous four years. This likely reflects rhetoric from Republican elites as well as general concerns about the integrity of the vote leading up to the 2020 election in the context of large-scale changes to voting due to the COVID-19 pandemic. After Biden won the election, only 10 percent of the Democrats sampled reported concerns about negative foreign influence, while Republicans had slightly higher levels of concern. The overall relatively lower levels of concern after the 2020 election again likely reflect the fact that the dominant narrative in 2020 was about fraud perpetrated by domestic actors.

Attentiveness to Meddling

Next, we explore partisan differences in attentiveness to information about meddling. Directional goals may affect not only how individuals respond to new information but also which sources of information they pay attention to.[36] Motivated reasoning suggests that individuals should search for (and pay closer attention to) information that is consistent with their directional goals rather than information that conflicts with those goals.

We examine this phenomenon using data from the 2018 and 2020 post-election surveys in the United States, which included a meddling experiment described briefly earlier in this chapter and in more detail in Chapter 5. The logic of motivated reasoning suggests that Republicans may have ignored our treatment in the experiment about Russia's attempts to meddle in the midterms (the "meddling" treatment) but could have been more attentive to our treatment about the lack of widespread Russian meddling (the "no meddling" treatment). This urge to resist information about Russian meddling in 2018 was likely higher than in 2020 since the Republican candidate who the Russian meddling would have supported did not win. Immediately following the experimental vignette, we asked respondents questions designed to gauge their perceptions of election credibility as well as the hypothesized moderators.

A subsequent follow-up question was designed to assess the extent of motivated reasoning. One observable implication of the selective attention individuals might pay to information that is incongruent with their partisan priors is that they may be unable to remember incongruent information and more likely to remember congruent information.[37] Therefore, our question probed how closely the respondent paid attention to the information revealed to them in the treatment text. It asked: "Now recall the information we gave you earlier in the survey about the midterm elections. Did US government security officials say that there was no indication of Russian interference in the midterms or did they say that Russia attempted to interfere in the midterms by spreading lies on the internet?" Only around half of the respondents in 2018 and 2020 correctly recalled the information in their randomly assigned vignette, which suggests that considerable motivated reasoning could have occurred.

---

[36] Kertzer, Rathbun, and Rathbun (2020) refer to these two mechanisms as "motivated skepticism" and "selective attention," respectively.
[37] Jerit and Barabas (2010).

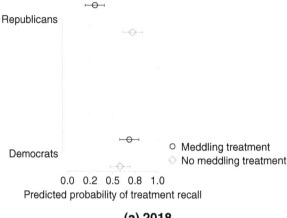

(a) 2018

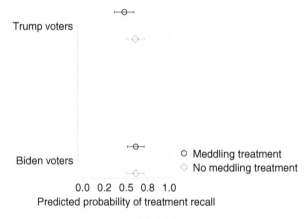

(b) 2020

Figure 7.11 Correct memory of meddling treatment by vote choice, United States, 2018 and 2020, post-election surveys
Note: This figure displays predicted probabilities with 95 percent confidence intervals. All predictions are based on logit models that contain control variables (see discussion in main text). The data come from the post-election surveys in 2018 and 2020. $N = 260$ and 300, respectively.

To test whether this was indeed the case, we regressed a variable indicating whether the respondent passed the attention check on their treatment assignment, the respondent's vote choice, and the interaction of the two. We also included our standard set of control variables, described earlier. Figure 7.11 plots the predicted probability of passing the attention check by treatment condition and vote choice.[38] It indicates notable partisan differences in attentiveness in 2018, but less substantial differences in 2020. Republican voters were significantly more likely to pass the "no meddling" attention check question than the "meddling" attention check, whereas Democratic voters were much more likely to pass the "meddling" attention check question than Republican voters, although there was not a significant difference in Democratic voters' probability of passing the attention check between the "meddling" and "no meddling" treatment conditions. Given recent Russian meddling in support of Republican presidential candidate Donald Trump, Republican voters' greater attention to the treatment when it was about the absence of meddling rather than its presence makes sense. Republicans seem to have been directionally motivated to reject information about meddling that might delegitimize their party's leader. While Trump voters were still less likely to pass the attention check if they were in the meddling treatment in 2020, the difference between those in the meddling vs. no meddling treatments was still significant but much smaller. This suggests there was potentially less motivated reasoning around Russian meddling in 2020 – four years after the 2016 Russian intervention.

This analysis suggests that individuals' directional motivations may affect their ability to retain information about meddling. In particular, respondents may have dismissed or ignored information that was inconsistent with their partisan beliefs about election meddling. When individuals engage in this type of information processing, they are less likely to update their political beliefs in response to new information.

Beliefs about Meddlers' Capabilities

Although, as noted earlier, we did not ask our standard question about foreign influence in the postelection survey in Georgia, we asked a related question that was designed to measure individual perceptions of meddlers' capabilities: "How likely do you think it is that Salome Zourabichvili won because of support from Russia?" (1 = "not likely at all" and 4 = "very likely"). If respondents believed Zourabichvili's victory was due to Russian meddling, this pattern would indicate that they thought the meddling was successful.

---

[38] The online appendix (www.cambridge.org/bushprather) reports the full results of this analysis.

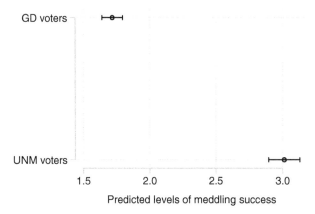

Figure 7.12 Georgian perceptions of successful Russian influence, 2018, post-second-round presidential election survey

Note: This figure displays point estimates with 95 percent confidence intervals. All predictions are based on an OLS model that contains control variables (see discussion in main text). The data come from the post-second-round presidential election survey. $N = 723$.

Russian meddling was the most appropriate case to consider when posing the question about meddling success. Although there was no credible public information about Russian meddling in support of Zourabichvili at the time of our surveys, as discussed in Chapters 3 and 5, there were fears prior to the election that GD was getting too close to Russia. Whereas Vashadze and his UNM party are vociferously pro-Western and pro-EU, Zourabichvili and GD have taken a more conciliatory (if not friendly) approach to Russia.[39] As such, Zourabichvili could have been considered Russia's preferred candidate.

We regressed the variable about perceived meddling success on respondents' treatment assignment, vote choice, and the interaction between the two. The regression included our standard set of control variables. Figure 7.12 presents the main results; the full results are available in the online appendix (www.cambridge.org/bushprather). The figure indicates that Zourabichvili voters were much less likely than Vashadze voters to perceive her success as due to Russian influence. This pattern suggests that Georgians' views about Russia's

[39] Economist (2018b).

capabilities as a meddler were shaped by whether their preferred candidate won the election. Again, this pattern is consistent with the idea that individuals engage in directional reasoning when assessing whether election meddling has occurred, although it could also reflect partisan differences in information sources.

7.5 Conclusion

This chapter demonstrated the powerful effect of voting for a winning or losing candidate on individuals' perceptions of election credibility. Winners were much more likely than losers to trust the results of all elections that had a clear winner and loser; their beliefs were not affected by information about either monitors or meddlers.

By contrast, foreign influences on elections can strongly affect the main election losers. Losers were not reassured by monitors' reports and were more likely to believe that foreign meddlers had influenced the election outcome. This result is normatively troubling, since democracy requires citizens who voted for the losing candidate to consent to being governed by the winner.[40] If election losers cannot be reassured by monitors when elections are clean and are more likely to believe foreign meddling is present even when there is little evidence that it has occurred, then these dynamics undermine one of the necessary conditions for democracy to survive.

Partisan differences in beliefs about (and responses to) meddling have important implications for policies designed to combat negative foreign influences, which must be initiated by election winners. Distressingly, if winners are more likely to dismiss information about foreign meddling and less likely to believe it has occurred, we would not expect them to take strong policy action to improve electoral security. As we have shown, they (and their supporters) are the least likely to acknowledge the existence or success of election meddling. This dynamic may explain, for example, why there was limited US policy action to respond to or enhance election security in the wake of the 2016 election, which we investigate further in Chapter 8.

---

[40] Anderson et al. (2005).

8 | *Elections with Foreign Influences*

Foreign influences on elections are newsworthy events. The media reports breathlessly when new information comes to light about foreign meddling. Monitoring missions, led by high-profile former politicians, hold televised press conferences to release their reports and inform the public about the praise and criticism of their country's election. Although some form of foreign influence on elections is the norm in contemporary politics, as we documented in Chapters 4 and 5, elections that have been influenced by foreign actors remain controversial.

This book has shown how foreign actors affect local perceptions of election credibility. They can, under the right conditions, influence local attitudes in significant ways. Yet, the conventional wisdom – that election monitors will enhance trust, whereas allegations of foreign meddling will diminish it – has limits. Important conditions related to the identity of the foreign actors, individual characteristics, and the electoral context moderate whether foreign actors have the anticipated effects. This chapter revisits the theory that we developed in Chapter 2 to explain the conditions under which foreign actors influence local trust in elections and reviews our findings from the empirical chapters (Chapters 4–7).

We then consider how our findings shed light on the strategic use of foreign interventions during elections on the part of both intervening and intervened-upon governments. For example, the effects we document in this book help us understand why countries invite various forms of foreign interventions into their elections, despite the encroachment on state sovereignty. We suggest that governments can strategically publicize foreign interventions that they anticipate will legitimize their rule without fear that such interventions (even election meddling) will alienate their supporters.

The chapter then examines how our theory might shed light on the effects of other types of foreign influences on domestic politics as well as the study's broader implications. We suggest that in forms of democracy promotion beyond monitoring, as well as peacekeeping and transnational human rights activism, foreign actors' effects on individuals are likely to depend on the characteristics of the actor, the individual, and the context. We propose ways in which future research can build on our findings to better understand the sources of credibility for the complex landscape of foreign actors seeking to influence domestic politics and the roles that foreign actors might play in triggering democratic backsliding and authoritarian resilience. Finally, we discuss the study's implications for policymakers and practitioners who seek to amplify high-quality information and combat misinformation related to election credibility.

8.1 Theory in Brief

In a credible election, people trust the results and believe the outcome reflects the will of the people. The starting point for our theory was the idea that individuals' perceptions of election credibility reflect two (sometimes conflicting) desires: to hold beliefs about election credibility that are (1) accurate and (2) consistent with their partisan commitments. The accuracy mechanism prompts people to rely on their personal experiences, the media, and other sources of information about elections, while the consistency mechanism prompts them to consider whether their preferred party won or lost the election.

Although both mechanisms can powerfully shape individuals' views about an election's credibility, voters still lack complete information, partly because it is difficult for them to personally observe every aspect of election quality. For instance, they only visit their own polling station (if that), and they cannot directly observe most aspects of the electoral cycle (e.g., voter registration, campaign finance, counting ballots), all of which could be subject to manipulation by politicians. Moreover, government officials have reasons to mislead the public about how fair the electoral playing field is. Candidates may pretend to be what Susan Hyde calls true democrats (committed to democracy and following the rules of the game) but actually be pseudo-democrats (secretly working to tilt the playing field in their favor).[1] Moreover, election losers have incentives to denounce fair elections.

---

[1] Hyde (2011).

Faced with these uncertainties and information asymmetries, foreign actors themselves as well as many scholars have argued that foreign influence can significantly affect local trust. The logic that we elucidate behind these arguments is that foreign actors provide information to the public about the electoral playing field and candidates. According to the conventional wisdom, election monitoring suggests to citizens that the electoral playing field is fair, whereas election meddling indicates it is not. These effects will occur, so the argument goes, because foreign interventions reveal information to the public about whether the candidates are true democrats, the quality of electoral institutions, or both.

Yet, we argued that the conventional wisdom fails to account for the dynamics that may lead citizens *not* to update in response to foreign interventions around elections. We draw on previous studies of public opinion to offer a unified "theory of the citizen" that takes into account both monitors' and meddlers' effects. Whereas the conventional wisdom offers observable implications about foreign actors' *average* effects on trust, our theory proposes more nuanced hypotheses that are conditional on three factors: (1) the identity of foreign actors, (2) individual characteristics, and (3) the electoral context. Before outlining the findings, we briefly review each factor in turn.

First, it is only when citizens believe foreign actors are able and willing to alter the electoral playing field that such outside influences will convey credible information to the public and cause citizens to re-evaluate their beliefs about election credibility. Therefore, individuals in the cases we studied responded to information only about some international monitors and some cases of foreign meddling – and not necessarily to the information that experts would consider to be the most reliable.

Second, citizens' characteristics – especially whether they supported the winning or losing candidate or party in the election – influence how receptive they are to the new information conveyed by foreign interventions around elections. Here, we return to the idea that both accuracy and consistency motivations influence the formation of beliefs about election credibility. In some cases, voters' prior views are influenced by the foreign actors or happen to coincide with the information provided by them. Election winners, for example, may already be so confident that an election was clean that they will not become more trusting when they learn that international observers have endorsed it. In other cases, citizens are motivated by partisan goals in their response to the information that foreign actors provide. For instance, election winners may be highly skeptical that foreign meddling has occurred because it would be inconsistent with their pre-existing partisan support for the winning party or candidate.

Third, the electoral environment determines whether there is sufficient uncertainty for foreign actors to influence citizens' beliefs. In highly certain environments, such as countries that have held fair (or unfair) elections over repeated cycles, the actions of foreign actors are unlikely to generate new insights into the electoral playing field. By contrast, when a country is holding a transitional election or some other type of election about which there is uncertainty, foreign actors are more salient.

Part of what makes our theory unique is that it does not emphasize the *foreignness* of influences on elections. Instead, the factors it identifies as most relevant – the perceived capabilities and biases of the information source, individuals' partisanship, and the electoral context – are the same ones we would expect to condition the effects of domestic sources of information about election credibility, such as media reports about election integrity. In this way, our theory contrasts with a prominent and growing perspective on the unintended negative consequences of international pressure related to human rights and related issues. Whereas that literature emphasizes how citizens' resistance to outside interference can generate a nationalist backlash,[2] we argue that various factors can lead the public to accept (if not welcome) foreign influences on elections – *even explicitly partisan and illegal involvement.*

8.2 Findings

We presented evidence from ten original surveys to test the predictions of our theoretical framework. These data enabled us to understand how information about monitoring and meddling affects perceptions of election credibility in general, and how these perceptions are influenced by characteristics of the intervener and the individual. Since our surveys were conducted in three countries with distinct regime types – a transitional democracy (Tunisia), a consolidated democracy

---

[2] For exemplars, see Gruffydd-Jones (2019); Terman (2019); Chaudhry (2021).

(the United States), and a partial democracy (Georgia) – we were further able to explore how the electoral environment shaped the impact of foreign actors. Although our survey evidence provided the core tests of the theory, we also drew on a variety of qualitative material identified through desk and field research, including news articles, election observer (EO) reports and manuals, intelligence reports, focus groups, and interviews with key informants (such as international and domestic election monitors, election management officials, and civil society organizations) to understand the nature of foreign influence in our case studies. When possible, we also drew on existing cross-national data to understand trends in foreign influences and perceptions of election credibility.[3] Table 8.1 summarizes our experimental findings, which we discuss in more detail in this section.

Challenging the conventional wisdom among foreign actors themselves as well as many scholars, information about international monitors' presence did not significantly increase perceptions of credibility on average (Chapter 4). We present evidence from Tunisia (though it failed to reach statistical significance) and the United States (in 2016, 2018, and 2020), however, that positive monitor reports increased trust more than negative reports. The effects were fairly modest in substantive terms. These limited effects of monitors cannot be explained by general skepticism of international observers, as we show that most global publics – including those in the countries we surveyed – have generally favorable views of them despite the criticism that they infringe on countries' sovereignty.

Similarly, information about the absence of meddling had ambiguous overall effects on perceptions of election credibility across our cases (Chapter 5). We show that there is substantial public concern about foreign meddling in many countries. Moreover, in our surveys, people who were concerned about foreign countries negatively influencing their elections tended to trust their elections less on average. Our experiments did not, however, find consistent evidence that priming people with information about foreign meddling decreased trust. Our clearest evidence of meddling's average effects came from an experiment in the United States in 2018 that primed people with

---

[3] These other datasets included the World Values Survey, National Elections Across Democracy and Autocracy dataset, and the Data on International Election Monitoring.

Table 8.1 *Summary of experimental findings*

	Variable	Prediction (Location Tested)	Findings
Average effects (conventional wisdom)	Monitors present	Increases credibility (Chapter 4)	Not supported
	Monitors' reports	Positive reports increase credibility more than negative reports (Chapter 4)	Mixed: supported in United States 2016, 2018, and 2020, but not supported in Tunisia or Georgia
	Meddling	Decreases trust (Chapter 5)	Not supported except in a hypothetical scenario; a "no meddling" treatment increased trust in US 2018 only
Conditional effects (new theory)	Foreign actors…		
	-Perceived as capable and unbiased	Accentuates effects of monitors (Chapter 6)	Supported (although only among uncertain respondents in Georgia)

	-Perceived as capable	Accentuates effects of meddlers (Chapter 6)	Supported
	Individuals… -Vote choice	Accentuates or diminishes effects of foreign actors (Chapter 7)	Mixed: supported for monitors in Tunisia and the United States (in 2016, 2018, and 2020) but not Georgia; supported for meddling in Georgia
		Shapes perceptions of foreign interventions (Chapter 7)	Supported
	-Uncertain	Accentuates effects of foreign actors (Chapters 4–7)	Supported
Nationalist backlash (alternative theory)	Any foreign influence	Decreases trust (Chapters 4-7)	Not supported

information about the *absence* of meddling (which enhanced trust) and an experiment about meddling in a hypothetical future election in Georgia (which reduced trust). We note, however, that the 2018 findings from the United States did not replicate in our 2020 survey, which was conducted in a context with stronger concerns about domestic threats to election credibility and weaker salience for foreign election meddling.

In summary, we find limited support for the conventional wisdom related to foreign actors' effects. Although our experiments' mostly null (or in some cases, mixed) average effects represent an important challenge to the conventional wisdom about foreign actors, we underscore the rarity of reporting null findings in social science publications. This type of selective reporting and publication bias is increasingly understood to be an important threat to progress within political science and related disciplines.[4] It is possible that the null effects we identified in Chapters 4 and 5 were artifacts of our research design; perhaps, we would have detected more significant effects of the presence of monitors or meddling if we had delivered the information about them in a different way. However, our treatments were similar to those in previous studies that found significant effects,[5] and were deployed in diverse settings, including at least one country (Tunisia, a transitioning democracy) considered to be a "most likely" case to find significant effects. As such, the fact that we did not find more consistent evidence that foreign interventions changed perceptions of election credibility on average should encourage at least some reconsideration of conventional assumptions about foreign actors' effects.

Following our theory, in subsequent chapters we examine how intervener identity and individual vote choice condition the effects of foreign actors. Chapter 6 presented the first important finding based on our new theory, which was that the characteristics of the foreign actor matter for both monitors and meddlers. When foreign actors are perceived as capable – and, in the case of monitors, unbiased – they are more likely to cause citizens to update their beliefs about election credibility. This pattern makes intuitive sense, since foreign actors that are not perceived as capable of affecting (or being willing

---

[4] See the discussion in Dunning et al. (2019, Ch. 3).
[5] Brancati (2014a); Tomz and Weeks (2020).

to affect) the electoral playing field would not provide information about election credibility. However, our study is the first to provide empirical evidence in support of this theoretical insight, and the specific actors that are perceived to be credible are somewhat unexpected. For instance, Tunisian respondents perceived observers from the Arab League – rather than those that are more trusted by the international community, such as EU or US monitors – as both relatively capable and unbiased.

Another important take-away from Chapter 6 concerned the comparison between international and domestic monitors. Drawing on some of the assumptions of the nationalist alternative explanation, practitioners often assume that domestic monitors will be perceived as more capable and legitimate. Yet, Tunisian respondents trusted international observers more than domestic ones. We found the opposite in the US surveys until we provided information about the observers' capabilities and political neutrality. These findings suggest that different types of monitors may perform complementary roles depending on the context, and caution against assumptions that foreign actors will necessarily have weaker effects than domestic actors. They also shed light on how the public may interpret information about the electoral playing field that is provided by other nonpartisan actors – including the media, electoral commissions, and courts.[6] Whether the public views these institutions as capable and biased will determine whether (and how) they affect perceptions of election credibility.

Chapter 7 established that the effect of foreign actors is conditional on individual vote choice. As expected, there was a substantial winner–loser gap in electoral trust: People who supported winning candidates and parties perceived elections as much more credible than those who backed the main losing candidates or parties. Foreign interventions around elections can further magnify this partisan divide. Across all three cases, individuals who supported the main losing candidates or parties tended not to be encouraged by monitors' positive reports and, especially in Tunisia and the United States, were responsive to their negative assessments. By contrast, winners were relatively unmoved by the good news contained in EO reports, perhaps because they already had such substantial confidence in the election. Similarly, we found that election losers were much more concerned about and attentive

---

[6] Chernykh and Svolik (2012).

to the possibility of foreign meddling than winners. The experimental evidence related to the conditional effect of vote choice on trust was more limited in the case of meddling, which may, however, be because one of our key experiments (in the United States in 2018) took place in the context of a legislative election that did not produce clear national winners and losers.

In addition to supporting various aspects of our theoretical framework, the evidence also undermines a plausible alternative theory about how foreign actors influence local attitudes. This alternative theory posits that individuals want their elections to be completely free of foreign influence, and will react negatively to any evidence of such influence due to a dynamic of nationalist backlash. However, we find that individuals in all of our surveys regarded many types of foreign influence positively, perhaps recognizing that some types of foreign interventions seek to make the electoral playing field more fair and that other types may help their preferred party. Moreover, individuals are generally hesitant to change their beliefs about election credibility in response to information about interventions from beyond a country's borders, even when it constitutes evidence of meddling – the most nefarious form of foreign influence on elections. Voters often tolerate meddling that is believed to support their party, despite the fact that it is widely considered to violate norms of both democracy and sovereignty.

Finally, we found that monitors and meddlers had their clearest real-time effects on perceptions of election credibility in Tunisia and the United States; their influence was less apparent in Georgia. This pattern is consistent with our theoretical framework since Georgia was not a particularly uncertain electoral environment in 2018 given its fairly stable status as a partial democracy. Interestingly, however, it was not just the transitional environment in our study that had sufficient uncertainty for foreign actors to shape trust. Since both monitors and meddlers affected perceptions of election credibility in the United States in significant ways, this book has shown how even in a consolidated democracy, foreign actors can increase or decrease trust. Americans' declining trust in and uncertainty surrounding elections, including as a consequence of the contested 2000 presidential election and subsequent politicians' statements about voter fraud, may be somewhat unusual in a long-standing democracy. Nevertheless, the example may be increasingly relevant for considering citizen trust in other consolidated democracies, such as Britain, that have also been targeted by Russian influence campaigns.[7]

8.3 The Strategic Use of Foreign Interventions

Understanding how foreign electoral interventions influence citizens' trust in elections helps explain several intriguing facets of state behavior. Chapter 1 began with two puzzles about foreign interventions around elections, which the theory and evidence we presented help to resolve.

The first puzzle was why countries frequently invite foreign actors to participate in their elections. For example, international monitors observe most countries' elections as standard practice. Most previous accounts of why states invite monitors focus on states' surprising decisions to willingly expose themselves to the scrutiny of credible international monitors. The dominant explanation in the literature is that doing so helps states adhere to prevailing international norms related to democracy.[8] Yet, why would states invite zombie observers to their elections from intergovernmental organizations (IGOs) such as the Commonwealth of Independent States (a Russia-led international organization) or the Shanghai Cooperation Organization?[9] It seems unlikely to generate benefits for states that are seeking to demonstrate their commitment to democracy. In fact, inviting such observers might do the opposite since mainly authoritarian states engage in this practice.

Our book helps explain why states might be motivated to invite zombie observers. Although most international audiences are unlikely to be persuaded by such groups' activities (and may even downgrade their assessment of elections if they are present), zombie monitors' actions and messages may resonate domestically. Our finding in Chapter 6 that an election monitoring mission from the Arab League (a largely undemocratic IGO) enhanced trust the most in Tunisia is consistent with this interpretation. Moreover, in Chapter 7, we found that monitors' negative reports tended to decrease election credibility among the main election losers. Since losers' acceptance of the election outcome

---

[7] Norris, Cameron, and Wynter (2019, 7).
[8] Hyde (2011); Kelley (2012b).
[9] Walker and Cooley (2013).

is key to maintaining stability during the post-election period, it may be important for autocrats to invite monitoring groups they know will not issue negative reports and threaten their survival.

It is perhaps even more puzzling that foreign meddlers often intervene in democratic elections with the tacit, if not explicit, support of the candidates or parties they intend to help. Yet, Chapters 5 and 7 did not provide consistent evidence that meddling prompts an outcry among the general public, which tends to view the practice through a highly partisan (as opposed to nationalist) lens. Even if meddling is known to have occurred, it is usually extremely difficult to establish whether it actually swung an election in favor of the preferred party. As such, it is relatively easy for winning partisans – who are highly motivated to process information about foreign meddling in ways that are consistent with their prior beliefs – to downplay even high-quality information about meddling when assessing election credibility.

This last point feeds into our answer to the second puzzle described in the introduction: Why governments do not take more action to prevent or punish meddling. As Chapter 7 demonstrated, public opinion again explains why: If a winning party or candidate has been helped by foreign meddling, they will usually face limited pressure from their supporters to combat such interference. Instead, their supporters will be inclined to deny such meddling occurred. This pattern seems to match events in the United States since 2016, when Russia intervened on behalf of presidential winner Donald Trump and did not provoke a substantial policy response, in part because enough Republican politicians presumed that they did not need to promote combating Russian interference to win re-election. Moreover, this dynamic offers an explanation for why states often meddle overtly: It may be less likely to provoke a backlash or policy response than previously understood. It may also be easier to influence the election outcome than covert meddling. In sum, our evidence about citizens' perceptions of election credibility suggests that *domestic political leaders can invite and otherwise strategically use foreign interventions in elections to advance their own political objectives.*

This conclusion raises a further question: How might the experimental treatment effects identified in our surveys change when the information contained in them is conveyed by political parties and other elites in the real world? After all, our surveys generally provided information about foreign actors' interventions to citizens directly, without introducing the additional complexity and realism of, for example, conveying that information in the form of a news article in which a domestic political leader also lauded or criticized foreign actors.[10]

To consider what might happen in such a situation, we consult the vast literature on how the public responds to information from partisan sources.[11] This literature suggests that information provided by a person's political party is more likely to affect his or her political opinions. Thus, when information about monitors and meddlers comes from a trusted partisan source, it is plausible that the type of effects we identified will be amplified. For example, election losers' trust could decline even more when monitors' negative reports are shared by their fellow partisans than when they are relayed in a fairly neutral manner, as in our survey experiments. In polarized political settings, people may be especially likely to access media sources that will exacerbate the partisan reactions to foreign actors that we documented in Chapter 7.

In the real world, individuals often encounter multiple – competing – sources of political information that could diminish the effects of foreign actors that we identified by creating a "fog" of disinformation about the electoral playing field.[12] A pseudo-democrat might, for example, attempt to undermine the credibility of critical international EOs by questioning their capabilities or objectivity; without this counternarrative, such monitors might diminish some individuals' trust by pointing out flaws in an election, but with it, monitors' negative reports could lose some of their punch. By contrast, in staunchly authoritarian settings, where the regime has control over the narrative, pseudo-democrats can promote knowledge of potentially trust-enhancing foreign interventions like zombie monitors and prevent coverage of trust-diminishing interventions like critical monitors.

While future research is needed to better understand these dynamics, our theory and findings help explain why domestic political actors behave how they do toward foreign actors. Government leaders and foreign actors anticipate some of the effects on the public that we

---

[10] Although note that it is not clear that using a different treatment format, in and of itself, would have increased the realism of the experimental scenario. See Kreps and Roblin (2019).

[11] For a recent review of this literature, see Bullock (2020).

[12] Merloe (2015, 90).

have identified and adjust their behavior accordingly. For instance, international monitors employ a variety of strategies to promote the perception that they are capable and politically neutral, including committing to the Declaration of Principles for International Election Observation and a Code of Conduct for International Election Observation; deciding which governmental and nongovernmental funding sources to accept; and choosing staff for missions that can enhance their reputation for expertise in terms of election integrity or regional knowledge.[13] Our findings from Chapter 6 help describe why, for example, the Carter Center might prefer to emphasize its technical capacity and objectivity, not its American headquarters, in its public-facing materials.[14] Given that the Carter Center seeks to contribute to public trust in elections, where warranted, our findings suggest that its approach makes sense.

8.4 Extending the Theory to Other Foreign Influences

Although this book developed a theory to understand how monitors and meddlers affect local trust in elections, its insights are relevant for thinking about how other types of foreign influences on domestic politics are likely to affect the public.[15] In today's interconnected world, foreign actors influence domestic politics in countless ways. We focus on three additional types of foreign influence: forms of democracy promotion beyond election monitoring, peacekeeping, and transnational human rights activism. In all three cases, and similar to monitors and meddlers, foreign actors seek to influence domestic politics through their effects on individual political attitudes

---

[13] Hyde (2012, 54–59).

[14] The Carter Center's website describes its role in observing elections as follows: "Impartial, credible EOs play a key role in shaping perceptions about the quality and legitimacy of electoral processes. The Carter Center has been a pioneer of election observation, monitoring more than 100 elections in Africa, Latin America, and Asia since 1989 and forging many of the techniques now common to the field. To ensure a meaningful, nonpartisan role for its election observation activities, the Carter Center must be invited by a country's election authorities and welcomed by the major political parties." See Carter Center (2020).

[15] As noted earlier in the chapter, variables such as the identity of the actor (and specifically, its perceived capabilities and biases), individual vote choice, and electoral environment are also relevant conditioning variables for domestic influences on elections.

and behaviors. Our theoretical framework therefore offers potential insights into the conditions under which foreign actors are most likely to have such effects.

8.4.1 Democracy Promotion

An obvious extension is to apply this book's theoretical framework to the various forms of democracy promotion that were not considered here, such as foreign aid to support civil society or IGO enforcement of democratic norms, both of which are now commonplace and sometimes occur around elections.[16] As discussed in Chapter 1, election monitoring is another form of democracy promotion, but it is distinct from some other types in that it always occurs around elections and is invited by the government.

A next step for the research agenda on how foreign actors influence local trust in elections would be to explore how citizens perceive these other types of democracy promotion. It is plausible that local citizens perceive certain forms of democracy promotion, such as assistance to political parties, as a type of meddling, but others, such as capacity-building activities for the electoral management body, as enhancing electoral integrity and more similar to high-quality monitoring. If that is the case, then our theory predicts that these other types of democracy promotion would have predictably negative or positive effects on trust in elections on average, and that those effects would depend on the characteristics of the intervener, the individual, and the electoral environment.

Future work might also extend our theory to consider how various forms of democracy promotion influence trust in government institutions beyond elections. Ordinary citizens face a similar information problem to the one that we described in Chapter 2 with regards to elections when they evaluate many other democratic institutions, such as courts, political parties, and the media: It is difficult to observe just how democratic such institutions are, and political actors have incentives to misrepresent themselves as more democratic than they are. Similar to election monitors' reports, when credible IGOs make statements about the rule of law or international nongovernmental organizations (NGOs) promulgate cross-national ratings of press

---

[16] Donno (2010); Bush (2015).

freedom, these actions provide relevant information to the public,[17] provided that the public regards those information sources as credible. Likewise, information that a foreign country has provided assistance to a local political party may exacerbate domestic polarization, and perhaps sow public doubt about the party's commitment to democracy among individuals who do not support it while failing to have a similar effect on its supporters.

8.4.2 *Peacekeeping*

Similar to international election monitoring and other forms of democracy promotion, international peacekeeping has become much more frequent since the 1980s. The end of the Cold War was associated with both an increase in intrastate conflict, which created a demand for international peacekeepers, and a decrease in great power tensions, which created a supply of them through international institutions such as the United Nations (UN). Post-Cold War peacekeeping became closely linked to democracy promotion as the settlements designed to bring an end to civil conflict began to rely on electoral participation provisions in which the various parties to the conflict made plans to compete in democratic elections instead of on the battlefield.[18] In response, international peacekeepers included various forms of democracy support in their missions.[19]

Peacekeepers attempt to prevent the recurrence of conflicts by gathering and providing credible information concerning the disarmament and demobilization process,[20] including about former combatants' compliance with standards established as part of peace processes.[21] In other words, peacekeepers seek to influence domestic audiences' political beliefs by providing credible information about the peace process. Although peacekeeping's effectiveness depends on more than domestic audiences' beliefs, former combatants' (and citizens') perceptions

---

[17] Bush (2017a).
[18] Matanock (2018).
[19] Paris (2004).
[20] Walter (2002); Fortna (2008, 94–95).
[21] Matanock (2017, 17).

of the peace process are thought to be an integral component of international interventions' success.[22]

Given these dynamics, our theory may shed light on the conditions under which international peacekeeping successfully mitigates local conflict. In particular, it suggests that in order for peacekeepers to provide credible information to domestic audiences about peace processes, they must be perceived as willing and able to do so. There is reason to suspect that there is significant variation within and across conflicts in individuals' likelihood to view peacekeepers as capable and unbiased, especially in an increasingly multi-actor international peacekeeping landscape.[23] For example, in Mali, a study found that a prime about UN peacekeepers encouraged interethnic cooperation in a trust game, whereas a prime about French peacekeepers had no such positive effect.[24] This pattern was driven by local perceptions that the UN is a fair broker between the warring Tuareg and Mandé ethnic groups, and that France (the former colonial power in Mali) is not. Yet, the UN's relatively positive local reputation in Mali does not travel to all settings; there is reason to think, for example, that it has been less well received in the Democratic Republic of Congo, and that this perception has hampered its success there.[25]

We offered tentative ideas in this book about the origins of individuals' beliefs about monitors and meddlers and highlighted the relevance of both accuracy and consistency goals. Similar goals likely shape beliefs about international peacekeepers. Civilians driven by accuracy goals may form such beliefs through either experience – those exposed to the services peacekeepers provide may find them trustworthy, whereas those exposed to abuse may not – or use heuristics such as peacekeeper nationality.[26] At the same time, consistent goals could cause civilians who believe their side has gotten an unfair deal in the peace process to question the peacekeepers' intentions. In either case, we expect these individual perceptions to condition peacekeepers' impact on local processes in much the same way as they condition the effect of foreign actors on election credibility.

---

[22] Autesserre (2014, 8).
[23] Brosig (2013).
[24] Nomikos (2021).
[25] Autesserre (2014).
[26] Bove and Ruggeri (2016); Gordon and Young (2017).

8.4.3 Transnational Human Rights Activism

In contrast to peacekeeping, which is the domain of states and IGOs, many of the primary human rights actors are NGOs, which work together in transnational advocacy networks to pressure states to improve their conduct.[27] These human rights advocates draw on an increasingly robust set of international treaties, courts, and norms pertaining to human rights.

Although states are traditionally understood as the targets of transnational human rights activism, individual attitudes and behaviors are also implicated. As Karisa Cloward notes about transnational activists' efforts to change norms related to female genital mutilation and early marriage, "many transnational campaigns promote norms for which individuals – not states – are the primary transgressors."[28] And even where states are the primary targets of activism, such as campaigns against torture, shifting public opinion influences the success of transnational human rights advocates. Indeed, a primary mechanism through which international human rights law is thought to improve states' human rights practices is by galvanizing domestic public mobilization in favor of compliance.[29]

Given the importance of shifting public attitudes on transnational human rights activism, it is important to consider whether our theory might have implications for this issue area. One obvious extension relates to how the local effects of foreign actors could depend on their identities. Like elections, transnational human rights involves many actors with diverse institutional characteristics.[30] Some organizations involved in transnational human rights campaigns that monitor and report on states' human rights violations have documented biases.[31] It is also plausible that human rights activists' identities or historical conduct could shape how audiences perceive them and thus condition their effects on domestic politics.

---

[27] Keck and Sikkink (1998).
[28] Cloward (2014, 495).
[29] Simmons (2009, 139–144). This observation has helped motivate a growing literature that examines how international human rights law affects public attitudes. For example, see Wallace (2013); Chilton and Versteeg (2016); Lupu and Wallace (2019).
[30] Hafner-Burton (2009).
[31] Hafner-Burton and Ron (2013).

Why is there is an apparent backlash against foreign interference in domestic politics on human rights issues, but not elections, as our study found? Although the evidence of the former is by no means uniform,[32] it is growing.[33] One possibility is that the countries studied by different scholars vary in their likelihood of backlash due to historical or other contextual factors, although as noted in Chapter 3, the publics in our case studies are relatively nationalist and so do not seem to be "hard" cases for identifying backlash effects. Another possibility is rooted in differences across issue areas. Transnational human rights activism sometimes touches on contested issues related to cultural practice (e.g., women's role in civic life), which may facilitate attempts to discredit activists by accusing them of cultural imperialism and enable government strategies like rhetorical adaptation designed to downplay charges of noncompliance.[34] By contrast, there may be greater agreement across and within countries about the core elements of election credibility,[35] which could make it more difficult to successfully question international efforts to promote free and fair elections writ large – even as the capabilities and biases of specific actors in this space may be (and are) questioned, as noted earlier.

8.5 Implications and Future Research

Having reviewed our central argument, our findings, and how our theory might apply to other issue areas, we now consider ways that future research might build on our study. We suggest that scholars might seek to understand the origins of perceptions of foreign actors and the long-term effects of foreign electoral interventions in both consolidated

---

[32] Exceptions or partial exceptions to this finding include Bush and Jamal (2015); Lupu and Wallace (2019); Anjum, Chilton, and Usman (2021). None of the cases considered in these studies (India, Jordan, and Pakistan) are ones in which scholars would typically characterize the public as especially welcoming of Western interference.

[33] Grossman, Manekin, and Margalit (2018); Gruffydd-Jones (2019); Terman (2019); Chaudhry (2021).

[34] Dixon (2017).

[35] Norris (2013a). Relatedly, whereas transnational human rights activism often deals with issues that relate to domestic customs (e.g., longstanding gender norms), elections are not linked to domestic tradition in the same way in most countries. As such, the public may be more welcoming of outside criticism of elections.

democracies and autocracies. We conclude the section by discussing some of our research's policy implications for building – or in some cases, rebuilding – trust in elections.

8.5.1 The Credibility of Foreign Actors

Our findings contribute to ongoing conversations about the legitimacy of IGOs and NGOs in world politics. Interest in this topic is growing in light of recent events, such as the Brexit vote in 2016 in the United Kingdom and the announcement the same year that Burundi, South Africa, and Gambia planned to leave the International Criminal Court, which seem to indicate a crisis of IGO legitimacy. A prominent framework within this literature "takes institutional features of [IGOs] as the analytical starting point" and then examines whether those features shift public attitudes.[36] This approach helps address how audiences might respond to the proliferation of international actors that serve similar functions (e.g., monitoring elections) but follow different procedures (e.g., more or less comprehensive missions) and have varying degrees of effectiveness (e.g., have more or less accurate reports).[37] As noted in Chapter 2, scholars refer to this phenomenon of overlapping IGOs and international NGOs as "international regime complexity."[38]

This book suggests additional directions for the study of IGO and NGO legitimacy. One intriguing finding that emerges from our book is that different audiences can attribute different levels of credibility to the same foreign actor. For example, international audiences of policymakers and journalists might value reports from high-quality US observers like the Carter Carter or appreciate the large-scale operations of domestic monitoring NGOs, but citizens in the observed countries – and even other global NGOs – do not seem to regard the same groups as especially credible.[39] This pattern supports the idea that expertise is fundamentally a social construct and varies according to the audience. Additional comparative studies – that include audiences from different countries as well as different types of audiences – will be needed to better understand who regards the various overlapping and competing foreign actors that influence domestic politics as legitimate and why.

---

[36] Tallberg and Zürn (2019, 601).
[37] Nielson, Hyde, and Kelley (2019, 700–701).
[38] Alter and Meunier (2009).
[39] Nielson, Hyde, and Kelley (2019).

Another path would be to use our observational findings about which foreign actors were perceived as the most capable – and, in the case of monitors, unbiased – to construct and test additional theories about the origins of individuals' perceptions of foreign actors. In Chapter 6, we showed that experimental treatments could cause foreign actors to be perceived as more or less capable and biased, which demonstrates that individuals' attitudes on these topics are at least somewhat malleable. This is an important point for policymakers and practitioners seeking to combat misinformation about elections and foreign actors, as we note later, since it means that foreign actors may have some control over how they are perceived.

But people also have some baseline opinions about foreign actors. As shown in Chapter 5, in the cases we studied, ordinary citizens believe there is a substantial amount of foreign influence in their elections, both positive and negative. What factors shape these beliefs? In Tunisia and Georgia, for example, individuals seemed to take a fairly dim view of American monitors, even though most scholars (for good reason) consider these observers to be reputable, though by no means perfect. We interpret this pattern as most likely reflecting opinions about the controversial political history of American organizations in both countries (as well as their broader regions). Further research will be needed to support this conclusion with more confidence. Nevertheless, it seems to support the idea that the research agenda on IGO and NGO legitimacy should pay greater attention to why citizens might be skeptical of these actors given the larger power relations in which they are embedded.[40]

8.5.2 *Democratic Backsliding*

Substantial concerns have emerged in the twenty-first century about democratic backsliding: In 2021, an essay from the American NGO Freedom House, which rates how democratic countries around the world are, announced "15th consecutive year of decline in global freedom."[41] The most common type of democratic breakdown in the post-Cold War era involves the gradual takeover by democratically elected

[40] Hurd (2019).
[41] Repucci and Slipowitz (2020).

executives.[42] Well-known examples of this phenomenon include Viktor Orbán in Hungary, Vladimir Putin in Russia, Recep Tayyip Erdoğan in Turkey, and Hugo Chávez and Nicolás Maduro in Venezuela. Many observers have wondered whether similar dynamics could occur in the United States.[43]

Milan Svolik's explanation of this phenomenon of executive-led democratic breakdown centers on the role of individual citizens: In polarized societies, voters are willing to tolerate some subversions of democracy, as long as they are committed by their fellow partisans.[44] If incumbent politicians believe (often correctly, as Svolik's surveys show) they will not be voted out of office for violating key democratic principles, they may be tempted to grab more and more power over time. The violations of democratic principles typically considered in the literature on democratic backsliding are domestic: attacks on the free press, packing the courts with partisan appointees or ignoring the rulings of independent courts, adopting laws that extend term limits, and so on.

This book posits that some forms of foreign influence – specifically, instances of foreign meddling – similarly undermine democracy by making the electoral playing field less fair. Moreover, it finds that election winners generally resist updating their political attitudes in response to bad news about election credibility when it comes in the form of information about meddling. In this way, we might consider a state's invitation of foreign meddling to be another case of an antidemocratic action for which partisan voters may be unwilling to punish politicians. That unwillingness poses a threat to democracies, even consolidated ones. This phenomenon has at least three worrisome implications on state behavior. First, it loosens the constraints on executives with authoritarian tendencies when it comes to inviting foreign meddling. Second, it encourages countries like Russia to meddle more often in elections, especially in polarized societies, if we assume that one of its motivations for meddling is to undermine democracy around the world. Third, it emboldens foreign meddlers to intervene in more overt and extensive ways if they believe that doing so will not cause a backlash in the target country.

---

[42] Svolik (2020).
[43] Levitsky and Ziblatt (2018); Carey et al. (2019); Kaufman and Haggard (2019).
[44] Graham and Svolik (2020); Svolik (2020).

Future studies might investigate how foreign interventions affect political behaviors that are more directly relevant to democracy. For reasons elaborated in Chapter 3, our research design focuses on identifying the relationship between foreign interventions and perceptions of election credibility. Further research might build on our findings to identify the effect of foreign interventions on individuals' behaviors, such as voting and participation in protests, using microlevel data. As we discussed in Chapter 1, our surveys showed that perceptions of election credibility are linked to self-reported voter turnout as well as a willingness to sign voting pledges. A future study could investigate the effect of awareness of foreign interventions using other forms of data about relevant political behaviors. For example, the effects of meddling on voting could be studied in the context of an election in which voters participated over a period of time (e.g., by using mail-in ballots), and there was a shock revelation of foreign meddling in support of a particular candidate mid-way through voting. This study's findings imply that such a revelation would not necessarily cause voters to turn away from the supported candidate and that its overall effects on voting would likely depend on whether people believed the meddler was capable, as well as their vote choices.

Another important topic for future research is public support for interventions in other countries' elections, building on our study of the United States as both an intervener and an intervention target. The American public is fairly diffident about most forms of democracy promotion,[45] and our study suggests that the same could be true when it comes to support for partisan electoral interventions. On the one hand, the absence of a strong nationalist backlash against foreign interventions implies that there may not be a large constituency that wants to retaliate for such actions, which is consistent with findings by Tomz and Weeks.[46] On the other hand, the public's relatively muted response may imply a lack of outrage should the US government choose to violate norms related to both democracy and sovereignty by meddling in another country's elections. Although future research is needed to understand the dynamics of public attitudes toward foreign electoral interventions, it is possible that they could fail to constrain antidemocratic actions abroad in the same way they do domestically.

---

[45] Brancati (2014b).
[46] Tomz and Weeks (2020).

8.5.3 Authoritarian Resilience

We also consider the likely implications of our findings for consolidated authoritarian regimes. As discussed in Chapter 3, we opted not to include a fully fledged autocracy as a case study, but there would be considerable value in extending the study of monitors and meddlers to such a setting since even closed autocracies typically hold elections in the twenty-first century. Although scholars usually consider elections in such settings to be instruments of authoritarian rule (e.g., that help the government monitor supporters and distribute patronage to them), autocratic elections can sometimes go awry and end up contributing to democratization by generating outrage over fraud.[47]

Our theoretical framework suggests that, all else equal, foreign actors' effects on perceptions of election credibility may be more muted in authoritarian environments since they tend not to feature a great deal of uncertainty about the fairness of the electoral playing field. Put differently, everyone knows that elections in a consolidated autocracy are not free and fair, which makes it more difficult for foreign actors to change citizens' minds. Nevertheless, we have noted examples throughout the book of authoritarian leaders attempting to use foreign influences to their advantage, such as when they invite zombie election monitors and widely publicize their activities to domestic audiences. As such, it is possible that when authoritarian governments can publicize foreign actors' interventions through blanket coverage on state-run media, they can still obtain some advantages in terms of reassuring the public despite the overall lack of uncertainty about the poor quality of elections. Future research can investigate this possibility.

A further concerning development in terms of authoritarian resilience is the "notable decline in foreign support for democracy around the world."[48] This decline has a variety of sources, including skepticism about democracy promotion in the wake of wars in Afghanistan and Iraq and the diffusion of restrictions on foreign funding for civil society, which make it more difficult for common forms of democracy promotion to occur.[49] Our findings imply that a diminished commitment to democracy promotion on the part of the United States, EU, and other IGOs could spell trouble for democracy globally

---

[47] Gandhi and Lust-Okar (2009, 414).
[48] Hyde (2020, 1192).
[49] Chaudhry (2021).

for additional reasons related to individuals' attitudes. On the one hand, if the international environment is less supportive of democracy, states will have fewer incentives to invite the types of foreign interventions that are most likely to advance democracy by influencing citizens' behaviors. For example, governments will be less inclined to invite high-quality international EOs to their elections – the type of monitors that (if trusted by citizens) could encourage productive forms of political engagement such as voting in democratic elections or protests in the aftermath of flawed elections. On the other hand, there will be fewer international checks on states that want to invite (or engage in) the types of foreign interventions that will make the electoral playing field less fair. We should therefore anticipate the continued growth of zombie monitoring and other forms of foreign meddling.

8.5.4 (Re-)building Trust in Elections

Finally, this book generated new insights into how citizens process information about election credibility as it is revealed to them through the actions of foreign actors. Its findings suggest several directions for policymakers, practitioners, and advocates interested in amplifying high-quality information and combatting low-quality information about elections. There are two basic problems that both require attention: Individuals may (1) ignore high-quality information and (2) be swayed by low-quality information. This section discusses each problem in turn.

Amplifying High-Quality Information

Reputable international monitors are now present at most elections around the world. Yet, information about their activities and reports does not reach all citizens – but not for lack of trying. As discussed in Chapter 4, EOs have developed a variety of strategies designed to attract media attention.

Monitors' publicity strategies are designed for the type of election they observe: an election in a developing democracy. The public is generally not aware of monitors' presence in consolidated democracies, even though monitors do get invited to elections there, and citizens may be uncertain about election credibility.[50] This overall pattern

---

[50] Eschenbächer (2010).

tracks with our survey data: We showed in Chapter 4 that international monitors had a lower profile in the United States than they did in Tunisia or Georgia. Media and nonprofit organizations in the United States that seek to disseminate high-quality information about election integrity should therefore consider drawing greater attention to monitors' reports. The same is true for other consolidated democracies facing problems of voter confidence in elections. This idea tracks with a recent recommendation from a group of academic experts in advance of the 2020 US presidential election: "Media organizations should engage in a public information effort to provide voters with accurate information about the process by which election officials count votes and determine election winners."[51] The urgency of such recommendations is partly rooted in the concern that when people lack trust in their elections, they will stop voting and disengage from the democratic process, which our survey evidence demonstrates is a reasonable concern (see Chapter 1).

Disseminating information about high-quality international monitors is not enough to enhance trust, however. The public must also perceive those monitors as able and willing to influence the electoral playing field. If EOs have such qualities but the public does not recognize them, then they will not enhance voter confidence in clean elections. The good news is that it may be possible for monitors to more effectively demonstrate their trust-enhancing characteristics to the public. For example, publicizing many of the steps that high-quality observation missions have already taken – such as sending lengthy and well-equipped technical missions or including observers of diverse nationalities to reduce the likelihood that they are politically biased – may help them establish their credibility among the public. Of course, it may not be easy for international EOs to change how they are perceived in countries where citizens hold strong opinions about other countries and international organizations. An alternative approach may therefore be for international actors to attempt to enhance the quality of lower quality observers that the public holds in high esteem or to support the emergence of promising new monitoring initiatives.

---

[51] Ad Hoc Committee for 2020 Election Fairness and Legitimacy (2020, vi).

Combating Low-Quality Information

This discussion also raises the question of whether (and how) inaccurate beliefs about election credibility can be corrected. As laid out in Chapter 2, our theory approaches the formation of beliefs about election credibility through two lenses: accuracy motivations and consistency motivations. When individuals respond to information in a way that reflects the latter, they are more likely to engage in motivated reasoning by ignoring high-quality information that is inconsistent with their prior partisan beliefs or embracing low-quality information that is consistent with these pre-existing beliefs. There is a debate about whether directional reasoning results more from individuals' dispositions or the situations in which they find themselves. To some extent, our findings support the notion that motivated reasoning related to elections is at least partly situational, since in Chapter 7 we find that the extent to which it occurs depends on whether there is a strong winner–loser dynamic.

Scholars of political behavior, especially in the United States, seek to correct misinformation and discourage individuals from engaging in directionally motivated updating.[52] Past research suggests that one way to correct directional reasoning is to inform individuals about an expert consensus, for instance from high-quality election monitors. In Tunisia, for example, there were many international observers, and their assessments of the election were similarly positive – a setting in which such an expert consensus might be effectively communicated to the public. By contrast, although the United States has a legal framework for domestic and international election observation, it is limited, and most US states only permit partisan observers.[53] Encouraging the practice of neutral, independent election observation even in advanced democracies may be a worthwhile step in the face of significant uncertainty about election integrity and contestation about the extent of foreign influence.

In much the same way that the public's faulty perceptions of EOs may be corrected by providing information about their true capabilities and biases, the same is possible for election meddlers. If the public is not taking election meddling seriously because they falsely believe foreign countries are not capable of changing the playing field,

---

[52] For a review, see Flynn, Nyhan, and Reifler (2017); Jerit and Zhou (2020).
[53] Vanka, Davis-Roberts, and Carroll (2018).

providing high-quality information about the extent of past meddling could clear up this misunderstanding. We expect it will be fairly difficult to counteract inaccurate opinions about foreign meddling, given that there is usually considerable uncertainty about whether it occurred and what effect it had on the election outcome. Moreover, given that election meddling is partisan, it is by definition the type of highly politicized issue on which we might expect consistency-driven updating to dominate.

8.6 Conclusion

This book has sought to explain how (and why) foreign actors influence local levels of trust in elections. Foreign influences on elections have been in the news a great deal lately, but researchers have thus far failed to comprehensively identify their effects on citizens in a way that recognizes the diverse forms of influence employed and the factors that might amplify or blunt their impact. This book advances our understanding by specifying the conditions under which foreign actors shape citizens' perceptions of election credibility, highlighting the role of the characteristics of the foreign actors, individual voters, and elections. Although foreign actors do not always transform citizens' views on elections, they can shape those views in measurable, concrete ways that have the potential to significantly alter countries' political trajectories in terms of democracy, peace, and stability. This book points out new ways to understand the connections between international and domestic politics. For policymakers, practitioners, and concerned citizens, it illustrates some of the important ways in which foreign actors can – and should – provide high-quality information about election integrity, and highlights serious dangers to avoid.

Bibliography

Ad Hoc Committee for 2020 Election Fairness and Legitimacy. 2020. "Fair Elections during a Crisis: Urgent Recommendations in Law, Media, Politics, and Tech to Advance the Legitimacy of, and the Public's Confidence in, the November 2020 U.S. Elections." UCI Law, April. Available at: www.law.uci.edu/faculty/full-time/hasen/2020ElectionReport.pdf.

Adams, John. 1787. "To Thomas Jefferson from John Adams, 6 December 1787." *Founders Online*, National Archives. Available at: www.founders .archives.gov/documents/Jefferson/01-12-02-0405. Original source: *The Papers of Thomas Jefferson*, volume 12, August 7, 1787–March 31, 1788, ed. Julian P. Boyd, Princeton: Princeton University Press, 1955, pp. 396–397.

Afrobarometer. 2015. "Merged Round 5 data (34 countries), 2011–2013 (last update: July 2015)." Available at: www.afrobarometer.org/data/ merged-round-5-data-34-countries-2011-2013-last-update-july-2015.

Agence France-Presse. 2018. "Outside Help Not Wanted, says DRC as Key Elections Loom." *Agence France-Presse*, August 24. Available at: www.news24.com/Africa/News/outside-help-not-wanted-says-drc-as-key-elections-loom-20180824.

Agence Tunis Afrique Presse. 2014a. "Arab League Election Observation Mission Expected Thursday in Tunis." December 16. Accessed via ProQuest.

Agence Tunis Afrique Presse. 2014b. "Tunisia Moves Forward at Steady Pace Towards Nascent Democracy." October 25. Accessed via Proquest.

Al Jazeera. 2021. "World Reacts to Tunisia's Political Turmoil." *Al Jazeera* (online), July 26, 2021. Available at: www.aljazeera.com/news/2021/7/26/ world-reacts-to-tunisia-political-turmoil.

Almond, Gabriel A. and Sidney Verba. 1963. *The Civic Culture: Political Attitudes and Democracy in Five Nations*. Newbury Park, CA: SAGE Publications.

Alter, Karen J. and Sophie Meunier. 2009. "The Politics of International Regime Complexity." *Perspectives on Politics* 7(1):13–24.

Alvarez, R. Michael, Lonna Rae Atkeson, Ines Levin and Yimeng Li. 2019. "Paying Attention to Inattentive Survey Respondents." *Political Analysis* 27(2):145–162.

Alvarez, R. Michael, Thad Hall and Morgan Llewellyn. 2008. "Are Americans Confident Their Ballots Are Counted?" *Journal of Politics* 70(3):754–766.

Anderson, Christopher, André Blais, Shaun Bowler, Todd Donovan and Ola Listhaug. 2005. *Losers' Consent: Elections and Democratic Legitimacy.* Oxford: Oxford University Press.

Andrew, Christopher and Vasili Mitrokhin. 2020. *The Sword and the Shield: The Mitrokhin Archive and the Secret History of the KGB.* New York: Basic Books.

Angrist, Michele Penner. 1999. "Parties, Parliament, and Political Dissent in Tunisia." *British Journal of Middle Eastern Studies* 4(4):89–104.

Anjum, Gulnaz, Adam Chilton and Zahid Usman. 2021. "United Nations Endorsement and Support for Human Rights: An Experiment on Women's Rights in Pakistan." *Journal of Peace Research* 58(3):462–478.

Ansolabehere, Stephen and Nathaniel Persily. 2008. "Vote Fraud in the Eye of the Beholder: The Role of Public Opinion in the Challenge to Voter Identification Requirements." *Harvard Law Review* 121(7): 1737–1774.

Arab Barometer. 2015. "Arab Barometer Wave III (2012–2014)." Available at: www.arabbarometer.org/survey-data/data-downloads/.

Associated Press. 2004. "Invisible Ink: How They Rigged the Vote." Republished in the *Sydney Morning Herald* (online), December 2. Available at: www.smh.com.au/world/invisible-ink-how-they-rigged-the-vote-20041202-gdk8j8.html.

Associated Press. 2017. "U.S. Tells 21 States That Hackers Targeted Their Voting Systems." *New York Times* (online), September 22. Available at: www.nytimes.com/2017/09/22/us/politics/us-tells-21-states-that-hackers-targeted-their-voting-systems.html.

Associated Press. 2018. "Salome Zurabishvili Wins Georgia Presidential Runoff." *New York Times* (online), November 29. Available at: www.nytimes.com/2018/11/29/world/europe/georgia-president-salome-zurabishvili.html.

Asunka, Joseph, Sarah Brierly, Miriam Golden, Eric Kramon and George Ofosu. 2019. "Electoral Fraud or Violence: The Effect of Observers on Party Manipulation Strategies." *British Journal of Political Science* 49(1):129–151.

Atwood, Richard. 2012. "How the EU Can Support Peaceful Post-Election Transitions of Power: Lessons from Africa." Expo/B/Afet/2012/06. Briefing Paper, Directorate-General for External Policies of the Union, Directorate B, Policy Department. Available at: www.europarl.europa.eu/RegData/etudes/note/join/2012/457110/EXPO-AFET_NT(2012)457110_EN.pdf.

Autesserre, Sèverine. 2014. *Peaceland: Conflict Resolution and the Everyday Politics of International Intervention*. Problems of International Politics Series. New York: Cambridge University Press.

Bader, Max. 2010. "Party Politics in Georgia and Ukraine and the Failure of Western Assistance." *Democratization* 17(6):1085–1107.

Barkan, Joel D. 2012. "Democracy Assistance: What Recipients Think." *Journal of Democracy* 23(1):129–137.

Barnes, Julian E. 2020. "Russia Continues Interfering in Election to Try to Help Trump, U.S. Intelligence Says." *New York Times* (online), August 7. Available at: www.nytimes.com/2020/08/07/us/politics/russia-china-trump-biden-election-interference.html.

Bartels, Larry M. 2002. "Beyond the Running Tally: Partisan Bias in Political Perceptions." *Political Behavior* 24(2):117–150.

Beaulieu, Emily. 2014a. *Electoral Protest and Democracy in the Developing World*. Cambridge: Cambridge University Press.

Beaulieu, Emily. 2014b. "From Voter ID to Party ID: How Political Parties Affect Perceptions of Election Fraud in the U.S." *Electoral Studies* 35(1):24–32.

Beaulieu, Emily and Susan D. Hyde. 2009. "In the Shadow of Democracy Promotion: Strategic Manipulation, International Observers and Election Boycotts." *Comparative Political Studies* 42(3):392–415.

Beissinger, Mark R. 2007. "Structure and Example in Modular Political Phenomena: The Diffusion of Bulldozer/Rose/Orange/Tulip Revolutions." *Perspectives on Politics* 5(2):259–276.

Beissinger, Mark R., Amaney A. Jamal and Kevin Mazur. 2015. "Explaining Divergent Revolutionary Coalitions: Regime Strategies and the Structuring of Participation in the Tunisian and Egyptian Revolutions." *Comparative Politics* 48(1):1–21.

Benstead, Lindsay, Kristen Kao and Ellen Lust. 2020. "Does It Matter What Observers Say? The Impact of International Monitoring on Electoral Legitimacy." *Mediterranean Politics*: 1–22, doi: 10.1080/13629395.2020.1730601.

Berger, Daniel, Alejandro Corvalan, William Easterly and Shanker Satyanath. 2013. "Do Superpower Interventions Have Short and Long Term Consequences for Democracy?" *Journal of Comparative Economics* 41(1):22–34.

Berinsky, Adam J. 2018. "Telling the Truth about Believing the Lies? Evidence for the Limited Prevalence of Expressive Survey Responding." *Journal of Politics* 80(1):211–224.

Berinsky, Adam J., Gregory A. Huber and Gabriel S. Lenz. 2012. "Evaluating Online Labor Markets for Experimental Research: Amazon.com's Mechanical Turk." *Political Analysis* 20(3):351–368.

Berinsky, Adam J., Michele F. Margolis and Michael W. Sances. 2014. "Separating the Shirkers from the Workers? Making Sure Respondents Pay Attention on Self-Administered Surveys." *American Journal of Political Science* 58(3):729–753.

Berlinski, Nicolas, Margaret Doyle, Andrew M. Guess, Gabrielle Levy, Benjamin Lyons, Jacob M. Montgomery, Brendan Nyhan and Jason Reifler. 2021. "The Effects of Unsubstantiated Claims of Voter Fraud on Confidence in Elections." *Journal of Experimental Political Science*: 1–16, doi:10.1017/XPS.2021.18.

Berman, Eli, Michael Callen, Clark Gibson, James D. Long and Arman Rezaee. 2019. "Election Fairness and Government Legitimacy in Afghanistan." *Journal of Economic Behavior & Organization* 168:292–317.

Bicchi, Federica. 2009. "Democracy Assistance in the Mediterranean: An Overview." *Mediterranean Politics* 14(1):61–78.

Birch, Sarah. 2008. "Electoral Institutions and Popular Confidence in Electoral Processes: A Cross-National Analysis." *Electoral Studies* 27(2): 305–320.

Birch, Sarah. 2010. "Perceptions of Electoral Fairness and Voter Turnout." *Comparative Political Studies* 43(12):1601–1622.

Birch, Sarah. 2011. *Electoral Malpractice.* Oxford: Oxford University Press.

Bjornlund, Eric. 2001. "Democracy, Inc." *The Wilson Quarterly* 25(3): 18–24.

Boubakri, Amor. 2012. The League of Arab States and the Electoral Gap. In *The Integrity of Elections: The Role of Regional Organizations*, ed. Raul Cordenillo and Andrew Ellis. Stockholm: International IDEA, pp. 77–92.

Boubekeur, Amel. 2009. "Lessons from Algeria's 2009 Presidential Election." Carnegie Middle East Center, April 13. Available at: www.carnegie-mec.org/2009/04/13/lessons-from-algeria-s-2009-presidential-election-pub-22983.

Bove, Vincenzo and Andrea Ruggeri. 2016. "Kinds of Blue: Diversity in UN Peacekeeping Missions and Civilian Protection." *British Journal of Political Science* 46(3):681–700.

Brancati, Dawn. 2014a. "Building Confidence in Elections: The Case of Electoral Monitors in Kosova." *Journal of Experimental Political Science* 1(1):6–15.

Brancati, Dawn. 2014b. "The Determinants of U.S. Public Opinion Towards Democracy Promotion." *Political Behavior* 36(4):705–730.

Brosig, Malte. 2013. "Introduction: The African Security Regime Complex – Exploring Converging Actors and Policies." *African Security* 6(3–4): 171–190.

Bubeck, Johannes and Nikolay Marinov. 2017. "Process or Candidate: The International Community and the Demand for Electoral Integrity." *American Political Science Review* 111(3):535–554.

Bubeck, Johannes and Nikolay Marinov. 2019. *Rules and Allies: Foreign Election Interventions.* Cambridge: Cambridge University Press.

Bugajski, Janusz. 2012. "Beware Russia's Hand in Elections in Georgia, Ukraine, Lithuania." *Christian Science Monitor* (online), October 1. Available at: www.csmonitor.com/Commentary/Opinion/2012/1001/ Beware-Russia-s-hand-in-elections-in-Georgia-Ukraine-Lithuania.

Bullock, John G. 2009. "Partisan Bias and the Bayesian Ideal in the Study of Public Opinion." *The Journal of Politics* 71(3):1109–1124.

Bullock, John G. 2020. Party Cues. In *Oxford Handbook of Electoral Persuasion*, ed. Elizabeth Suhay, Bernard Grofman and Alexander H. Trechsel. New York: Oxford University Press, pp. 129–150.

Bullock, John G., Alan S. Gerber, Seth J. Hill and Gregory A. Huber. 2015. "Partisan Bias in Factual Beliefs about Politics." *Quarterly Journal of Political Science* 10(4):519–578.

Bunce, Valerie J. and Sharon L. Wolchik. 2007. "Defeating Dictators: Electoral Change and Stability in Competitive Authoritarian Regimes." *World Politics* 62(1):43–86.

Bush, Sarah Sunn. 2015. *The Taming of Democracy Assistance: Why Democracy Promotion Does Not Confront Dictators.* Cambridge: Cambridge University Press.

Bush, Sarah Sunn. 2016. "When and Why is Civil Society Support 'Made-in-America'? Delegation to Non-State Actors in American Democracy Promotion." *Review of International Organizations* 11(3):361–385.

Bush, Sarah Sunn. 2017a. "The Politics of Rating Freedom: Ideological Affinity, Private Authority, and the Freedom in the World Ratings." *Perspectives on Politics* 15(3):711–731.

Bush, Sarah Sunn. 2017b. "Varieties of International Influence and the Middle East." *PS: Political Science & Politics* 50(3):668–671.

Bush, Sarah Sunn and Amaney Jamal. 2015. "Anti-Americanism, Authoritarian Regimes, and Women's Political Representation: Evidence from a Survey Experiment in Jordan." *International Studies Quarterly* 59(1): 34–45.

Bush, Sarah Sunn and Lauren Prather. 2017. "The Promise and Limits of Election Observers in Building Election Credibility." *Journal of Politics* 79(3):921–935.

Bush, Sarah Sunn and Lauren Prather. 2018. "Who's There? Election Observer Identity and the Local Credibility of Elections." *International Organization* 72(3):659–692.

Bush, Sarah Sunn and Lauren Prather. 2019. "Do Electronic Devices in Face-to-Face Interviews Change Survey Behavior? Evidence from a Developing Country." *Research & Politics* 6(2):1–7.

Bush, Sarah Sunn and Lauren Prather. 2020. "Foreign Meddling and Mass Attitudes Toward International Economic Engagement." *International Organization* 74(3):584–609.

Cantú, Francisco and Omar García-Ponce. 2015. "Partisan Losers' Effects: Perceptions of Electoral Integrity in Mexico." *Electoral Studies* 39:1–14.

Carey, John M., Gretchen Helmke, Brendan Nyhan, Mitchell Sanders and Susan Stokes. 2019. "Searching for Bright Lines in the Trump Presidency." *Perspectives on Politics* 17(3):699–718.

Carothers, Thomas. 1997. "The Observers Observed." *Journal of Democracy* 8(3):17–31.

Carothers, Thomas and Andrew O'Donohue. 2019. Introduction. In *Democracies Divided: The Global Challenge of Political Polarization*, ed. Thomas Carothers and Andrew O'Donohue. Washington, DC: Brookings Institution Press, pp. 1–13.

Carter Center. 2020. "Democracy Program." Available at: www.cartercenter.org/peace/democracy/index.html.

Cecire, Michael. 2013. "Georgia's 2012 Elections and Lessons for Democracy Promotion." *Orbis* 57(2):232–250.

Center for Insights in Survey Research, International Republican Institute. 2017. "Survey of Public Opinion in Georgia." Available at: www.iri.org/sites/default/files/iri_poll_presentation_georgia_2017.03-general.pdf.

Central Election Commission (Georgia). 2018a. "International Observer Organizations Registered at the CEC for October 28, 2018 Presidential Elections." August 15. Available at: www.bit.ly/2OpdhjP.

Central Election Commission (Georgia). 2018b. "Local Observer Organizations Registered at the CEC for October 28, 2018 Presidential Elections." August 15. Available at: www.bit.ly/33qmWxs.

Chapman, Terrence and Stephen Chaudoin. 2020. "Public Reactions to International Legal Institutions: The ICC in a Developing Democracy." *Journal of Politics* 82(4):1305–1320.

Chaudhry, Suparna. 2021. "The Assault on Civil Society: Explaining State Repression of NGOs." *International Organization* p. forthcoming.

Chaudhry, Suparna, Marc Dotson and Andrew Heiss. 2021. "Who Cares About Crackdowns? Exploring the Role of Trust in Individual Philanthropy." *Global Policy* 12(S5):45–58.

Cherif, Youssef. 2014. "Tunisia's Elections Amid a Middle East Cold War." *MENA Source* blog, Atlantic Council, October 22. Available at: www.atlanticcouncil.org/blogs/menasource/tunisian-elections-amid-a-middle-eastern-cold-war.

Cherif, Youssef. 2017. "Tunisia's Fledgling Gulf Relations." *Sada* blog, Carnegie Endowment for International Peace, January 17. Available at: www.carnegieendowment.org/sada/67703.

Chernykh, Svitlana and Milan W. Svolik. 2012. "Can International Election Monitoring Harm Governance?" *Journal of Politics* 74(2):501–513.

Chilton, Adam S. and Mila Versteeg. 2016. "International Law, Constitutional Law, and Public Support for Torture." *Research & Politics* 3(1):1–9.

Chivers, C.J. 2005. "Communists of Moldova Appear to Win, Even if They're Weaker." *New York Times*, March 7, p. A8.

Chong, Alberto, Ana L. De La O, Dean Karlan and Leonard Wantchekon. 2015. "Does Corruption Information Inspire the Fight or Quash the Hope? A Field Experiment in Mexico on Voter Turnout, Choice, and Party Identification." *Journal of Politics* 77(1):55–71.

Church Committee. 1975. "Covert Action in Chile 1963–1973: Staff Report of the Select Committee to Study Governmental Operations with respect to Intelligence Activities, United States Senate." Available at: www.intelligence.senate.gov/sites/default/files/94chile.pdf.

Claassen, Ryan L., David B. Magleby, J. Quin Monson and Kelly D. Patterson. 2013. "Voter Confidence and the Election-Day Voting Experience." *Political Behavior* 35(2):215–235.

Clayton, Mark. 2014. "Ukraine Election Narrowly Avoided 'Wanton Destruction' from Hackers." *Christian Science Monitor*, June 17, p. 6.

Cloward, Karisa. 2014. "False Commitments: Local Misrepresentation and the International Norms Against Female Genital Mutilation and Early Marriage." *International Organization* 68(3):495–526.

Coats, Daniel R. 2019. "Statement for the Record: Worldwide Threat Assessment of the U.S. Intelligence Community." Office of the Director of National Intelligence, January 29. Available at: www.dni.gov/files/ODNI/documents/2019-ATA-SFR---SSCI.pdf.

Cohn, Nate. 2018. "Why Democrats' Gain Was More Impressive Than It Appears." *New York Times* (online), TheUpShot, November 7. Available at: www.nytimes.com/2018/11/07/upshot/2018-midterms-blue-wave-democrats.html.

Copelovitch, Mark and Jon C. W. Pevehouse. 2019. "International Organizations in a New Era of Populist Nationalism." *Review of International Organizations* 14(2):169–186.

Coppedge, Michael, John Gerring and Carl Henrik Knutsen, Staffan I. Lindberg, Jan Teorell, David Altman, Michael Bernhard, M. Steven Fish, Adam Glynn, Allen Hicken, Anna Lührmann, Kyle L. Marquardt, Kelly McMann, Pamela Paxton, Daniel Pemstein, Brigitte Seim, Rachel Sigman, Svend-Erik Skaaning, Jeffrey Staton, Agnes Cornell, Lisa

Gastaldi, Haakon Gjerløw, Valeriya Mechkova, Johannes von Römer, Aksel Sundtröm, Eitan Tzelgov, Luca Uberti, Yi ting Wang, Tore Wig and Daniel Ziblatt. 2019. "V-Dem Codebook v9." Varieties of Democracy (V-Dem) Project. Available at: www.v-dem.net/media/filer_public/e6/d2/e6d27595-9d69-4312-b09f-63d2a0a65df2/v-dem_codebook_v9.pdf.

Coppock, Alexander. 2021. *Persuasion in Parallel.* Chicago Studies in American Politics. Chicago: University of Chicago Press.

Corstange, Daniel and Nikolay Marinov. 2012. "Taking Sides in Other People's Elections: The Polarizing Effect of Foreign Intervention." *American Journal of Political Science* 56(3):655–670.

Dafoe, Allan, Baobao Zhang and Devin Caughey. 2018. "Information Equivalence in Survey Experiments." *Political Analysis* 26(4):399–416.

Davis, Julia [@JuliaDavisNews]. 2021. "Russia's state TV plays another clip of Tucker Carlson, quoting Putin's questions about the Capitol insurrectionists. Kremlin propagandists conclude: 'We hit the mark. Putin was heard. Bullseye.' They add that this proves they should continue influencing public opinion in the US." *Twitter*, June 17. Available at: www.twitter.com/JuliaDavisNews/status/1405676978888482820.

Daxecker, Ursula E. 2012. "The Cost of Exposing Cheating: International Election Monitoring, Fraud, and Post-Election Violence in Africa." *Journal of Peace Research* 49(4):503–516.

Daxecker, Ursula and Gerald Schneider. 2014. Election Monitoring: The Implications of Multiple Monitors for Electoral Integrity. In *Advancing Electoral Integrity*, ed. Pippa Norris, Richard W. Frank and Ferran Martínez i Coma. Oxford: Oxford University Press, pp. 73–93.

Daxecker, Ursula, Jessica Di Salvatore and Andrea Ruggeri. 2019. "Fraud is What People Make of It: Election Fraud, Perceived Fraud, and Protesting in Nigeria." *Journal of Conflict Resolution* 63(9):2098–2127.

Debre, Maria J. and Lee Morgenbesser. 2017. "Out of the Shadows: Autocratic Regimes, Election Observation and Legitimation." *Contemporary Politics* 23(3):328–347.

Declaration of Principles for International Election Observation. 2005. Commemorated October 27, 2005, at the United Nations, New York.

DeConde, Alexander. 1958. *Entangling Alliance: Politics & Diplomacy Under George Washington.* Durham, NC: Duke University Press.

Director of National Intelligence. 2018. "Joint Statement from the ODNI, DOJ, FBI and DHS: Combating Foreign Influence in U.S. Elections." Press release, October 19. Available at: www.dni.gov/index.php/newsroom/press-releases/item/1915-joint-statement-from-the-odni-doj-and-dhs-combating-foreign-influence-in-u-s-elections.

Dixon, Jennifer M. 2017. "Rhetorical Adaptation and Resistance to International Norms." *Perspectives on Politics* 15(1):83–99.

Dodsworth, Susan. 2019. "Double Standards: The Verdicts of Western Election Observers in Sub-Saharan Africa." *Democratization* 26(3):
382–400.

Donno, Daniela. 2010. "Who is Punished? Regional Intergovernmental
Organizations and the Enforcement of Democratic Norms." *International
Organization* 64(4):593–625.

Donno, Daniela. 2013. *Defending Democratic Norms: International Actors
and the Politics of Electoral Misconduct*. Oxford: Oxford University
Press.

Dorell, Oren. 2017. "Russia Engineered Election Hacks and Meddling in
Europe." *USA Today* (online), January 29. Available at: www.usatoday
.com/story/news/world/2017/01/09/russia-engineered-election-hacks-euro
pe/96216556/.

Draper, Robert. 2020. "Unwanted Truths: Inside Trump's Battles with
U.S. Intelligence Agencies." *New York Times* Magazine (online), August
16. Available at: www.nytimes.com/2020/08/08/magazine/us-russia-
intelligence.html.

Drennan, Justine. 2015. "Should International Groups Be Monitoring
Sudan's Elections?" *Foreign Policy* (online), April 14. Available at: www
.foreignpolicy.com/2015/04/14/should-international-groups-be-monitorin
g-sudans-elections/.

Driscoll, Jesse and Daniel F. Hidalgo. 2014. "Intended and Unintended Consequences of Democracy Promotion Assistance to Georgia after the Rose
Revolution." *Research & Politics* 1(1):1–13.

Dunning, Thad, Guy Grossman, Macartan Humphreys, Susan D. Hyde,
Craig McIntosh and Gareth Nellis. 2019. *Information, Accountabil-
ity, and Cumulative Learning: Lessons from Metaketa I*. Cambridge:
Cambridge University Press.

Economist. 2018a. "Lexington: A Legitimacy Problem." July 21, p. 35.

Economist. 2018b. "Pragmatic but Principled." January 13, p. 29.

Edelstein, David M. 2011. *Occupational Hazards: Success and Failure in
Military Occupation*. Ithaca, NY: Cornell University Press.

Eil, David and Justin M. Rao. 2011. "The Good News-Bad News Effect:
Asymmetric Processing of Objective Information about Yourself." *American Economic Journal: Microeconomics* 3(2):114–138.

El Sheikh, Mayy. 2014. "Egypt: Sisi Wins with 97 Percent." *New
York Times*, 4 June. Available at: www.nytimes.com/2014/06/04/world/
middleeast/egypt-sisi-wins-with-97-percent.html.

Enikolopov, Ruben, Vasily Korovkin, Maria Petrova, Konstantin Sonin and
Alexei Zakharov. 2013. "Field Experiment Estimate of Electoral Fraud in
Russian Parliamentary Elections." *Proceedings of the National Academy
of Sciences* 110(2):448–452.

Erlanger, Steven. 2006. "U.S. Spent $1.9 Million to Aid Fatah in Palestinian Elections." *New York Times*, January 23, p. A11.

Erlich, Aaron and Nicholas Kerr. 2016. "The Local Mwananchi has Lost Trust?: Design Transition and Legitimacy in Kenyan Election Management." *Journal of Modern African Studies* 54(4):671–702.

Eschenbächer, Jens-Hagen. 2010. "Assessing Elections in Established Democracies - Why ODIHR Sends Observers and Experts to Countries Across the Entire OSCE Region." OSCE Office for Democratic Institutions and Human Rights, June 28. Available at: www.osce.org/odihr/elections/104137.

European Union Election Observation Mission. 2019. "Republic of Mozambique: Final Report, General and Provincial Assembly Elections, 15 October 2019." Available at: www.epgencms.europarl.europa.eu/cmsdata/upload/83ba3820-1453-469d-9597-466e4fcc0a19/Mozambique_general&provincial-elections__15-October-2019_EOM_final_report (EN).pdf.

Evanina, William. 2020. "Statement by NCSC Director William Evanina: Election Threat Update for the American Public." Office of the Director of National Intelligence, August 7. Available at: www.odni.gov/index.php/newsroom/press-releases/item/2139-statement-by-ncsc-director-william-evanina-election-threat-update-for-the-american-public.

Fabian, Jordan. 2018. "U.S. Warns of 'Ongoing' Election Interference by Russia, China, Iran." *The Hill* (online), October 19. Available at: www.thehill.com/policy/national-security/412292-us-warns-of-ongoing-election-interference-by-russia-china-iran.

Fandos, Nicholas and Michael Wines. 2018. "Russia Tried to Crack Voting Systems in at Least 18 States, Senators Say." *New York Times*, May 9, p. A18.

Fawn, Rick. 2006. "Ballot Over the Box: International Election Observation Missions, Political Competition, and Retrenchment in the post-Soviet Space." *International Affairs* 82(6):1133–1153.

Fearon, James D. 2011. "Self-Enforcing Democracy." *Quarterly Journal of Economics* 126(4):1661–1708.

Feldman, Noah. 2014. "Can Arabs Do Democracy?" *Bloomberg News* (online), October 23. Available at: www.bloomberg.com/opinion/articles/2014-10-23/can-arabs-do-democracy.

Ferraz, Claudio and Frederico Finan. 2008. "Exposing Corrupt Politicians: The Effects of Brazil's Publicly Released Audits on Electoral Outcomes." *Quarterly Journal of Economics* 123(2):703–745.

Flynn, D.J., Brendan Nyhan and Jason Reifler. 2017. "The Nature and Origins of Misperceptions: Understanding False and Unsupported Beliefs About Politics." *Political Psychology* 38(S1):127–150.

Forero, Juan. 2006. "Seeking United Latin America, Venezuela's Chavez is a Divider." *New York Times*, May 20, p. A1.

Fortna, Virginia Paige. 2008. *Does Peacekeeping Work? Shaping Belligerent's Choices after Civil War*. Princeton: Princeton University Press.

Freedom House. 2014. "Tunisia Country Report." In *Freedom in the World 2014*. Available at: www.freedomhouse.org/report/freedom-world/2014/tunisia.

Freedom House. 2019. "Georgia Country Report." In *Freedom in the World 2019*. Available at: www.freedomhouse.org/report/freedom-world/2019/georgia.

Freedom House. 2021a. "Georgia Country Report." In *Freedom in the World 2021*. Available at: www.freedomhouse.org/country/georgia/freedom-world/2021.

Freedom House. 2021b. "Tunisia Country Report." In *Freedom in the World 2021*. Available at: www.freedomhouse.org/country/tunisia/freedom-world/2021.

Freedom House. 2021c. "United States Country Report." In *Freedom in the World 2021*. Available at: www.freedomhouse.org/country/united-states/freedom-world/2021.

Freyburg, Tina and Solveig Richter. 2015. "Local Actors in the Driver's Seat: Transatlantic Democracy Promotion Under Regime Competition in the Arab World." *Democratization* 22(3):496–518.

Friedberg, Aaron L. 2005. "The Future of U.S.–China Relations: Is Conflict Inevitable?" *International Security* 30(2):7–45.

Friedman, Uri. 2016. "American Democracy is More Than One Election." *The Atlantic* (online), November 8. Available at: www.washingtonpost.com/opinions/republicans-more-concerned-with-partisanship-than-russian-meddling/2017/03/20.

Fumagalli, Matteo. 2014. "The 2013 Presidential Election in the Republic of Georgia." *Electoral Studies* 35:362–405.

Gabriel, Trip. 2016. "Few Answering Call by Trump to Watch Polls." *New York Times*, October 19, p. A1.

Gaines, Brian J., James H. Kuklinski and Paul J. Quirk. 2007. "The Logic of the Survey Experiment Reexamined." *Political Analysis* 10(1):1–20.

Gall, Carlotta. 2014. "Islamist Party in Tunisia Concedes to Secularists." *New York Times*, October 27, p. A9.

Gandhi, Jennifer and Ellen Lust-Okar. 2009. "Elections Under Authoritarianism." *Annual Review of Political Science* 12:403–422.

Gavin, Michelle D. 2019. "African Leaders Must Act to Stop Electoral Fraud in Congo." *Foreign Policy* (online), January 9. Available at: www.foreignpolicy.com/2019/01/09/african-leaders-must-act-to-stop-electoral-fraud-in-congo/.

Gerasimov, Valery. 2016. "The Value of Science is in the Foresight: New Challenges Demand Rethinking the Forms and Methods of Carrying out Combat Operations." *Military Review* January-February:23–29.

Gerber, Alan and Donald Green. 1999. "Misperceptions about Perceptual Bias." *Annual Review of Political Science* 2(1):189–210.

Gerber, Alan S., Gregory A. Huber, David Doherty, Conor M. Dowling and Seth Hill. 2013. "Do Perceptions of Ballot Secrecy Influence Turnout? Results from a Field Experiment." *American Journal of Political Science* 57(3):537–551.

Gettleman, Jeffrey. 2007. "Riots Batter Kenya as Rivals Declare Victory: Supporters of Presidential Challenger Take to Streets as Election Lead Shrinks." *New York Times*, December 30, p. 3.

Gibson, Clark C. and James D. Long. 2007. "The Presidential and Parliamentary Elections in Kenya, December 2007." *Electoral Studies* 29(3):497–502.

Gill, Timothy M. 2018. "Americans Shouldn't Be Shocked by Russian Interference in the Election. The US Does It, Too." *The Washington Post* (online), Made by History, March 7. Available at: www.washingtonpost .com/news/made-by-history/wp/2018/03/07/americans-shouldnt-be-shocked-by-russian-meddling-in-the-election-the-u-s-does-it-too/.

Global Americans. 2018. "Keeping Up Appearances: All Eyes on Venezuela at the OAS General Assembly." Global Americans Report. Available at: www.theglobalamericans.org/reports/eyes-venezuela-oas-general-assembly/.

Gonzales, Richard and Matthew S. Schwartz. 2019. "Surprise Winner Of Congolese Election Is An Opposition Leader." NPR, January 9. Available at: www.npr.org/2019/01/09/683830171/surprise-winner-of-congolese-election-is-an-opposition-leader.

Gordon, Grant M. and Lauren E. Young. 2017. "Cooperation, Information, and Keeping the Peace: Civilian Engagement with Peacekeepers in Haiti." *Journal of Peace Research* 54(1):64–79.

Gourevitch, Peter G. 1978. "The Second Image Reversed." *International Organization* 32(4):881–912.

Graham, Chris. 2018. "'Split Decision': How US Newspapers Reacted to the Midterm Elections." *The Telegraph* (online), November 7. Available at: www.telegraph.co.uk/news/2018/11/07/split-decision-us-newspapers-reacted-midterm-elections/.

Graham, Matthew H. and Milan W. Svolik. 2020. "Democracy in America? Partisanship, Polarization, and the Robustness of Support for Democracy in the United States." *American Political Science Review* 114(2): 392–409.

Gray, Julia. 2013. *The Company States Keep: International Economic Organizations and Investor Perceptions*. Cambridge: Cambridge University Press.

Grier, Peter. 2017. "Election Meddling: When Russia Returns, Will the U.S. be Ready?" *Christian Science Monitor* (online), March 31. Available at: www.csmonitor.com/USA/Politics/2017/0331/Election-meddling-When-Russia-returns-will-the-US-be-ready.

Groll, Elias. 2018. "Is China Really Meddling in U.S. Elections?" *Foreign Policy* (online), October 2. Available at: www.foreignpolicy.com/2018/10/02/theres-little-evidence-of-trumps-claim-of-chinese-political-meddling/.

Grossman, Guy, Devorah Manekin and Yotam Margalit. 2018. "How Sanctions Affect Public Opinion in Target Countries: Experimental Evidence From Israel." *Comparative Political Studies* 51(14): 1823–1857.

Grubman, Nate and Aytuğ Şaşmaz. 2021. "The Collapse of Tunisia's Party System and the Rise of Kais Saied." *Middle East Report Online*, August 17. Available at: www.merip.org/2021/08/the-collapse-of-tunisias-party-system-and-the-rise-of-kais-saied/.

Gruffydd-Jones, Jamie J. 2019. "Citizens and Condemnation: Strategic Uses of International Human Rights Pressure in Authoritarian States." *Comparative Political Studies* 52(4):579–612.

Guess, Andrew, Jonathan Nagler and Joshua Tucker. 2019. "Less Than You Think: Prevalence and Predictors of Fake News Dissemination on Facebook." *Science Advances* 5(1):eaau4586.

Haerpfer, Christian, Ronald Inglehart, Alejandro Moreno, Christian Welzel, Kseniya Kizilova, Jaime Diez-Medrano, Marta Lagos, Pippa Norris, Eduard Ponarin and Bi Puranen, et al. 2014. "World Values Survey: Round Six - Country-Pooled Datafile Version." Available at: www.worldvaluessurvey.org/WVSDocumentationWV6.jsp.

Hafner-Burton, Emilie M. 2009. "The Power Politics of Regime Complexity: Human Rights Trade Conditionality in Europe." *Perspectives on Politics* 7(1):33–37.

Hafner-Burton, Emilie M. and James Ron. 2013. "The Latin Bias: Regions, the Anglo-American Media, and Human Rights." *International Studies Quarterly* 57(3):474–491.

Hafner-Burton, Emilie M., Stephan Haggard, David A. Lake and David G. Victor. 2017. "The Behavioral Revolution and International Relations." *International Organization* 71(S):S1–S31.

Hafner-Burton, Emilie M., Susan D. Hyde and Ryan S. Jablonski. 2014. "When Do Governments Resort to Election Violence?" *British Journal of Political Science* 44(1):149–169.

Hall, Thad E., J. Quin Monson and Kelly D. Patterson. 2009. "The Human Dimension of Elections: How Poll Workers Shape Public Confidence in Elections." *Political Research Quarterly* 62(3):507–522.

Hamid, Shadi, Peter Mandaville and William McCants. 2017. "How America Changed Its Approach to Political Islam." *The Atlantic* (online), October 4. Available at: www.theatlantic.com/international/archive/2017/10/america-political-islam/541287/).

Hamilton, Alexander. 1788. "Federalist No. 68." In *The Federalist Papers*, Avalon Project. Available at: www.avalon.law.yale.edu/18th_century/fed68.asp.

Hassan, Amro and Laura King. 2014. "Egypt, International Groups Weigh Value of Observers for Election." *Los Angeles Times*, May 20, p. A3.

Hendawi, Hamza. 2014. "Egypt: El-Sissi wins election by landslide." *AP News* (online). Available at: www.apnews.com/article/ada7c51bf2e042949a2a63fd8b2b45f8.

Hermann, Richard K. 2017. "How Attachments to the Nation Shape Beliefs About the World: A Theory of Motivated Reasoning." *International Organization* 71(S1):S61–S84.

Hjelmgaard, Kim. 2020. "This Group Monitors Foreign Elections. Its Latest Challenge: American Democracy." *USA Today* (online), October 22. Available at: www.usatoday.com/story/news/world/2020/10/22/q-a-what-leader-osce-election-monitoring-group-thinks-us-voting/5976926002/.

Huntington, Samuel P. 1991. *The Third Wave: Democratization in the Late Twentieth Century*. Norman, OK: University of Oklahoma Press.

Hurd, Ian. 2019. "Legitimacy and Contestation in Global Governance: Revisiting the Folk Theory of International Institutions." *Review of International Organizations* 14(4):717–729.

Hyde, Susan D. 2007. "The Observer Effect in International Politics: Evidence from a Natural Experiment." *World Politics* 60(1):37–63.

Hyde, Susan D. 2011. *The Pseudo-Democrat's Dilemma: Why Election Observation Became an International Norm*. Ithaca, NY: Cornell University Press.

Hyde, Susan D. 2012. Why Believe International Election Monitors? In *The Credibility of Transnational NGOs: When Virtue is Not Enough*, ed. Peter A. Gourevitch, David A. Lake and Janice Gross Stein. Cambridge: Cambridge University Press, pp. 37–61.

Hyde, Susan D. 2015. "Experiments in International Relations: Lab, Survey, and Field." *Annual Review of Political Science* 18:403–424.

Hyde, Susan D. 2020. "Democracy's Backsliding in the International Environment." *Science* 369(6508):1192–1996.

Hyde, Susan D. and Nikolay Marinov. 2012. "Which Elections Can Be Lost?" *Political Analysis* 20(2):191–210.

Hyde, Susan D. and Nikolay Marinov. 2014. "Information and Self-Enforcing Democracy: The Role of International Election Observation." *International Organization* 68(2):329–359.

Ichino, Nahomi and Matthias Schündeln. 2012. "Deterring or Displacing Electoral Irregularities? Spillover Effects of Observers in a Randomized Field Experiment in Ghana." *Journal of Politics* 74(1):292–307.

Imai, Kosuke, Luke Keele, Dustin Tingley and Teppei Yamamoto. 2011. "Unpacking the Black Box of Causality: Learning about Causal Mechanisms from Experimental and Observational Studies." *American Political Science Review* 105(4):765–789.

Inglehart, Ronald, Christian Haerpfer, Alejandro Moreno, Christian Welzel, Kseniya Kizilova, Jaime Diez-Medrano, Marta Lagos, Pippa Norris, Eduard Ponarin and Bi Puranen, et al. 2020. "World Values Survey: Round Seven - Country-Pooled Datafile Version." Madrid, Spain & Vienna, Austria: JD Systems Institute & WVSA Secretariat. Available at: doi:10.14281/18241.1.

Instance Supérieure Indépendante pour les Élections (Tunisia). 2014a. "Statistiques des Observateurs Étrangers." Available at: www.isie.tn/wp-content/uploads/2015/01/Statistiques-des-Observateurs-%C3%89tranger s.pdf.

Instance Supérieure Indépendante pour les Élections (Tunisia). 2014b. "Statistiques des Observateurs Nationaux." Available at: www.isie.tn/wp-content/uploads/2015/01/Statistiques-des-Observateurs-Nationaux.pdf.

Instance Supérieure Indépendante pour les Élections (Tunisia). 2014c. "Taux de participation durant le 1er tour des élections présidentielles." Available at: www.isie.tn/isie_documents/taux-participation-election-presidentielles-tour-1-fr/.

International IDEA. 2021. "COMPULSORY VOTING." Available at: www .idea.int/data-tools/data/voter-turnout/compulsory-voting.

International Republican Institute. 2015. "Tunisia Presidential Elections: November 23 and December 21, 2014." Available at: www.iri.org/ Tunisia_2014_Presidential/1/assets/common/downloads/publication.pdf.

InterPressNews. 2018a. "Kakha Kaladze - Some of the NGOs directly fit into the National Movement's 'MessageBox' (translation)." InterPressNews, November 20. Available at: www.bit.ly/2MJUOPc.

InterPressNews. 2018b. "Nukri Kantaria - 'Dream' will not allow the representation of the Russian mentality 'matryoshka' inside Saakashvili, Merabishvili and other criminals of different caliber (translation)." Inter-PressNews, October 31. Available at: www.bit.ly/2BkpVf4.

Jablonski, Ryan. 2014. "How Aid Targets Votes: The Impact of Electoral Incentives on Foreign Aid Distribution." *World Politics* 66(2): 293–330.

Jamal, Amaney A. 2012. *Of Empires and Citizens: Pro-American Democracy or No Democracy at All?* Princeton, NJ: Princeton University Press.

Jamal, Amaney A., Robert O. Keohane, David Romney and Dustin Tingley. 2015. "Anti-Americanism and Anti-Interventionism in Arabic Twitter Discourse." *Perspectives on Politics* 13(1):55–73.

Jamieson, Kathleen Hall. 2020. *Cyberwar: How Russian Hackers and Trolls Helped Elect a President; What We Don't, Can't, and Do Know*. Revised ed. New York: Oxford University Press.

Jawad, Pamela. 2008. "Conflict Resolution through Democracy Promotion? The Role of the OSCE in Georgia." *Democratization* 15(3):611–629.

Jerit, Jennifer and Jason Barabas. 2010. "Partisan Perceptual Bias and the Information Environment." *Journal of Politics* 74(3):672–684.

Jerit, Jennifer and Yangzi Zhou. 2020. "Political Misinformation." *Annual Review of Political Science* 23:77–94.

Jochem, Torsten, Ilia Murtazashvili and Jennifer Murtazashvili. 2020. "Can the Design of Electoral Institutions Improve Perceptions of Democracy in Fragile States? Evidence from Afghanistan." *Journal of Global Security Studies* 5(3): 443–462.

Kahlaoui, Tarek. 2013. The Powers of Social Media. In *Making of the Tunisian Revolution: Contexts, Architects, Prospects*, ed. Nouri Gana. Edinburgh: Edinburgh University Press, pp. 147–158.

Kakachia, Kornely and Bidzina Lebanidze. 2019. "Georgian Dream Meets Georgia's Nightmare." *Foreign Policy* (online), June 25. Available at: www.foreignpolicy.com/2019/06/25/georgian-dream-meets-georgias-nightmare/.

Katzenstein, Peter J. and Robert O. Keohane. 2007. Varieties of anti-Americanism: A Framework for Analysis. In *Anti-Americanisms in World Politics*, ed. Peter J. Katzenstein and Robert O. Keohane. Ithaca, NY: Cornell University Press, pp. 9–38.

Kaufman, Robert R. and Stephan Haggard. 2019. "Democratic Decline in the United States: What Can We Learn from Middle-Income Backsliding?" *Perspectives on Politics* 17(2):417–432.

Kavakli, Kerim Can and Patrick M. Kuhn. 2020. "Dangerous Contenders: Election Monitors, Islamist Opposition and Terrorism." *International Organziation* 74(1):145–164.

Keating, Joshua. 2012. "Connie Mack Declares War on U.N. Over Its Nonexistent Election Monitors." *Foreign Policy* (online), October 26. Available at: www.foreignpolicy.com/2012/10/26/connie-mack-declares-war-on-u-n-over-its-nonexistent-election-monitors/.

Keck, Margaret E. and Kathryn Sikkink. 1998. *Activists Beyond Borders: Advocacy Networks in International Politics*. Ithaca, NY: Cornell University Press.

Kelley, Judith G. 2004. *Ethnic Politics in Europe: The Power of Norms and Incentives*. Princeton, NJ: Princeton University Press.

Kelley, Judith G. 2009a. "D-Minus Elections: The Politics and Norms of International Election Observation." *International Organization* 63(4):765–787.

Kelley, Judith G. 2009b. "The More the Merrier? The Effects of Having Multiple International Election Monitoring Organizations." *Perspectives on Politics* 7(1):59–64.

Kelley, Judith G. 2010. "Election Observers and Their Biases." *Journal of Democracy* 21(3):158–172.

Kelley, Judith G. 2011. "Do International Election Monitors Increase or Decrease Opposition Boycotts?" *Comparative Political Studies* 44(11):1527–1556.

Kelley, Judith G. 2012a. "International Influences on Elections in New Multiparty States." *Annual Review of Political Science* 15:203–220.

Kelley, Judith G. 2012b. *Monitoring Democracy: When International Election Observation Works and Why it Often Fails*. Princeton, NJ: Princeton University Press.

Kerr, Nicholas. 2013. "Popular Evaluations of Election Quality in Africa: Evidence from Nigeria." *Electoral Studies* 32(4):819–837.

Kerr, Nicholas. 2018. "Election-Day Experiences and Evaluations of Electoral Integrity in Unconsolidated Democracies: Evidence from Nigeria." *Political Studies* 66(3):667–686.

Kerr, Nicholas and Anna Lührmann. 2017. "Public Trust in Elections: The Role of Election Administration Autonomy and Media Freedom." *Electoral Studies* 50:50–67.

Kertzer, Joshua D., Brian Rathbun and Nina Srinivasan Rathbun. 2020. "The Price of Peace: Motivated Reasoning and Costly Signaling in International Relations." *International Organization* 74(1):95–118.

Kertzer, Joshua D. and Dustin Tingley. 2018. "Political Psychology in International Relations: Beyond the Paradigms." *Annual Review of Political Science* 21:319–339.

Khemara, Sok. 2018. "International Community Condemns Cambodia Elections as 'Setback to Democracy'." *Voice of America* (online), July 30. Available at: www.voacambodia.com/a/international-community-condemns-cambodia-elections-as-setback-to-democracy-/4505764.html.

King, Gary, Robert O. Keohane, and Sidney Verba. 1994. *Designing Social Inquiry: Scientific Inference in Qualitative Research*. Princeton, NJ: Princeton University Press.

Kirchick, James. 2012. "Blindsided." *Foreign Policy* (online), October 12. Available at: www.foreignpolicy.com/2012/10/12/blindsided/.

Kirkpatrick, David D. and David E. Sanger. 2011. "A Tunisian–Egyptian Link That Shook Arab History." *New York Times*, February 13, p. A1.

Kocher, Matthew Adam, Adria K. Lawrence and Nuno P. Monteiro. 2018. "Nationalism, Collaboration, and Resistance: France under Nazi Occupation." *International Security* 43(2):117–150.

Kreps, Sarah and Stephen Roblin. 2019. "Treatment Format and External Validity in International Relations Experiments." *International Interactions* 45(3):576–594.

Kunda, Ziva. 1990. "The Case for Motivated Reasoning." *Psychological Bulletin* 108(3):480–498.

Laakso, Liisa. 2002. "The Politics of International Election Observation: The Case of Zimbabwe in 2000." *The Journal of Modern African Studies* 40(3):437–464.

Lake, David A. 2016. *The Statebuilder's Dilemma: On the Limits of Foreign Intervention*. Ithaca, NY: Cornell University Press.

Lake, David A. and Robert Powell. 1999. International Relations: A Strategic-Choice Approach. In *Strategic Choice and International Relations*, ed. David A. Lake and Robert Powell. Princeton, NJ: Princeton University Press, pp. 3–38.

Latinobarómetro. 2014. "Latinobarómetro 2012–2013." Available at: www.latinobarometro.org/latContents.jsp.

LeBas, Adrienne. 2018. "Can Polarization Be Positive? Conflict and Institutional Development in Africa." *American Behavioral Scientist* 62(1): 59–74.

Leeper, Thomas J. and Kevin J. Mullinix. 2018. "Oxford Bibliographies in Political Science." In *Motivated Reasoning*, ed. Sandy Maisel. New York: Oxford University Press. Available at: www.oxfordbibliographies.com/view/document/obo-9780199756223/obo-9780199756223-0237.xml.

Levin, Dov H. 2016. "When the Great Power Gets a Vote: The Effects of Great Power Electoral Interventions on Election Results." *International Studies Quarterly* 60(2):189–202.

Levin, Dov H. 2019a. "Partisan Electoral Interventions by the Great Powers: Introducing the PEIG Dataset." *Conflict Management and Peace Science* 31(6):88–106.

Levin, Dov H. 2019b. "A Vote for Freedom? The Effects of Partisan Electoral Interventions on Regime Type." *Journal of Conflict Resolution* 63(4):839–868.

Levin, Dov H. 2020. *Meddling in the Ballot Box: The Causes and Effects of Partisan Electoral Interventions*. Oxford: Oxford University Press.

Levitsky, Steven and Daniel Ziblatt. 2018. *How Democracies Die*. New York: Crown.

Levitsky, Steven and Lucan A. Way. 2010. *Competitive Authoritarianism: The Origins and Evolution of Hybrid Regimes in the Post-Cold War Era*. Problems of International Politics Series. New York: Cambridge University Press.

Little, Andrew T. 2012. "Elections, Fraud, and Election Monitoring in the Shadow of Revolution." *Quarterly Journal of Political Science* 7(3): 249–283.

Little, Andrew T. 2019. "The Distortion of Related Beliefs." *American Journal of Political Science* 63(3):675–689.

Lührmann, Anna. 2019. "United Nations Electoral Assistance: More than a Fig Leaf?" *International Political Science Review* 40(2):181–196.

Lührmann, Anna, Marcus Tannenberg and Staffan I. Lindberg. 2018. "Regimes of the World (RoW): Opening New Avenues for the Comparative Study of Political Regimes." *Politics and Governance* 6(1): 1–18.

Lupu, Noam. 2015. "Party Polarization and Mass Partisanship: A Comparative Perspective." *Political Behavior* 37(2):331–356.

Lupu, Yonatan and Geoffrey P.R. Wallace. 2019. "Violence, Nonviolence, and the Effects of International Human Rights Law." *American Journal of Political Science* 63(2):411–426.

Marinov, Nikolay. 2013. "Voter Attitudes when Democracy Promotion turns Partisan: Evidence from a Survey-Experiment in Lebanon." *Democratization* 20(7):1297–1321.

Markey, Patrick and Tarek Amara. 2014. "Tunisia's Islamists Down But Not Out After Election Defeat." *Reuters*, October 30. Available at: www .reuters.com/article/us-tunisia-election/tunisias-islamists-down-but-not-ou t-after-election-defeat-idUSKBN0IJ1LP20141030.

Martin, Jonathan and Alexander Burns. 2014. "Officials Fight Trump's Claims of a Rigged Vote." *New York Times*, October 17, p. A1.

Masters, Jonathan and Mohammed Aly Sergie. 2010. "The Arab League." Council on Foreign Relations Backgrounder, February 19. Available at: www.cfr.org/backgrounder/arab-league/.

Matanock, Aila M. 2017. "Bullets for Ballots: Electoral Participation Provisions and Enduring Peace after Civil Conflict." *International Security* 41(4):93–132.

Matanock, Aila M. 2018. "External Engagement: Explaining the Spread of Electoral Participation Provisions in Civil Conflict Settlements." *International Studies Quarterly* 62(3):656–670.

Mayer, Jane. 2018. "How Russia Helped Swing the Election for Trump." *New Yorker* (online), September 24. Available at: www.newyorker.com/ magazine/2018/10/01/how-russia-helped-to-swing-the-election-for-trump.

McCarthy, Justin. 2018. "Most Americans Confident in Accuracy of Upcoming Elections." *Gallup News* (online), November 5. Available at: www.news.gallup.com/poll/244373/americans-confident-accuracy-upcoming-elections.aspx.

McFaul, Michael. 2007. "Ukraine Imports Democracy: External Influences on the Orange Revolution." *International Security* 32(2):45–83.

McGraw, Kathleen M., Edward Hasecke and Kimberly Conger. 2003. "Ambivalence, Uncertainty, and Processes of Candidate Evaluation." *Political Psychology* 24(3):421–448.

McGraw, Kathleen M., Milton Lodge and Patrick Stroh. 1990. "On-line Processing in Candidate Evaluation: The Effects of Issue Order, Issue Importance, and Sophistication." *Political Behavior* 12: 41–58.

McIntire, Mike and Jeffrey Gettleman. 2009. "A Chaotic Kenya Vote and a Secret U.S. Exit Poll." *New York Times*, January 31, p. A1.

Mearsheimer, John J. 2021. "Liberalism and Nationalism in Contemporary America." *PS: Political Science & Politics* 54(1):1–8.

Melia, Thomas O. 2018. "Russia and America Aren't Morally Equivalent." *The Atlantic* (online), February 27. Available at: www.theatlantic.com/international/archive/2018/02/election-meddling-democracy-promotion/5 54348/.

Melikishvili, Elene. 2018. "Voter Apathy in Georgia's Presidential Election." Geopoliticus blog, Foreign Policy Research Institute, October 30. Available at: www.fpri.org/article/2018/10/voter-apathy-in-georgias-presidential-election/.

Merloe, Patrick. 2015. "Election Monitoring Vs. Disinformation." *Journal of Democracy* 26(3):79–93.

Michel, Casey. 2015. "The Rise of the Zombie Monitors." *The Diplomat* (online), April 30. Available at: www.thediplomat.com/2015/04/the-rise-of-the-zombie-monitors/.

Milbank, Dana. 2017. "Republicans Read Trump's Cue Cards on Russia and Wiretapping." *Washington Post* (online), March 20. Available at: www.washingtonpost.com/opinions/republicans-more-concerned-with-pa rtisanship-than-russian-meddling/2017/03/20/040d66d2-0dba-11e7-9d5a -a83e627dc120_story.html.

Miller, James E. 1983. "Taking Off the Gloves: The United States and the Italian Elections of 1948." *Diplomatic History* 7(1):35–55.

Milligan, Susan. 2019. "A Growing Lack of Faith in Elections." *U.S. News & World Report* (online), May 10. Available at: www.usnews.com/news/the-report/articles/2019-05-10/after-russian-election-interference-americans-are-losing-faith-in-elections/.

Mitchell, Lincoln A. 2004. "Georgia's Rose Revolution." *Current History* 103:342–348.

Mitchell, Lincoln A. 2006. "Democracy in Georgia Since the Rose Revolution." *Orbis* 50(4):669–676.

Mitchell, Lincoln A. 2009. *Uncertain Democracy: U.S. Foreign Policy and Georgia's Rose Revolution*. Philadelphia: University of Pennsylvania Press.

Moaddel, Mansoor. 2015. "A Panel Survey of Value Orientations and Political Actions in Tunisia, 2013–2015." College Park, University of Maryland.

Moehler, Devra C. 2009. "Critical Citizens and Submissive Subjects: Election Losers and Winners in Africa." *British Journal of Political Science* 39(2):345–366.

Morgenbesser, Lee. 2018. "Fake Monitors Endorse Cambodia's Sham Election." *Foreign Policy* (online), July 30. Available at: www.foreignpolicy.com/2018/07/30/fake-monitors-endorse-cambodias-sham-election/#.

Morin, Rebecca. 2016. "Trump Campaign Launches Drive to Recruit 'Election Observers'." *Politico* (online), August 13. Available at: www.politico.com/story/2016/08/donald-trump-election-observers-226981.

Mudge, Lewis. 2020. "A Perfect Storm is Brewing in Burundi: WHO Experts Expelled, Election Observers Blocked." Human Rights Watch, May 14. Available at: www.hrw.org/news/2020/05/14/perfect-storm-brewing-burundi.

Mueller, III, Robert S. 2018. "Report on the Investigation into Russian Interference in the 2016 Presidential Election." Volume I of II. U.S. Department of Justice, Washington, DC. Available at: www.justice.gov/storage/report.pdf.

Mullinix, Kevin J., Thomas J. Leeper, James N. Druckman and Jeremy Freese. 2015. "Evaluating Online Labor Markets for Experimental Research: Amazon.com's Mechanical Turk." *Journal of Experimental Political Science* 2(2):109–138.

Myre, Greg (narrator). 2020. "Whistleblower Alleges DHS Told Him to Stop Reporting on Russia Threat." NPR, *All Things Considered*, September 9. Available at: www.npr.org/2020/09/09/911188416/whistleblower-alleges-dhs-tried-to-alter-intelligence-to-match-trumps-claims.

Myrick, Rachel. 2021. "Do External Threats Unite or Divide? Security Crises, Rivalries, and Polarization in American Foreign Policy." *International Organization*, pp. 1–38, doi:10.1017/S0020818321000175.

National Democratic Institute. 2013. "Outreach and External Communication: A Field Guide for the West Africa Election Observers Network." Available at: www.ndi.org/sites/default/files/Outreach%20and%20Communication_WAEON_EN.pdf.

National Democratic Institute. 2014. "Preliminary Statement of the NDI Observer Delegation to Tunisia's 2014 Legislative Elections." Press Release, October 27. Available at: www.ndi.org/sites/default/files/NDI%20Tunisia%202014%20Legislative%20Elections%20Preliminary%20Statement%20%5BEN%5D%20%282%29_0.pdf.

National Democratic Institute. 2017. "NDI: Public attitudes in Georgia, June 2017." Available at: www.caucasusbarometer.org/en/nj2017ge.

National Democratic Institute. 2018a. "Democracy Assistance is Not Election Meddling: Distinguishing Support from Sabotage." Available at: www.ndi.org/democracy-assistance-not-election-meddling-distinguishing-support-sabotage.

National Democratic Institute. 2018b. "Statement of the National Democratic Institute Pre-Election Delegation to Georgia." Tbilisi, Georgia, July 27. Available at: www.ndi.org/sites/default/files/NDI%20Georgia_PEAM%20statement_July%2027%202018_ENG.pdf.

National Democratic Institute. 2019. "Moldova: Overview." Available at: www.ndi.org/eurasia/moldova.

National Intelligence Council. 2021. "Foreign Threats to the 2020 US Federal Election." Intelligence Community Assessment (ICA 2020–00078D), Unclassified Version, March 10. Available at: www.dni.gov/files/ODNI/documents/assessments/ICA-declass-16MAR21.pdf.

Nielson, Daniel L., Susan D. Hyde and Judith G. Kelley. 2019. "The Elusive Sources of Legitimacy Beliefs: Civil Society Views of International Election Observers." *Review of International Organizations* 14(4):685–715.

Nomikos, William G. 2021. "Peacekeeping and the Enforcement of Intergroup Cooperation: Evidence from Mali." *Journal of Politics*: 1–36, doi: 10.1086/715246.

Norris, Pippa. 2013a. "Does the World Agree about Standards of Electoral Integrity? Evidence for the Diffusion of Global Norms." *Electoral Studies* 32(4):576–588.

Norris, Pippa. 2013b. *Why Electoral Integrity Matters*. Cambridge: Cambridge University Press.

Norris, Pippa. 2018. "Do Doubts about Electoral Integrity Undermine Satisfaction with Democracy? The U.S. in Cross-National Perspective." *International Political Science Review* 40(1):5–22.

Norris, Pippa, Sarah Cameron and Thomas Wynter. 2018. Challenges in American Elections. In *Electoral Integrity in America: Securing Democracy*, ed. Pippa Norris, Sarah Cameron and Thomas Wynter. New York: Oxford University Press, pp. 3–29.

Norris, Pippa, Sarah Cameron and Thomas Wynter. 2019. Challenges of Electoral Integrity. In *Electoral Integrity in America: Securing Democracy*, ed. Pippa Norris, Sarah Cameron and Thomas Wynter. New York: Oxford University Press, pp. 3–29.

Nugent, Elizabeth R. 2020. *After Repression: How Polarization Derails Democratic Transition*. Princeton, NJ: Princeton University Press.

Nyhan, Brendan and Jason Reifler. 2010. "When Corrections Fail: The Persistence of Political Misperceptions." *Political Behavior* 32(2):303–330.

O'Donnell, Jefcoate and Robbie Gramer. 2018. "Cameroon's Paul Biya Gives a Master Class in Fake Democracy." *Foreign Policy* (online), October 22. Available at: www.foreignpolicy.com/2018/10/22/cameroons-paul-biya-gives-a-master-class-in-fake-democracy/.

Office for Democratic Institutions and Human Rights. 2014. "Georgia Presidential Election, 27 October 2013. OSCE/ODIHR Election Observation Mission Final Report." Available at: www.osce.org/odihr/elections/110301.

Office for Democratic Institutions and Human Rights. 2016. "United States of America, General Elections, 8 November 2016. OSCE/ODIHR Election Observation Mission Final Report." Available at: www.osce.org/odihr/elections/usa/294196?download=true.

Office for Democratic Institutions and Human Rights. 2018. "United States of America, Mid-term Congressional Elections, 6 November 2018. OSCE/ODIHR Election Observation Interim Report." Available at: www.osce.org/odihr/elections/usa/401243?download=true.

Office of the Director of National Intelligence. 2017. "Background to 'Assessing Russian Activities and Intentions in Recent US Elections': The Analytic Process and Cyber Incident Attribution." Office of the Director of National Intelligence, Washington, DC. Available at: www.dni.gov/files/documents/ICA_2017_01.pdf.

O'Rourke, Lindsey A. 2018. *Covert Regime Change: America's Secret Cold War*. Cornell Studies in Security Affairs Ithaca, NY: Cornell University Press.

OSCE Parliamentary Assembly. 2020. "Fundamental freedoms respected in competitive Georgian elections, but allegations of pressure and blurring of line between party and state reduced confidence." Available at: www.oscepa.org/en/news-a-media/press-releases/2020/fundamental-freedoms-respected-in-competitive-georgian-elections-but-allegations-of-pressure-and-blurring-of-line-between-party-and-state-reduced-confidence-and-international-observers-say.

O'Sullivan, Donie. 2018. "Facebook removes more pages, as FBI warns Russia still targeting American voters." *CNN.com*, November 5. Available at: www.cnn.com/2018/11/05/app-politics-section/facebook-pages-russia-target/index.html.

Paris, Roland. 2004. *At War's End: Building Peace After Civil Conflict*. New York: Cambridge University Press.

Perlroth, Nicole and David E. Sanger. 2019. "Iranian Hackers Target Trump Campaign as Threats to 2020 Mount." *New York Times* (online), October 4. Available at: www.nytimes.com/2019/10/04/technology/iranian-campaign-hackers-microsoft.html.

Pevehouse, Jon C. 2005. *Democracy from Above: Regional Organizations and Democratization*. Cambridge University Press.

Pevehouse, Jon C. W. and Felicity Vabulas. 2019. "Nudging the Needle: Foreign Lobbies and US Human Rights Ratings." *International Studies Quarterly* 63(1):85–98.

Pew Research Center. 2018. "Global Attitudes & Trends, Spring 2018 Questionnaire." Available at: www.pewresearch.org/global/dataset/spring-2018-survey-data/.

Pew Research Center. 2020. "Americans See Spread of Disease as Top International Threat, Along With Terrorism, Nuclear Weapons, Cyberattacks." April 13. Available at: www.pewrsr.ch/2UAkuCq.

Pratt, Tyler. 2018. "Deference and Hierarchy in International Regime Complexes." *International Organization* 72(3):561–590.

Pratt, Tyler. 2020. "Vertically Differentiated Cooperation: Explaining Policy Change in International Regime Complexes." Working Paper.

Prior, Markus, Gaurav Sood and Kabir Khanna. 2015. "You Cannot Be Serious: The Impact of Accuracy Incentives on Partisan Bias in Reports of Economic Perceptions." *Quarterly Journal of Political Science* 10(4): 489–518.

Przeworski, Adam. 2006. Self-Enforcing Democracy. In *Oxford Handbook of Political Economy*, ed. Barry R. Weingast and Donald A. Wittman. New York: Oxford University Press, pp. 312–328.

Rabe, Stephen. 2005. *U.S. Intervention in British Guiana: A Cold War Story.* Chapel Hill, NC: University of North Carolina Press.

Radio Free Europe/Radio Liberty. 2018. "Thousands In Georgia Protest Alleged Election Fraud." *RadioFree Europe RadioLiberty*, December 2. Available at: www.rferl.org/a/thousands-in-georgia-protest-alleged-election-fraud/29633223.html.

Radnitz, Scott. 2012. "The Politics of Foreign Intrigue." PONARS Eurasia Policy Memo No. 243. Program on New Approaches to Research and Security in Eurasia. Available at: www.ponarseurasia.org/sites/default/files/policy-memos-pdf/pepm_243_Radnitz_Sept2012.pdf.

Repucci, Sarah and Amy Slipowitz. 2020. "Democracy Under Siege." Available at: www.freedomhouse.org/report/freedom-world/2021/democracy-under-siege.

Robertson, Graeme. 2017. "Political Orientation, Information and Perceptions of Election Fraud: Evidence from Russia." *British Journal of Political Science* 47(3):589–608.

Robinson, William I. 1996. *Promoting Polyarchy: Globalization, US Intervention, and Hegemony. Cambridge Series in International Relations.* Cambridge: Cambridge University Press.

Rogers, Tim. 2006. "Chávez Plays Oil Card in Nicaragua." *The Christian Science Monitor*, May 5, p. 01.

Rosas, Guillermo. 2010. "Trust in Elections and the Institutional Design of Electoral Authorities: Evidence from Latin America." *Electoral Studies* 29(1):74–90.

Rose, David. 2008. "The Gaza Bombshell." *Vanity Fair* 50(4):192–197.

Rose, Richard and William Mishler. 2009. "How Do Electors Respond to an 'Unfair' Election? The Experience of Russians." *Post-Soviet Affairs* 25(2):118–136.

Rundlett, Ashlea and Milan W. Svolik. 2016. "Deliver the Vote! Micromotives and Macrobehavior in Electoral Fraud." *American Political Science Review* 110(1):180–197.

Rusnac, Corneliu. 2018. "Moldova Election Campaign Starts, Some Fear Russia Influence." *Associated Press* (online), December 18, 2018. Available at: www.apnews.com/797b237cb33448319b4751de66c146a5.

Rustavi2. 2018a. "NDI Observation Mission is in Georgia - 16 representatives of observers to observe presidential elections (translation)." Rustavi2, October 23. Available at: www.rustavi2.ge/ka/news/116742.

Rustavi2. 2018b. "Soldiers vs. Salome Zourabichvili - Military Says Country Should Not Have a Betrayed Commander-in-Chief (translation)." Rustavi2, November 12. Available at: www.rustavi2.ge/ka/news/118600.

Sabatini, Christopher. 2018. "Who is Left to Credibly Judge Latin America's Elections?" *New York Times* (online), June 7. Available at: www.nytimes.com/2018/06/07/opinion/latin-america-elections.html.

Sadiki, Larbi. 2002. "Bin Ali's Tunisia: Democracy by Non-Democratic Means." *British Journal of Middle Eastern Studies* 29(1):57–78.

Sances, Michael W. and Charles Stewart. 2015. "Partisanship and Confidence in the Vote Count: Evidence from U.S. National Elections since 2000." *Electoral Studies* 40:176–188.

Saul, Stephanie and Reid Epstein. 2020. "Trump is Pushing a False Argument on Vote-by-Mail Fraud. Here are the Facts." *New York Times* (online), September 28. Available at: www.nytimes.com/article/mail-in-voting-explained.html.

Schaffner, Brian F. and Samantha Luks. 2018. "Misinformation or Expressive Responding? What an Inauguration Crowd Can Tell Us about the source of Political Misinformation in Surveys." *Political Opinion Quarterly* 82(1):135–147.

Seawright, Jason. 2016. *Multi-Method Social Science: Combining Qualitative and Quantitative Tools*. Strategies for Social Inquiry. Cambridge: Cambridge University Press.

Seawright, Jason and John Gerring. 2008. "Case Selection Techniques in Case Study Research." *Political Research Quarterly* 61(2):294–308.

Seldin, Jeff. 2018. "Report Puts Russia, China and Iran in Line for Sanctions for Election Meddling." *Voice of America* (online),

December 21. Available at: www.voanews.com/usa/us-politics/
report-puts-russia-china-and-iran-line-sanctions-election-meddling.

Seldin, Jeff. 2021. "US: Russia, Iran Meddled in November's Election;
China Held Back." *Voice of America (VOA)* (online), March 16.
Available at: www.voanews.com/usa/us-politics/us-russia-iran-meddled-
novembers-election-china-held-back.

Shimer, David. 2020. *Rigged: America, Russia, and One Hundred Years of
Covert Electoral Interference*. New York: Alfred A. Knopf.

Shulman, Stephen and Stephen Bloom. 2012. "The Legitimacy of Foreign Intervention in Elections: The Ukrainian Response." *Review of
International Studies* 38(2):445–471.

Sides, John, Michael Tesler and Lynn Vavrek. 2019. *Identity Crisis: The
2016 Presidential Campaign and the Battle for the Meaning of America*.
Princeton: Princeton University Press.

Simmons, Beth A. 2009. *Mobilizing for Human Rights: International Law
in Domestic Politics*. New York: Cambridge University Press.

Simpser, Alberto and Daniela Donno. 2012. "Can International Election
Monitoring Harm Governance?" *Journal of Politics* 74(2):501–513.

Sinclair, Betsy, Steven S. Smith and Patrick D. Tucker. 2018. "'It's Largely
a Rigged System': Voter Confidence and the Winner Effect in 2016."
Political Research Quarterly 71(4):854–868.

Snyder, Jack. 2020. "Backlash Against Human Rights Shaming: Emotions in
Groups." *International Theory* 12(1):109–132.

Stone, Randall W. 2004. "The Political Economy of IMF Lending in Africa."
American Political Science Review 98(4):577–591.

Stone, Randall W. 2011. *Controlling Institutions: International Organizations and the Global Economy*. Cambridge: Cambridge University Press.

Svolik, Milan W. 2019. "Polarization versus Democracy." *Journal of
Democracy* 30(3):20–32.

Svolik, Milan W. 2020. "When Polarization Trumps Civic Virtue: Partisan
Conflict and the Subversion of Democracy by Incumbents." *Quarterly
Journal of Political Science* 15(1):3–31.

Szakal, Vanessa. 2014. "Continued – International Observation Delegations
for Tunisia's 2014 Elections." *Nawaat*, October 21. Available at: www
.nawaat.org/portail/2014/10/21/continued-international-observation-dele
gations-for-tunisias-2014-elections/.

Taber, Charles S. and Milton Lodge. 2006. "Motivated Skepticism in the
Evaluation of Political Beliefs." *American Journal of Political Science*
50(3):755–769.

Tallberg, Jonas and Michael Zürn. 2019. "The Legitimacy and Legitimation
of International Organizations: Introduction and Framework." *Review of
International Organizations* 14(4):581–606.

Tavana, Daniel and Alex Russell. 2014. "Previewing Tunisia's Parliamentary & Presidential Elections." October, Project on Middle East Democracy. Available at: www.pomed.org/wp-content/uploads/2014/10/Tunisia-Election-Guide-2014.pdf.

Terman, Rochelle. 2019. "Rewarding Resistance: Theorizing Defiance to International Shaming." Working Paper.

Thompkins, Gwen (narrator). 2007. "Protesters Dispute Kibaki Victory in Kenya Election." NPR, *Morning Edition*, December 31. Available at: www.npr.org/templates/story/story.php?storyId=17716242.

Timberg, Craig and Tony Romm. 2019. "It's Not Just the Russians Anymore as Iranians and Others Turn Up Disinformation Efforts Ahead of 2020 Vote." *Washington Post* (online), July 25. Available at: www.washingtonpost.com/technology/2019/07/25/its-not-just-russians-anymore-iranians-others-turn-up-disinformation-efforts-ahead-vote/?wpisrc=al_news__alert-national–alert-world–alert-politics&wpmk=1.

Tingley, Dustin. 2017. "Rising Power on the Mind." *International Organization* 71(S1):S165–S188.

Tomz, Michael and Jessica L.P. Weeks. 2020. "Public Opinion and Foreign Electoral Intervention." *American Political Science Review* 114(3): 856–873.

Trager, Eric. 2017. "The Muslim Brotherhood is the Root of the Qatar Crisis." *The Atlantic* (online), July 2. Available at: www.theatlantic.com/international/archive/2017/07/muslim-brotherhood-qatar/532380/.

Transparency International Georgia. 2018. "Transparency International Georgia is Leaving the Interagency Commission in Protest." October 9. Available at: www.transparency.ge/en/post/transparency-international-georgia-leaving-interagency-commission-protest.

Tucker, Joshua. 2007. "Enough! Electoral Fraud, Collective Action Problems and Post Communist Colored Revolutions." *Perspectives on Politics* 5(3):535–551.

Vachudova, Milada Anna. 2005. *Europe Undivided: Democracy, Leverage and Integration After Communism*. Oxford: Oxford University Press.

Vanka, Nandi, Avery Davis-Roberts and David Carroll. 2018. Transparency. In *Electoral Integrity in America: Securing Democracy*, ed. Pippa Norris, Sarah Cameron and Thomas Wynter. New York: Oxford University Press, pp. 134–150.

Vickery, Chad, David Ennis, Katherine Ellena and Alyssa Kaiser. 2018. "When Are Elections Good Enough? Validating or Annulling Election Results." International Foundation for Electoral Systems, October. Available at: www.ifes.org/sites/default/files/2018_ifes_when_are_elections_good_enough_final.pdf.

Vilmer, Jean-Baptiste Jeangène. 2018. "Successfully Countering Russian Electoral Interference: 15 Lessons Learned from the Macron Leaks." CSIS Briefs, June. Available at: www.csis-website-prod.s3.amazonaws.com/s3fs-public/publication/180621_Vilmer_Countering_russiam_electoral_influence.pdf.

Viser, Matt. 2020. "Joe Biden Warns that President Trump 'is going to try to steal this election'." *The Washington Post* (online), June 11. Available at: www.washingtonpost.com/politics/joe-biden-warns-that-president-trump-is-going-to-try-to-steal-this-election/2020/06/11/a48f88cc-ab98-11ea-9063-e69bd6520940_story.html.

Volz, Dustin. 2018. "No Significant Foreign Interference Seen on Midterm Vote." *Wall Street Journal* (online), November 7. Available at: www.wsj.com/articles/u-s-on-alert-for-election-interference-says-nothing-significant-spotted-1541521048.

Volz, Dustin and Jim Finkle. 2016. "U.S. Indicts Iranians for Hacking Dozens of Banks, New York Dam." *Reuters*, March 24. Available at: www.reuters.com/article/us-usa-iran-cyber/u-s-indicts-iranians-for-hacking-dozens-of-banks-new-york-dam-idUSKCN0WQ1JF.

von Borzyskowski, Inken. 2019a. *The Credibility Challenge: How Democracy Aid Influences Election Violence*. Ithaca, NY: Cornell University Press.

von Borzyskowski, Inken. 2019b. "The Risks of Election Observation: International Condemnation and Post-Election Violence." *International Studies Quarterly* 63(3):654–667.

Walker, Christopher and Alexander Cooley. 2013. "Vote of the Living Dead." *ForeignPolicy.com*, October 31. Available at: www.foreignpolicy.com/2013/10/31/vote-of-the-living-dead.

Wallace, Geoffrey P.R. 2013. "International Law and Public Attitudes toward Torture: An Experimental Study." *International Organization* 67(1):105–140.

Walter, Barbara F. 2002. *Committing to Peace: The Successful Settlement of Civil Wars*. Princeton: Princeton University Press.

Ward, Alex. 2018. "It's Not Just Russia. China, North Korea, and Iran Could Interfere in 2018 Elections, Too." *Vox.com*, August 20. Available at: www.vox.com/2018/8/20/17759574/midterm-russia-china-north-korea-iran-hack-cyber.

Washington, George. 1793. "Farewell Address." In *George Washington Papers, Series 2, Letterbooks -1799: Letterbook 24, April 3, 1793 - March 3, 1797*, Library of Congress. Available at: www.loc.gov/resource/mgw2.024/?sp=229&st=text.

Way, Lucan. 2016. "The Authoritarian Threat: Weaknesses of Autocracy Promotion." *Journal of Democracy* 27(1):64–75.

Way, Lucan Ahmed and Adam Casey. 2018. "Russian Foreign Election Interventions Since 1991." PONARS Eurasia Policy Memo No. 520. Program on New Approaches to Research and Security in Eurasia. Available at: www.ponarseurasia.org/sites/default/files/policy-memos-pdf/Pepm520_Way-Casey_March2018.pdf.

Weingast, Barry R. 1997. "The Political Foundations of Democracy and the Rule of Law." *American Political Science Review* 91(2):245–263.

Wellman, Elizabeth Iams, Susan D. Hyde and Thad E. Hall. 2017. "Does Fraud Trump Partisanship? The Impact of Contentious Elections on Voter Confidence." *Journal of Elections, Public Opinion, and Parties* 28(3):330–348.

Williamson, Scott. 2021. "Elections, Legitimacy, and Compliance in Authoritarian Regimes: Evidence from the Arab World." *Democratization*: 1–22, doi:10.1080/13510347.2021.1929180.

Wilson, Tom, David Blood and David Pilling. 2019. "Congo Voting Data Reveal Huge Fraud in Poll to Replace Kabila." *Financial Times* (online), January 15. Available at: www.ft.com/content/2b97f6e6-189d-11e9-b93e-f4351a53f1c3.

Winters, Matthew S. and Rebecca Weitz-Shapiro. 2017. "Can Citizens Discern? Information Credibility, Political Sophistication, and the Punishment of Corruption in Brazil." *Journal of Politics* 79(1):60–74.

WorldPublicOpinion.org. 2009. "World Publics Strongly Favor International Observers for Elections, Including Their Own." WorldPublicOpinion.org. Available at: www.worldpublicopinion.net/world-publics-strongly-favor-international-observers-for-elections-including-their-own.

Worth, Robert. 2013. "Egypt is Arena for Influence of Arab Rivals." *New York Times*, 10 July, p. A1.

Yarhi-Milo, Keren. 2014. *Knowing the Adversary: Leaders, Intelligence, and Assessment of Intentions in International Relations*. Princeton, NJ: Princeton University Press.

Yee, Vivian. 2021. "As Tunisia's President Cements One-Man Rule, Opposition Grows." *New York Times* (online), September 27. Available at: www.nytimes.com/2021/09/27/world/middleeast/tunisia-president-dictator.html.

Zaller, John and Stanley Feldman. 1992. "A Simple Theory of the Survey Response: Answering Questions versus Revealing Preferences." *American Journal of Political Science* 36(3):579–616.

Zhang, Chan and Frederick G. Conrad. 2014. "Speeding in Web Surveys: The Tendency to Answer Very Fast and Its Association with Straightlining." *Survey Research Methods* 8(2):127–135.

Index

Milton Keynes UK
Ingram Content Group UK Ltd.
UKHW020840110324
439289UK00018B/137